# Watching over Yellowstone

# Watching over Yellowstone

## The US Army's Experience in America's First National Park, 1886–1918

Thomas C. Rust

University Press of Kansas

Published by the University Press of Kansas (Lawrence, Kansas 66045), which was organized by the Kansas Board of Regents and is operated and funded by Emporia State University, Fort Hays State University, Kansas State University, Pittsburg State University, the University of Kansas, and Wichita State University



Names: Rust, Thomas C., 1969– (Historian), author.
Title: Watching over Yellowstone : The US Army's Experience in America's First National Park, 1886–1918 / Thomas C. Rust.
Description: Lawrence : University Press of Kansas, 2020. | Series: Modern war studies | Includes bibliographical references and index.
Identifiers: LCCN 2019045938
ISBN 9780700629404 (cloth)
ISBN 9780700629619 (paper)
ISBN 9780700629411 (epub)
Subjects: LCSH: Yellowstone National Park—History. | United States. Army. Cavalry—History. | United States. Army. Cavalry, 1st. Troop M—History. | Military administration—Yellowstone National Park—History. | National parks and reserves—United States—Management—History. | United States. National Park Service—History. | United States. Army—Biography. | Soldiers—United States—Biography.
Classification: LCC F722 .R87 2020 | DDC 978.7/52031—dc23
LC record available at https://lccn.loc.gov/2019045938.

British Library Cataloguing-in-Publication Data is available.

Printed in the United States of America

10 9 8 7 6 5 4 3 2 1

The paper used in this publication is recycled and contains 30 percent postconsumer waste. It is acid free and meets the minimum requirements of the American National Standard for Permanence of Paper for Printed Library Materials Z39.48-1992.

# Contents

*To all those who served in places they didn't want or expect to—like Charles in Korea or Bill at Fort Riley*

# Foreword

Over the years there have been many accounts of the army's tenure as the first guardians of Yellowstone between 1886 and 1918. Few provided details of the story behind the scenery. Some provided a less than accurate portrayal of what actually happened, especially as relating to the soldiers.

*Watching over Yellowstone* is not only an excellent read; it is a very accurate historical accounting that vividly describes the trials and tribulations associated with the human hardships of those soldiers who served during that time period in Yellowstone.

This is a well-written book. It will be apparent to anyone who reads it, that life as a soldier, stationed in the hinterlands of Yellowstone in the late 1800s and early 1900s, with the purpose of protecting the park, was a story of great hardship, challenge, and survival . . . both physically and mentally.

The ardent students and scholars of Yellowstone's history will find this a compelling story. The general reader will be fascinated by the details of soldiers' lives in Yellowstone over 100 years ago. Days were tedious much of the time, especially during the long, harsh winters, though conflict, to the point of death, sometimes occurred.

I am not aware of a book about Yellowstone that has captured the essence of the life of the lower-ranked soldiers. The author strives and succeeds in telling the story from the bottom up. While not always putting the army in a romantic or glamorous light, the true story needed to be told.

In 1886, Capt. Moses Harris and the soldiers of Troop M, First US Calvary, arrived in what is now called Mammoth Hot Springs, Yellowstone National Park, and established Fort Yellowstone.

In 1986, 100 years after Captain Harris arrived, I was assigned as the Chief Ranger of Yellowstone National Park. I spent the next twelve years overseeing the national park rangers and protecting Yellowstone. During that time I immersed myself getting to know the natural and cultural resources of the park. Having traveled thousands of miles by horseback and skis throughout the park during that time, I forged a sense of what it took to support and oversee soldiers and their post . . . and in today's terms, rangers and their stations. Even in modern times, it is challenging to successfully carry out the duties of being a ranger or ranger supervisor in Yellowstone. I can only imagine the challenges soldiers and officers faced 130 years ago. There are many insights gained from those who went before.

Some of the world's most iconic natural and cultural resources are in Yellowstone. Considering the exploitation of wildlands in the United States over the past 130 years, it is amazing that Yellowstone has survived and is still a wild place.

While far from perfect, there is little doubt that the US Army and its soldiers played a critical role in preserving America's premier national park and *Watching over Yellowstone.*

*Dan Sholly*
Chief Ranger
Yellowstone National Park
1985–1998

# Preface

Like most historians who write about Yellowstone National Park, I have an emotional affinity for it. I was fortunate enough to be born and grow up in Bozeman, Montana, just ninety miles from its west entrance. Day trips through "the Park" (as if there were any other parks) were a typical family experience. I have seen Old Faithful nearly every year of my life, hiked and camped in the backcountry, and caught countless fish in its lakes and streams. For most of the 1990s, I worked as a "savage" or a non-NPS park employee in the park at Bridge Bay Marina and Lake Lodge while working on my two master's degrees. It was then that the seeds for this project were planted. Always needing to read something, I read Aubrey Haines's work *The Yellowstone Story*, which partially covered the military era. Another year it was all the rage among employees to read Lee Whittlesey's book *Death in Yellowstone*, which also contained stories about the soldiers in the park. Being in graduate school (though committed to writing about another topic for my thesis), I thought there must be more to the story. Graduate school had enlightened me to the idea of looking at a problem from a more "bottom-up" perspective, a concept that I fully embraced on a master's thesis about Fort Ellis, Montana. I knew, having read Haines's and Whittlesey's work, that the same approach could be applied to the military in Yellowstone, so I filed that idea away for a future opportunity.

Even though it took nearly a quarter of a century before that seed would germinate, working in Yellowstone unconsciously helped prepare me for writing this book in other ways. The first year I worked in the park, I was on the front-desk staff at Bridge Bay Marina—in my opinion, one of the choice locations in the park. Well over half the staff had worked there for multiple years, and several people work there still. Everyone loved the park and especially the Lake area. We were a pretty tight group, but I found out later that several other "savages" thought we were a bit elitist. The next year I became the assistant controller at Lake Lodge. During my training I was taught how to do "payouts," when employees quit their job (or were fired) and left the park, receiving their pay in cash rather than waiting for the final paycheck. I distinctly remember the jolt of thinking that people would willingly stop working in the park. However, after talking with the much larger and less tight-knit employees of the lodge, I realized that Yellowstone is not the same for everyone. Some people loved it, others hated it, several grew tired of it, many both loved and hated it at the same time. Talking with my fellow "savages," I learned that some people from more urban areas couldn't handle the isolation, even if they thought they could. One acquaintance from New York City couldn't handle the quiet. Some dislike the demanding demeanor of the tourists. Others didn't like their fellow employees. Their experiences in the park were very different from what I had ever imagined.

I would be lying if I said that I didn't recollect those complaints and experiences as I wrote about the soldiers. I encourage my students to be aware of their own thought processes. Working for a concessionaire, with its large impersonal corporate structure and diverse workforce, certainly had a tone of familiarity to it as I researched the soldiers who worked in the park. Of course, the employees I worked with chose to come to Yellowstone, while for many of the soldiers it was merely another posting, albeit a unique one, over which they had virtually no choice. Yet, the diversity of experiences, the isolation, the friction with tourists, the disenchantment with the job were all familiar and hopefully drove me to ask questions that I might not otherwise have asked.

However, I also tell my students not to lull themselves into a false sense of familiarity. While it is natural to gravitate to the familiar, by doing so, we make the past what we want it to be rather than exploring it on its own terms. The people of the past acted differently, had different morals, and even thought differently than we do today. Common constructs taken for granted by later generations, labels that describe those constructs, and external and internal expectations are unique to place and time. Despite the false feeling of Yellowstone's timelessness, the past is a very different place, and the mindsets and pressures then are not the same as they are today. The historian needs to keep that in mind, especially when researching a place to which they are emotionally drawn as I am to Yellowstone Park.

I think that is true for others as well. Chapter 4 of this work is based mainly on an article that I wrote for the *Montana Magazine of Western History*, published in the fall of 2017. When I discussed it with one person, they commented that it felt "negative"; they had been surprised at finding that the soldiers not only didn't like their jobs but weren't always doing their jobs well. I knew that most of the historians who had studied the army in Yellowstone had sung its praises for bringing some order out of the early chaos of the park and laying the foundation for the National Park Service. All that was true, but the record clearly showed that the soldiers had struggled as well. Many didn't like the park since the duties really weren't part of a soldier's job. Others didn't like the isolation. Some didn't like the "disrespect shown the uniform" by tourists. Others did like their job or their comrades. The rest, perhaps the majority, simply did what they were ordered—as soldiers are wont to do, making the best of the situation. While I wasn't (and currently am not) trying to paint a negative picture of the military experience in the park, I am not "whitewashing" it either. As archaeologist Ken Karsmizki, who excavated several soldier stations in the park, wrote: "Although this part of the history of the U.S. Army in Yellowstone is not the best side of the soldiers' story, a study of the past events does not limit its pursuit to the positive characteristics of the events of the past."[1]

Actually, in my opinion, while I try to be as balanced and fair as possible, the disappointments of the soldiers, their struggles, and their unenthusiastic behavior only serve to emphasize what a sacrifice they made in bringing order to the park. Throughout history soldiers have often found their duties unappealing; they don't always find their posting to their liking; they find their reality vastly different from what they had enlisted for. Yet their country asked them to perform a task for a reason that they may not have been enthusiastic about. That is part of what makes serving in the military special. It requires self-sacrifice. From 1886 to 1918 hundreds of men served in Yellowstone Park and performed duties that truly were greater and more important than some of the duties the country has asked of other soldiers. They may not have realized it at the time, but their sacrifice preserved Yellowstone (not to mention the other national parks). Yet we must remember that it was a sacrifice, and the only way to do that is to recognize their struggles as well as their triumphs. As I sit on the porch of Lake Lodge writing this preface, I fully realize that my experience in and with Yellowstone was made possible only through their sacrifice. If we remember that, in my opinion, that is the "best side" of their story.

# Acknowledgments

No research endeavor is done in a vacuum, and this was no exception. I have had the assistance of numerous people who have helped shape this work. First and foremost, my wife, Aimee, and my children Bridger, Jackson, and Madison have supported my efforts and tolerated my distractions and trips to Yellowstone to perform my research. The faculty and staff of Montana State University Billings have provided the resources and time to complete this work, including a sabbatical in 2017 that allowed me time to focus exclusively on this project. Of particular note are the fantastic staff (especially Samantha Thatcher—the interlibrary loan technician) at the MSUB Library who were able to get the resources I needed; the fantastic staff at the Yellowstone Heritage Center including archivist Anne Foster and Robin Park in the museum curator's office; and the excellent front desk staff at the Yellowstone Park Heritage Center in Gardiner. I especially want to thank the Yellowstone archaeologist, Beth Horton, who granted me access to some of the reports on the soldier stations, which proved invaluable. Lastly, thanks to the reviewers and editorial staff at the University Press of Kansas for their diligent work on the manuscript. Of course, any shortcomings are entirely my own.

# "To Correct and Remedy the Existing State of Things"

Captain Moses Harris arrived at his new command on August 20, 1886. As his company, Troop M of the First United States Cavalry, settled in on the flat below Mammoth Hot Springs, he sought out David W. Wear, the man he was to replace as the acting superintendent of Yellowstone National Park. Harris had traveled with his command from Fort Custer near Hardin, Montana, via train to Billings, on to Livingston, and south to Cinnabar, where they disembarked. From there they marched on foot as their horses had not yet arrived. However, the political road that led Captain Harris and Troop M to Mammoth was much longer and more convoluted. It was a last resort by the government to impose a semblance of order on the nation's first national park, and several people openly hoped that the deployment of troops would fail, ending the national park experiment.

Yellowstone National Park had been created fourteen years earlier, on March 1, 1872, when President Ulysses S. Grant signed the Yellowstone National Park Protection Act into law. The bill was relatively uncontroversial at the time. The Northern Pacific Railroad had lobbied in support of the bill, hoping to capitalize on tourist travel to the West along with its soon-to-be-completed transcontinental railroad. The bill empowered the secretary of the interior to create "such regulations that shall provide for the preservation, from injury or spoliation, of all timber, mineral deposits, natural curiosities, or wonders within said park, and their retention in their natural condition." He could also grant leases "for building purposes for terms not to exceed ten years, of small parcels of ground . . . for the accommodation of visitors." Only Senator Cornelius Cole opposed the bill. "I do not see the reason or propriety of setting apart a large tract of land of that kind," he said during the congressional debate. "The natural curiosities there cannot be interfered with by anything that man can do. The geysers will remain, no matter where the ownership of the land may be, and I do not know why a settler could be excluded." The expected costs of administering the park also concerned him. He wrote to Secretary of the Interior Carl Schurz, claiming that he should "not apply for an appropriation for several years at least."[1]

Cole's concerns were prophetic as Congress failed to appropriate the necessary funds to fulfill the park's mission to "provide for the preservation, from injury or spoliation, of all timber, mineral deposits, natural curiosities within." There was not enough money to even pay the salary of the park's first superintendent, Nathaniel P. Langford, forcing him to keep his job as national bank examiner for the Montana Territory. Only nominal funding was designated in the coming years, but Congress did not see a pressing need for more investment given the political climate of the day. The depression of 1873 stopped the march of the Northern Pacific Railroad across the West and slowed the anticipated travel from the East, giving even less incentive for Congress to financially support the park.

Consequently, for the first ten years of the park's existence, relatively few visitors came through the park, but those who did were remarkably destructive. They vandalized the thermal features by carving their names on them, breaking parts off to take a souvenir specimen home, or throwing everything from soap to tin cans into the geysers or pools. Poachers were rampant in the park and harvested game, sometimes for the food to feed visitors or local families, other times for profit. Buffalo heads could fetch $300 apiece, and elk teeth were particularly valuable. Slowly the annual number of tourists increased, yet Congress was reluctant to increase appropriations for suitable protection of the wonders of the park.[2]

That would change on September 8, 1883, when former President Ulysses S. Grant drove the golden spike into the completed Northern Pacific Railroad. With the completed route the company's long history of promoting Yellowstone Park loomed heavily over the park's administration. The railroad had already reached Livingston, Montana, the year before and started a branch line to the edge of the park. Jay Cooke, the head of the company, promised miners on the northeast corner of the park that he would bring the railroad to them, even if it meant going through the park.[3] The number of tourists was expected to steadily increase and so were the depredations to features and game. Any substantial increase in visitors would strain the limited law enforcement as well as the rudimentary tourist accommodations and facilities. At the same time, obtaining a lease and operating businesses in the park would be more attractive to other entrepreneurs. The first two

"The Nimrod of Yellowstone" by an unknown artist. This illustration was part of an article that appeared in the July 11, 1878, issue of the *Daily Graphic*, highlighting the unrestrained destruction of game in Yellowstone Park. (National Park Service photo)

Lieutenant General Philip Sheridan and party in Yellowstone Park, 1883. *Left to right*: John Schuyler Crosby, Lt. Col. Michael V. Sheridan, Lt. Gen. Philip H. Sheridan, Anson Stager, unidentified, President Arthur, unidentified, unidentified, Robert Todd Lincoln, and George G. Vest. Unidentified men may be Daniel G. Rollins, James F. Gregory, W. P. Clark, W. H. Forwood, and/or George G. Vest, Jr. (Library of Congress)

superintendents, Langford and Philetus Norris, had done an admirable job of administering the park with chronically limited resources, but the landscape would be rapidly changing with the arrival of the railroad.

On April 1, 1882, Norris was replaced as superintendent by Patrick H. Conger, a former US marshal from Iowa. He faced the dual problems of increased visitation and limited means to enforce rules and regulations. A small group of entrepreneurs approached him and proposed a solution. Henry Douglas and Carroll Hobart of North Dakota teamed up with New York financier Rufus Hatch to create the Yellowstone Park Improvement Company (YPIC). Hatch was heavily invested in the Northern Pacific Railroad and had the support of the railroad lobby. They asked Secretary of the Interior Henry Teller for 4,400 acres of leased land in the park in order to run a near monopoly of accommodations and services. Teller asked for Conger's input but was disappointed that the park's new superintendent opposed the lease because it was too large and he feared that granting privileges to a single company would make the public "restive," especially at the bargain price of only two dollars an acre. However, in Secretary Teller's mind, granting a monopoly to the YPIC would make the company responsible for the park's features and protect them "with the least possible expense to the government."[4]

Secretary Teller and Superintendent Conger were not the only ones concerned about the impact of the railroad's arrival. Lieutenant General Philip Sheridan toured the park in the summers of 1881 and 1882. For all his faults, he was a forceful proponent for the park. He had fame and notoriety from the Civil War and the Indian wars in the West and was in line to become the general of the army upon the impending retirement of General Sherman. Sheridan was shocked and dismayed at the wanton slaughter of game animals in the park, and when he learned of the proposed lease to the YPIC, he "regretted exceedingly to learn that the national park had been rented out to private parties." He felt that "improvements in the park should be national, the control of it in the hands of an office of the government." The obstinate general proposed that "if authorized to do so, I will engage to keep out skin hunters and all other hunters, by use of troops from Forts Washakie on the south, Custer on the east, and Ellis on the north, and, if necessary, I can keep sufficient troops in the Park to accomplish this object."[5] He worked successfully at gaining allies including the governor of the Montana Territory, John S. Crosby, Missouri Senator George Vest of the Senate Committee on Territories, and he even invited President Arthur on an expedition through the park in the following year, 1883, so he could see the problems firsthand.

The YPIC lease became a national issue when George Bird Grinnell, the owner and editor of the magazine *Forest and Stream*, made combating the lease a crusade. His worst fear was that the park would become an over-commercialized blight as had happened at Niagara Falls. "The Park is at present all our own. How would the readers like to see it become a second Niagara—a place where one goes only to be fleeced, where patent medicine advertisements stare one in the face, and the beauties of nature have all been defiled by the greed of man?" Together, Grinnell, Sheridan, and especially Vest, became a powerful lobby for the government to find a way to preserve the park without bowing to private commercial interests. The secretary of the interior scrapped the proposed megalease, and the YPIC received only seven smaller leases near important features. They began construction of the National Hotel near Mammoth Hot Springs as well as other hotels at various locations. However, Superintendent Conger's resistance to the proposed massive lease created a relationship of animosity between him and the concessionaires that continued for the rest of his tenure.[6]

"Desecration of our national parks—A scene that may be witnessed if the Yellowstone Park is leased to speculators." Wood engraving by W. A. Rogers published in *Harper's Weekly* 27 (January 20, 1883), 46. (Library of Congress)

The problem of policing the park remained a critical issue as depredations continued nearly unabated. Congress considered extending the park and putting it entirely in the legal jurisdiction of the Montana territorial courts, and Wyoming's US attorney general sought permission to extend the jurisdiction of that territory's courts over the park as well. The quagmire led Senator Vest to form a select committee of senators to investigate, but he also asked the secretary of the interior to "call upon the proper military authorities for such force as may be necessary" to protect the park and its natural wonders. Again, Congress failed to act, and Rep. Anson McCook of

New York attempted to amend the budget for the park and allow the secretary of the interior to call upon the secretary of war for troops, just as General Sheridan had suggested. The people causing the problems in the park "have a profound respect for the power of the General Government as represented by the officers and men of the Army," claimed McCook during the debate. He found a surprising ally in Rep. James Blount of Georgia. A conservative Democrat and former Confederate officer, Blount had witnessed firsthand the use of troops as constables during Reconstruction. He was a rabid white supremacist and openly criticized the racial policies of the federal government during Reconstruction, particularly the US Army's enforcement of them.[7] His support for using the army to patrol and enforce laws in Yellowstone, therefore, is quite impressive. Undoubtedly, he could attest to the effectiveness of troops in such duty, but his support demonstrates that his previous criticisms were based on racial ideology more than any ideological position he held regarding the use of the military for enforcing constitutional authority.

Other politicians, particularly Democrats, were not so flexible in their thinking regarding the use of soldiers to enforce civilian laws. Occasionally troops had been used in such a way, the most protracted period being during Reconstruction and most recently during the railway strike of 1877. Southern Democrats were particularly bitter regarding the army's role during Reconstruction. Northern Democrats disliked the fact that the army was called into labor strife, such as the strike in 1877, in the name of "law and order" but seemingly always on the side of business against workers. Neither soldiers nor officers enjoyed such duty either. Not only was it not seen as a soldier's duty, but it also created internal conflicts. Officers did not like the confused chain of command that resulted from local politicians demanding their services, and enlisted men often sympathized more with the laboring classes than management. In the south both officers and enlisted men frequently disagreed with the racial policies they had to enforce. All of this led Congress to severely limit the army's ability to enforce civilian law with the Posse Comitatus Act of 1878.[8] The fact that a southern Democrat like Blount and a northern Republican like McCook would agree on using the troops in the park demonstrates how desperate the situation in the park had become.

McCook's amendment failed to pass, but the bill's several other revisions paved the way for the army to take over the park's administration at a later date. Senator Vest added a provision that paid the superintendent and ten assistant superintendents to actively patrol the park. The number, minimal for such a large area, acknowledged the growing need to enforce the laws and regulations. Yet, recognizing the herculean task, the bill also stipulated that the secretary of the interior could request the secretary of war to "make the necessary details of troops to prevent trespassers or intruders from entering the park for the purpose of destroying the game or objects of curiosity therein, or for any other purpose prohibited by law, and to remove such persons from the park if found therein." Therefore, a safety net for the park existed in which, if the duties of preserving and protecting the park proved too much for the Department of the Interior, it could seek the aid of the War Department. Still, many members of Congress were growing impatient with the park idea in general, and a minority even advocated returning the whole of it back to the territories or selling it off entirely.[9] The immediate question seemed settled when the sundry bill passed, but Congress had done little more than kick the proverbial can down the road for a few more years. The Department of the Interior now had at least some resources to administer the park and did not need to request the army's help just yet. Since there was no sunset clause in the amendment that authorized the request of troops, the request could come at any time in the future. Until then, eleven people were sanctioned to patrol the park and enforce the laws.

However, Conger's assistant superintendents were mostly political appointees from the East, ill-suited for the rugged conditions in Yellowstone. The acerbic relationship between Conger and the concessionaires continued to sour as the YPIC was slowly sliding into bankruptcy. The situation became bad enough that the acting secretary of the interior, M. L. Joslyn, sent an agent from the General Land Office to investigate the management of the park. His report was scathing. He concluded that Conger "either failed to comprehend the importance of the duties of this office or had intentionally disregarded the same."[10] For his part, Conger denied the allegations and shifted the blame back to Congress, claiming that the laws and the apparatus for enforcing them were entirely inadequate. He told his superiors that "some legislation is needed immediately to correct and remedy the existing state of things." Yet criticism steadily grew in both Washington and in the territories around the park. Montana Territorial Governor John Crosby noted that the assistant superintendents were as useful as "a Sioux Indian would be in charge of a locomotive." The Wyoming territorial legislature simply took matters into its own hands by extending its own laws into the park and giving the governor the authority to appoint judges and constables to oversee it.[11]

Wanton killing of park game openly continued unabated despite the best efforts of the premilitary superintendents as shown by this 1880 photo of numerous elk carcasses at the train station just outside the park. (Yellowstone National Park Museum Collection)

Things changed in the fall of 1884 when the secretary of the interior asked Conger for his resignation and replaced him with the political appointee Robert E. Carpenter. The new superintendent joined forces with the concessionaires to resurrect the idea of large-scale leases. The Yellowstone Park Improvement Company had gone bankrupt in the spring and large leases could provide the ability to reap the profits needed to get the company out of receivership. However, Carpenter's tenure in the park was short: he was quickly replaced by David W. Wear after the Cleveland administration took office.

The newly seated 49th Congress finally investigated the park management with a special House committee. The new secretary of the interior, Lucius Quintus Cincinnatus Lamar, ran his own concurrent investigation as well. Both reports noted that Wyoming's legal jurisdiction over the park was problematic at best. Since the judges could personally keep the fines they imposed, there was the temptation of corruption. That resulted in "ridiculous"

Senator George Vest, D-Missouri. (Library of Congress)

and "Draconian" enforcement of the park regulations. The judges also demonstrated their gross incompetence. Notably, Lewis E. Payson, a sitting US representative and former judge from Illinois, was accused of a minor infraction within the park and was brought before one of the Wyoming justices of the peace. The accused had to repeatedly clarify legal procedures for the judge, who demonstrated his apparent incompetence. The Interior Department's report advocated the nullification of the Wyoming statutes claiming authority over the park and the imposition of federal control by Congress.[12] Wyoming conceded before the US government could act by repealing its law on March 10, 1886, leaving the park once again entirely under federal control.

Senator Vest once again attempted to introduce a bill to strengthen the superintendent's ability to enforce the rules and regulations of the park. The reports of both the House and the Interior Department noted that Wear had replaced the incompetent assistant superintendents with "experienced mountain men to enforce the laws," often to excellent effect. However, the long shadow of the previous misadministration loomed large, and opposition to the park idea as a whole was steadily growing, especially in the House of Representatives. The House Committee on Appropriations reduced the budget for the park from $40,000 to $20,000 for the fiscal year ending in June of 1887. That effectively eliminated the salaries of the superintendent and his assistant superintendents, essentially forcing the secretary of the interior to enact the provisions of the 1883 bill that allowed him to seek help from the secretary of war.[13] Efforts by Secretary Lamar and Senator Vest retained the budget at $40,000 in the Senate version of the bill, but the conference committee reduced the sum to $20,000.

When the House and Senate debated the bill for final approval, the deliberations were spirited. Some wanted to do away with the park entirely. Others thought that military control was the best and most economical answer. Senator Vest, who had previously supported military control of the park in 1882, now felt that those who supported the use of soldiers in the park were the instruments of the railroads and wanted to exploit it. Those who were supporting the use of army troops in Yellowstone had previously supported an earlier bill to either grant a railroad easement through the northern part of the park or remove the northern part of the park altogether, giving it entirely to the railroad. Vest had strongly opposed those efforts and gained powerful enemies who were now all but forcing the secretary of the interior to seek military aid. In addition, ideologically Vest had always been a strong advocate of states' rights, even before the Civil War and especially during the Missouri secession crisis; during the war he had served in both houses of the Confederate national legislature.[14] His natural inclinations, therefore, probably lay with limited use of federal authority over local control whenever possible.

As he fought against the military administration of the park, Vest claimed the soldiers were not trained for the type and rigors of work needed in Yellowstone's isolated backcountry. "It requires mountaineers, men experienced in the mountains," Vest contended. "Soldiers would be more than useless for that sort of work." Beyond their lack of training and skill, he questioned the morality of the soldiers, stating that they "would allow anybody to go in there and kill game and destroy the objects of curiosity" because "we know the character of the men in the regular Army." Turning control of the park over to the army, he now believed, would mean "virtually an end of the Yellowstone National Park." Frustrated at the whole debate, he lambasted his fellow senators about their "cheap talk thrown in here for the purpose of prejudicing the public against the Yellowstone National Park." Sensing defeat, he concluded that "if the house conferees are able to hold their position and to cut off these salaries . . . and put this park into the hands of the

Captain Moses Harris and Company M of the First United States Cavalry arriving at Mammoth Hot Springs, beginning the military administration of Yellowstone National Park, August 1886. Official reports indicate that the soldiers arrived before their horses, so this photograph probably depicts the unit a few days after their official arrival. (National Park Service photo)

military, it is but another form for repealing the act which created the park itself."[15]

In the end Senator Vest failed to maintain civilian control of the park as the bill passed on August 4, 1886, with the reduced sum. Two days later the secretary of the interior, unable to pay the salaries of park officials, had little choice but to formally request the help of the secretary of war as provided for in the bill of 1883. The request was then forwarded to the original champion of the cause, Lt. Gen. Philip Sheridan, now the top general of the United States Army. He ordered that Troop M of the First United States Cavalry with "Captain Moses Harris commanding—station Fort Custer, M.T.—be ordered to perform the duties in Yellowstone National Park that recently devolved upon the Superintendent of Yellowstone National Park and his assistants" with Special Order No. 79 from the headquarters of the Department of Dakota.[16]

After he arrived, Captain Harris toured the park with former Superintendent Wear, not knowing how long his troops would be stationed in the park. It was unclear even whether they were to winter in the park or return to Fort

Custer at the end of the summer. Nobody knew when, or whether, Congress would reverse course again and allow the return of the park to civilian control. In the end a full generation passed before the army would finally retreat from the park. It was a time of great transformation not only for Yellowstone but also the army. During the time that the military administered Yellowstone, the Indian Wars concluded and America became an imperial power—fighting wars in Cuba and two in the Philippines, putting down the Boxer Rebellion in China, invading Mexico to chase Pancho Villa, and entering World War I. During the time that the army permanently stationed troops in Yellowstone, they also took and relinquished control of Yosemite, Sequoia, Grant, and Glacier National Parks. The army that left the park in 1918 did not resemble the troops that Harris marched into Mammoth Hot Springs in 1886 in either organization or mission.

The stability brought by the military was tangible and historians have noted as much in the studies of the military era in Yellowstone Park. They have focused on a "top-down" perspective, primarily examining the letters and records of commanding officers and their successful efforts at creating an administrative foundation for the future of the National Park Service. Most studies provide at least anecdotal stories about soldier life in the park, but few examine in detail or analyze the true experience of the common soldier in the park and their role in the development of the park.[17] While the top-down approach of examining the military years in Yellowstone highlights the administrative success, a "bottom up" or social history, provides a more complete picture of the army's experience in the park by highlighting the trials the soldiers faced, their successes, and the impact they had on developing the foundations for the National Park Service ranger program.

The study of the US military through a social-history lens has yielded significant advances in our understanding of the relationship between those who serve in the armed forces and society at large, and such a viewpoint promises to be equally beneficial in analyzing the military in Yellowstone. While the widespread perception of the army has promoted an idealized image of the American soldier as representative of a cross section of society at any given time, that has rarely been the case. Even in times of conscription during a war, the wealthy have used paid substitutes, bounties, and deferments to avoid service. Rarely has the army represented the racial and social makeup of the country. During times of peace, the army was more representative of the lower socioeconomic classes than of general society. Recent works in the social history of the soldiers in society have produced significant scholarship regarding the implications of this, particularly during times of war. Many questions that historians have asked are pertinent to military experience in Yellowstone and the other national parks that they would administer. Who were the soldiers, and why had they enlisted in the army? What were the normative forces that created their society, and how did they interact with one another? What values did the soldiers embrace, and how did they display them? How did they understand and execute their mission, especially one for which they had not trained? How did they interact with society, particularly in a place such as Yellowstone where they were in such close contact not only with the public but also most commonly the social elite? Answering these questions deepens our understanding of the military experience in Yellowstone Park.

As the historian Richard Kohn reminds us, "There have been many different military forces in our history, most of which have changed over the course of their existence," and scholarship generally has focused on the rise and impact of large forces during times of war.[18] The peacetime military is insufficiently studied, and the military between the end of the Indian Wars and the advent of World War I especially so. Examining the soldier's experience in Yellowstone provides insight into this period of the army's history, as it transitioned from a force that had traditionally fought only on the North American continent to an instrument of the country's global ambitions. Moreover, the rapid change wrought by the industrialization of America spurred the Progressive Movement's ideas of scientific management, conservation, emphasis on greater participatory democracy, and weakening of the Victorian social hierarchy. The crucible of Yellowstone Park, where soldiers and wealthy tourists were in close proximity and even paradoxical relationships, provides a window into the military's relationship with society and the changes America was experiencing at the time.

Studying the ordinary soldier's experience is not always easy. In the army overall, and the unit stations in the Yellowstone in particular, the written sources are often biased toward the much smaller and more elite officer class than the more massive enlisted ranks. In the late Victorian era officers fancied themselves men of letters and learning, publishing their accounts in magazines and newspapers of the time. Even when Frederic Remington visited the park, his writings focused more on interactions with the officers, keeping the enlisted men in the background. It is not that these sources are not valuable, as they do give impressions of enlisted men, at least through the eyes of their commanders, but orders, circulars, and reports provide a glimpse into the world of the ordinary soldier. Inspection reports, while they often focus on deficiencies, are particularly insightful and deliver valuable data about the soldier's world.

Rich source material for enlisted men and their society is found in the court-martial cases of soldiers who violated the military code of conduct. Summary courts-martial, or those for minor offenses, list charges and the specifics of cases and provide a window into much of the less "official" behavior of the soldiers. The general court-martial cases are those of more serious offenses and have recorded testimony that is exceptionally valuable and can be mined for details about the soldiers' experience. Using them as case studies, historians can see how people interacted with one another, examine their complicated relationships, examine how they related with their social setting, and from there understand better the experience of people who rarely left significant written records. The method has been pioneered by historians of early-modern Europe to great effect in what is known as "microhistory," but it has not yet been fully realized by historians of the United States in general or the United States' military specifically.[19]

Taken together and combined with the writings of local civilians around the park and tourists within it, a picture emerges that is more nuanced than the traditional history of the military era in Yellowstone. The soldiers, who had no training for the duties they were asked to perform, faced a prodigious task. Often isolated from officers and the official command structure, they performed their assigned duties as best they could in an often hostile physical and social environment. Their society, based on order and discipline, provided much of what the park needed. At the same time, the unique context of the park created situations when that order and discipline broke down. There was a complex mixture of men in the army who sometimes embraced their mission and at other times were critical of it, but perhaps were most often uninterested. As the archaeologist Ken Karsmizki, who excavated several of the soldier stations in the park, noted, "Although this part of the history of the U.S. Army in Yellowstone is not the best side of the soldiers' story, a study of the past events does not limit its pursuit to the positive characteristics of the events of the past."[20]

Nonetheless, the soldiers performed their duties as they understood them. The masculine values embraced by the soldiers promoted confrontation, both with tourists and with each other when isolated from the watchful eyes of the commanders. It became clear early on to both the Department of War and the Department of the Interior that the soldiers were an imperfect solution to park management. The military experience as seen through the soldiers' eyes highlights their inadequacies. Still, understanding those shortfalls is important as it reveals what was needed for the more permanent solution to park management. The army could and did meet many needs of the park at the turn of the century, creating the basis of law enforcement and protecting its wonders. But in the end, when the army retreated from Yellowstone in 1918, its successor, the National Park Service, was shaped by the successes of the military superintendents. The National Park Service's ranger corps, however, was equally shaped by both the success and the struggles of the soldiers who had served in the park for over a generation.

CHAPTER ONE

# "The Work Is Not a Military Duty"

## The Constabulary Soldier in Yellowstone Park

As Capt. Moses Harris surveyed his new command in 1886, he faced several issues. Several forest fires were ravaging the park: "The most destructive one . . . [was] in full view from the Mammoth Hot Springs Hotel and about seven miles distant." He noted that "this fire was started maliciously," and he suspected that many other fires were started by "unscrupulous hunters, who, being prevented from hunting the Park, resorted to this method of driving the game beyond the Park limits." Other fires "were probably caused by the carelessness of camping parties." He lamented that the park was surrounded by "all sorts of worthless and disreputable characters" and that his men needed to be constantly "watching any suspected parties" who might be poaching because they were visiting "the portions of the Park not frequented by ordinary tourists." The tourist areas also needed "watchful supervision" because, as he could personally attest, "without exaggeration . . . not one of the notable geyser formations in the Park has escaped mutilation or defacement in some form." He concluded that the current rules and regulations, issued in 1881, were simply "no longer applicable under the changed conditions of the Park."[1]

Bringing order from the chaos would be the charge of the troops under his command. Yet the duties were more constabulary in nature than martial. The US Cavalry trained for open field maneuvers against a determined military foe with a similar mindset. "It is generally expected of cavalry," the *Cavalry Drill Regulations,* the official drill manual for the cavalry stated, "to be bold and daring. . . . A sudden and bold charge which surprises the enemy is not only successful but the loss is small in proportion to its success." Drills were organized by squad (five to eight men), platoon (four to six squads or twenty to forty-eight men), the troop or company (two to three platoons or 40 to 144 men), the squadron (two to four troops or 80 to 576 men), the regiment (three squadrons of over 240 to 1,728 men), and the division (three or more regiments). Even individual horsemanship drills were done in units no smaller than a squad. The skilled use of the carbine, pistol, and saber was crucial for combat since the object of cavalry was "to ride the enemy down and complete his overthrow with the saber and pistol."[2] The soldiers of Troop M, First United States Cavalry, would not find much of their training effective in preparing them for duty in the park. Training manuals do not refer to fighting forest fires, stalking individual poachers in pairs or groups of three, or policing and protecting popular tourist attractions. In short, Harris's command would need to learn a new set of skills and develop a new attitude to meet the situations they encountered.

Even beyond the official skills needed to enforce park regulations, the troopers' identity and normative behaviors, which to that point were centered on being soldiers, would need to be adjusted to something more similar to that of police officers. This was no ordinary deployment, and even so any deployment of troops requires an adjustment that often lasts several weeks before the unit can sustain an effective operation. The goal of regular military training is to automate the unit as much as possible through drills to make the transition as smooth as possible, but routines are nonetheless disrupted and unit relationships often change.[3] But for the troops stationed in Yellowstone throughout the military years, this adjustment was compounded by adjusting to a mission for which they had not trained and for which the cavalry did not necessarily have the ideal set of primary or transferable skills. In this new environment with a distinctive mission, they had to learn an entirely new skill set and negotiate a modified self and social identity shaped by both their intrapersonal attitudes and the external social forces unique to the park.

By 1886 Troop M of the First United States Cavalry had moved around the West before their deployment to the park. After nearly thirty years in various posts along the Pacific coast, they moved to Arizona to fight the Apaches in 1881 before being stationed at the Presidio along the San Francisco Bay in 1882. In June of 1884, they were moved to Fort Custer near modern-day Hardin, Montana. There they remained until August 1886 when Captain Harris took them to Yellowstone Park with a mission fundamentally different from both the combat with Apaches or garrison duties at the Presidio or Fort Custer. Each transfer of station caused significant transitions when routines, habits, and behaviors changed as the soldiers underwent substantial cognitive, social, and emotional challenges. Some transitions required more

Stereoscopic view of the first military camp near the Liberty Cap at Mammoth Hot Springs shortly after Captain Harris's arrival in 1886. By the fall of that year, it became clear that the army would have a long-term presence in the park, and construction began on more permanent accommodations. (Library of Congress)

extended periods than others, but even in a modern context, deployments and transfers can undermine military effectiveness for several weeks until new habits and norms are established.[4]

The deployment to the park would be more complex and take greater individual efforts as the troop entered a location without an established physical fort that required the specific daily "garrison duties." The soldiers were housed in tents at Mammoth or one of the six separate posts throughout the park, which amounted to little more than small log cabins. How long their deployment would last was also unclear, further hindering the soldiers' ability to establish new routines and norms quickly. By September Captain Harris sought clarification on whether his command would be spending the

Camp Sheridan circa 1900. Even though this photograph dates from a much later period, by the fall of 1886, the army had begun to construct more permanent accommodations for the park garrison. Construction of the new post, named Fort Yellowstone, began in 1891, but the buildings of the original Camp Sheridan continued to be used. (National Park Service photo)

winter in the park. He finally was directed to construct "such temporary shelter for the command as may be necessary for the comfort of the troops."[5]

The transition to the park permeated all levels of Troop M. Fort Custer, which housed four companies of cavalry and two of infantry, was a large and busy place with over three hundred soldiers and one hundred buildings. Garrison duties required at the post followed a well-established routine commensurate with such a large post. In addition, social interactions were dictated by the context of the post. Enlisted men lived in quarters that housed entire companies of over sixty men. They could enjoy all the amenities of an established post, including a canteen and regular amusement opportunities such as the post baseball team, the Fort Custer Comic Opera and Burlesque Co., and various fraternal societies such as the Masonic Lodge, the Maennerchor Club, the Custer Social Club, the Ancient Order of Hibernians, and the Independent Order of Good Templars.[6] Officers lived with their families in well-appointed quarters and socialized with each other at dinners, dances, and outings. The routine life at Fort Custer was probably similar in many respects to that of their stationing at the Presidio in San Francisco, though certainly the city there provided many more off-duty opportunities and temptations than did the plains of southeastern Montana.

In the early days of Troop M's station in Yellowstone, neither officers nor enlisted men enjoyed any of these comforts, though some would come in time. In essence, the troop left Fort Custer on what would appear to be a typical field deployment, albeit with a rather unique mission. The routine of garrison duties disrupted, engaging in an exceptional mission for which they had not trained or drilled, the soldiers were forced to establish new routines during their time of transition. While field maneuvers would be familiar from their training, their social interactions with each other were dictated by the context of the assignment. From a large barracks housing dozens of men, the enlisted men found themselves living in tents with four to six other men. Some men found themselves stationed at the six isolated cabin outposts in small groups of usually fewer than four, removed at a considerable distance from the rest of the command.

Officers' social routines differed significantly from their previous station at Fort Custer. Even though historians have generally seen Captain Harris in a favorable light since he established effective management over the chaos heretofore rampant in the park, his fellow officers and men thought he was "a most disagreeable man" who "had no friends [in the troop], but all were his enemies." He rarely walked alone at night "for fear someone would attack him." Even the other officers only spoke to him regarding official business, never informally or about things other than their immediate mission.[7] Things did not change substantially once the new, crude buildings were constructed in the fall of 1886. The dinners and social gatherings of officers' families at Fort Custer became a distant memory and would take time to reestablish themselves as the command grew.

The small one-company outpost took shape over the late fall and winter of 1886–1887 and was named Camp Sheridan. The social atmosphere evolved congruently with the post. A far cry from the Presidio or Fort Custer, the small camp would have to develop its own unique social norms and routines. As it became clear that the assignment would be rather long term it also required significant mental adjustment by both officers and enlisted men. The park mission required them to assume a set of occupational tasks and an identity entirely different from that of a soldier. Rather than fighting cavalrymen, the soldiers became a constabulary force whose mission was more similar to that of police officers tasked with law enforcement or laborers who fought wildfires. The officers, especially the commanding officer, also had the additional tasks of managing the government leases of the concessionaires and creating a coherent game management policy that included monitoring and managing game and fish. Of course, much of the labor for these policies would be provided by the enlisted men, again, far outside what they had been trained for.

The immediate experience of the enlisted men of Troop M had been in fighting the Apaches in the Southwest, and their mental outlook reinforced the general self-identity of many if not most enlisted men, especially those who had reenlisted or were noncommissioned officers. They identified themselves as artisans, skilled in the art of war and soldiering. Rather than tools that produced material goods, they used arms in specific ways that others could not. Unlike the public at large, many soldiers perceived themselves as proficient craftsmen.[8] They saw manual labor as beneath their status and felt free to openly complain if they were relegated to nothing more than government laborers.

Private James Purvis, stationed with the First Cavalry at Fort Custer, complained about soldiers doing excessive manual labor. By the mid-1880s, the army's mission of Indian fighting was waning. Purvis was keenly aware of this trend as he despondently noted that "if there have been no battles to fight of later years . . . the soldiers of the Regular Army have not been idle. They have performed a vast amount of manual and clerical labor," which he lamented had made soldiers "less skilled in the use of the rifle." Four months before Troop M was deployed to the park, he objected to officers trying to make of soldiers "laborers when they are supposed to represent soldiery." He added that it would be best if the army hired "enough [civilian] laborers to do all of the work of a post. . . . The objection to labor on the part of a soldier is not on account of laziness or a dislike for work, but simply because it is not his profession." If a soldier continues to perform labor tasks, according to Private Purvis, "he loses pride, and after a little while he is neither soldier nor laborer."[9] In other words, if a soldier was too much removed from his trained skill, he lost his identity.

In Yellowstone the soldiers were required to perform duties that were not, as Purvis would state, "soldiery," and they would likely have sympathized with his assessment. In 1890 Capt. Frazier Boutelle, Harris's successor, explicitly stated such. He noted two major duties in the park. "It is probably generally understood that the troops in the Park are engaged in the protection of the curiosities," but he continued that the protection "cuts so small a figure compared with the work on fires as not to be worth mentioning." Indeed, the soldiers in the park found themselves in a situation where their training and skills were called upon in ways not typical for the army. "The work is probably not a military duty and certainly not desirable." He did, however, note that the army's main attribute was crucial in fighting fires in the park since "none other than thoroughly organized and disciplined men could be called upon to ride all night and fight a fire all the next day, as has been done and done cheerfully." Whether Boutelle actually had the pulse of his men's morale or was merely putting a good face on things, his admission that the command was outside of its traditional training is quite telling. A park tourist guide written by G. L. Henderson had a different take on the situation. He noted that "the soldiers do not like the new function of preserving a national park. They say it is not a soldier's work."[10]

Even officers were not immune from grumbling about being assigned park duty. "I was selected for [park duty] without being consulted and came here against my wish," Boutelle complained to the secretary of the interior. However, he decided to make the best of the situation as a good soldier would. "My selection may have been unfortunate but being here I take great interest in my work, and as has been the rule of my life, do as well as I can." Still, the job was not soldiering and neither enlisted men nor officers were practicing their chosen profession or skill. While people, especially enlisted men, may have had a variety of motivations to enlist, their expectations after enlistment focused mainly on martial pursuits. The organizational higher command also wanted soldiers to preserve their soldierly skills. Maintaining the balance between military preparedness and performing the unusual duties in the park became a constant struggle. Annual inspections mentioned the troops' need for more military drill, and as early as 1889 even Captain Harris noted that the park's unique duties resulted in an "impairment of military efficacy in the force so employed." The problem never fully resolved itself over the army's tenure in the park. Nearly two decades later, Colonel S. M. B. Young claimed that "the majority [of soldiers] . . . appear to resent being required to sub serve both military interests and the interests of the park."[11]

Even when the soldiers engaged in drills to keep their martial skills sharp, they could be called away at a moment's notice. On July 10, 1893, Lieutenant Nance was drilling the troops at Mammoth Hot Springs when at about 1:20 p.m. the soldiers at the Norris Soldier Station telegrammed that they had spotted a fire and "needed a half-dozen men to help extinguish it." Captain

Boutelle, the post commander, "immediately stopped drill" and sent a sergeant and six men to the scene. He then received a supplementary telegram "saying the fire was beyond control"; he "ordered the balance of the troop to start at once, and ordered Capt. Scott down from the Lower Basin with his troop."[12] If the troops identified themselves as soldiers first, beyond the rapid deployment at a moment's notice, leaving a military drill for mere "labor" duty was probably not entirely welcome even as a break from the routine.

Firefighting was perhaps the most laborious and challenging of all the tasks the soldiers were asked to perform. "The seriousness of a fire here can only be understood by those who have observed the almost impenetrable thickness of the pine forests with their dense masses of fallen and decaying trees," wrote Boutelle.[13] Worse yet, the cavalryman's training did not directly address fire suppression, although some secondary skills, primarily organization, teamwork, and the ability to follow orders, certainly were assets. Still, the labor was backbreaking, especially at high altitude. Captain Boutelle described it in colorful detail.

> A detachment of Troop K, First Cavalry, left this post at half-past 1 o'clock one morning in August and by 6 o'clock was at a point in Gibbon Canyon 28 miles away, where it joined a detachment of Troop A, First Cavalry, which had been at work all the previous day on a fire on top of one of the sides of Gibbon Canyon. Climbing to the fire was so severe that two men had epileptic fits from the effort. The fire was in the timber and the ground covered with fallen dry trees. It took me just an hour to walk around it in making an examination with a view to determining whether it was possible to do anything with it. Concluding that it was worth the trial, I called up all available men—twenty-nine in number—and by night a clearing was made entirely around the fire. All combustible matter was scraped away to the earth. The fire was surrounded and controlled. There was no water on the height, and the only way to do anything was to keep the fire within bounds and let the interior burn out. High winds prevailed almost every afternoon while this fire was burning, and at times the flames would jump the cut-off and get beyond control, but as soon as the wind subsided another cut was made, and at the end of three weeks the fire was out.[14]

Not only were the troops inadequately trained, they did not have the appropriate implements as they were not part of the typical cavalryman's kit. The "work was doubly hard from the want of proper tools," Boutelle added. "Up to a late date last season there was no fire equipment in the Park. The

Fires were particularly challenging to put out in early Yellowstone with its rugged terrain and thick undergrowth as this photo from the early twentieth century shows. (Yellowstone National Park Museum Collection)

few axes and shovels supplied the troops for garrison purposes were the only tools available." The previous year he had requested folding rubber buckets, axes, shovels, and a water wagon to bring water to fires distant from the rivers and stream. Yet, it was not acted upon by either the War Department or the Department of the Interior the next year when he had to repeat "my recommendation of last year, that there be supplied at least two tanks and the necessary number of draught animals for the transportation of water." He had to point out that "it very often happens that fires get into the dead roots of trees where it cannot be reached by shovels or axes. Such fires have to be watched for days or until burned out, while a few buckets of water would extinguish them at once." A water wagon would be especially useful fighting fires at "too great a distance from streams for the water to [be] carried by hand" in buckets, which he also did not have.[15]

The lack of attention by the Interior Department was unfortunate as the 1890 fire season was particularly difficult and tested the army to its limits. "Last season," wrote Boutelle, "was probably the most dry known in the history of Montana and Wyoming. Forest fires raged uncontrolled on every side of the Park and destroyed millions of acres of valuable timber."[16] Whether started by nature, careless campers, or poachers, nothing seemed to stop them. The *Helena Independent* lauded Captain Boutelle for putting all the men under his command into fighting the fires, even calling on the road building crews from the Army Corps of Engineers. The effort was herculean and Mother Nature did not help. One fire even "jumped [the Yellowstone River] where it was 300 yards wide." A fire in the northern part of the park swelled when "one of those Rocky Mountain gales that frequently sweep down from the snow-clad pyramid . . . swept [the fire] down the Yellowstone Valley, dispersing it over a continent . . . with resistless fury, leaving a charred desert in its wake." Another fire along the Madison River "shot over every gap and barrier that the soldiers and road builders had worked so hard for days to set up." The reporter felt for the soldiers. "These poor devils, who are fighting these fires, ruin suits of clothes every day that they are engaged in the thankless task of preserving the evergreen glades of Wonderland." Beyond that, the job was dangerous. "When one of these mountain gales leaps into a fire all that man can do is flee from its path and wait until the wind exhausts itself."[17]

The toll on the soldiers of fighting the fires was extreme. "I had exhausted all men and implements under my control," Boutelle wrote the secretary of the interior. As the fires raged on, he again renewed his pleas for the necessary equipment. "On the 27th of July, I telegraphed to the Interior Department for permission to purchase buckets and axes for use in extinguishing fires," but he received no response while the fires continued their fury. He vented his frustration to a party of tourists, exclaiming that "I didn't know what I should do . . . and was afraid that the Park would burn in spite of every possible effort." Despairingly, he added that "I had applied for rubber buckets and had failed to get them; that I supposed the Secretary [of the Interior] had not funds." After expressing his vexations, one gentleman in the party, a "Mr. J. Lewis, of Mauchunk, Pa., exclaimed that 'if this great United States government or the Secretary of the Interior has not money to buy you a few rubber buckets for the protection of this wonderful and beautiful country, I have.'" He handed Boutelle $40 on the spot, and "in three days I was supplied with two dozen buckets, which were of incalculable service during the remainder of the season." In his report to the secretary of the interior, Boutelle cathartically added: "Would that Congress would take such an interest in the protection of the Park before it is too late."[18]

Early "tramping" campers in Yellowstone, date unknown. During the military era, tourists staying in the park fell into three categories. The hotel tourists were the most wealthy and could afford the posh accommodations. The next level of tourists stayed in one of the many "permanent" camps, such as the Wylie or Shaw & Powell camps. The least regulated visitors stayed in roadside camps such as this. Unsupervised, they often violated park rules, particularly with regard to campfires. (National Park Service photo)

The best way to fight forest fires was to prevent as many as possible from starting in the first place. One of the more common sources was the careless use of campfires. To prevent these from igniting the timber, soldiers stationed around the park would patrol the roads in their assigned region, "carrying with them a bucket and a shovel with which to thoroughly extinguish any smoldering embers that may be found in the abandoned camps of tourists." Again, cleaning up after careless tourists could hardly be considered a soldier's traditional duties, but it was one that certainly was necessary to prevent having to fight large fires. These patrols would "continue on their way until they [met] similar patrols from the neighboring station when after a short halt, they retraced their steps in the afternoon to their own proper home." The monotonous routine nevertheless produced "good results" according to commanders. If campers were still present near any fire violations arrests were "promptly made . . . with the result of making subsequent parties more careful."[19]

Confronting a careless tourist was easier than confronting many of the locals living around the park, who used fire as a weapon against the government's restrictions on their perceived interests. Even when Captain Harris brought the first troops into the park, he noted that outgoing Superintendent Wear claimed that at least one "fire was started maliciously by some of his personal enemies," though Harris could not independently verify that. When Congress debated segregating the northern portion of the park for a railroad line to Cooke City and the military acting superintendent Captain Boutelle openly opposed it, rumor had it that many locals would retaliate, claiming that "they would burn over the entire Park." Boutelle admitted that "there are men in the country of just such character, yet I have small fear that they will actually carry out their threats." However, local poachers had no compunctions about starting fires intentionally to continue their practice of hunting the park's game. These were "unscrupulous hunters, who, being prevented from hunting in the Park, resort to this method of driving the game beyond the Park limits."[20] The fires may also have been in retaliation for interfering in hunting, such as one likely started by a "Thomas Garfield" in 1889 near Norris Hot Springs after he had been expelled earlier for trapping beaver.[21] If he started the fire, it would be located too far in the interior to drive game beyond the park boundaries. In addition, his modus operandi was trapping not hunting. The fire, therefore, should best be seen as a type of revenge against the soldiers and military administration.

Resistance to the military was nearly immediate by many local residents. "From what I can learn," reported Captain Harris, "the Park, until recent years, was considered by many in the neighborhood as little else than a fine hunting ground." The infringement of local access to the park for hunting or other activities that locals deemed their natural right spurred resistance to the military's ability to protect the game. As late as 1897, Acting Superintendent Capt. George Anderson complained that "a certain sentiment of hostility toward the Park and of antagonism toward efforts of the authorities to protect the wild animals from destruction has existed and continues to exist among the ranchers and people of the settlements near the park boundaries." The conflict between the army and the resident populace was born at a time when the idea of conservation was only starting to be discussed. Progressive ideas of restricting use with scientific management for the greater good or even simple preservation ran counter to the traditions of local use. "This feeling of hostility," added Captain Anderson, "seems to be due to the idea, which prevails widely, that a reservation of any park of the public domain for the perpetual benefit of the whole people is an invasion and an abridgment of the private rights of the people of the adjoining region."[22] The antagonistic relationship with much of the populace brought the soldiers directly into conflict with local citizens, an "enemy" for whom they had no training.

The cavalry's training in unit tactics and deployment also provided little or no experience in the cat-and-mouse game that poachers played with the soldiers. Even with larger numbers, between one and four companies of soldiers (64 and 356 men at ideal strength), Yellowstone's vast and isolated wilderness could not be easily patrolled, and the long borders were frequently crossed without detection. In fact, the army's lack of training and skill forced the commanders to hire civilian scouts to compensate for the soldiers' lack of training. These scouts "were accustomed to the mountains," knew the terrain, and had a similar skill set to that of the poachers. In 1898 the military acting superintendent vented his frustration to the secretary of the interior that the soldiers were not prepared to patrol for poachers. "My great problem is to get uncommissioned officers to put in charge of the men who are able and disposed to cope with the class of men who form the poaching population."[23] In other words, the soldiers were inadequately trained or did not possess the motivation to combat the poachers. Scouts had the required skills, and they could carry the mental burden of finding the poachers, relegating the soldiers who accompanied them to little more than armed "muscle." Soldiers naturally would learn the backcountry skills from the scouts, but units rotated in and out of the park with such frequency that acquiring these skills likely had only limited effect. Even though soldiers came and went, the scouts remained a more stabilizing force.

Capturing a notorious poacher showed that the soldiers themselves were in a more supportive role. In March of 1894, Ed Howell, the infamous poacher from Cooke City, crossed into the park and passed the Soda Butte Soldier Station during the night to avoid detection. Scout Felix Burgess and a sergeant pursued him through the wilderness. They found his camp with a small lodge and a cache of six bison scalps hanging in the trees. Hearing shots, the two men found Howell and his dog in an open clearing working on cleaning his prey. Burgess daringly crossed the open terrain with only a pistol to apprehend Howell, literally red-handed, while the sergeant waited at the tree line providing cover. The sergeant accompanied Burgess in escorting Howell to Mammoth, providing the added security of numbers if he tried to escape. As they marched Howell out, Emerson Hough, a reporter for the magazine *Forest and Stream*, was in the park and reported the story. Yet,

Captured poacher Edward Howell (far right with his dog curled up by his feet) and soldiers, 1894. After being captured, the notorious poacher and his guard encountered a reporter for *Forest and Stream*. His capture, and the reported light punishment he received, prompted Congress to create strong legal codes for the park through the Lacey Act. (Yellowstone National Park Museum Collection)

since there was no technical way to try Howell for his crimes at that time, all the army could do was confine him in the guardhouse at Mammoth for a while and then expel him. Hough's reporting gained national attention and is largely responsible for passage of the Lacey Act, which provided for enforcement of the laws through legal punishments and the appointment of a judge to administer justice. John Meldrum would be the first to be appointed the US commissioner in the park.[24]

Once the military arrived and patrolling increased, poachers created a "shadow landscape" of trails, shelters, cabins, and stashes of equipment in the dense forests off the main roads. Commanders required that scouts and soldiers at the various stations go out on patrol at infrequent and unpredictable times "in order that all may become acquainted with the country and habits and habitats of the game, and the tricks and cunning ways of the poachers." The military also constructed its own network of "snowshoe" cabins throughout the backcountry, which differed from the regular soldier stations occupied along the main routes. The backcountry snowshoe cabins were not permanently occupied but used while patrolling in the backcountry on an ad hoc basis to provide shelter and house provisions for soldiers or scouts in case of inclement weather. "All persons are enjoined to use the rations in the snowshoe cabins only in case of necessity; never under any

Officers from Fort Yellowstone pose with the bison heads confiscated from Ed Howell in 1894. (Yellowstone National Park Museum Collection)

circumstances to waste any of them and always to leave the cabins and their contents secure and in good condition. The ax and shovel must be left inside, the comforts hanged [*sic*] up, the cooking utensils left clean and dry and the food in its box secure from mice, etc. Enough dry wood for one night should always be left in the cabin."[25]

Both the soldiers and poachers knew they were searching for each other in a type of cat-and-mouse game in the park's backcountry. The military officers undoubtedly used their training in strategy and tactics to good effect as did the noncommissioned officers and scouts. Patrols disguised routes to keep from being predictable. They often split up and approached destinations from several directions. When they pitched camp for the evening, it was often simply a ruse, and they would move silently under cover of darkness to another camp. "My idea for doing this at night," reported one scout, "is to keep the hunting class of people thinking the camps were still out where they were." But these guerrilla tactics in the backcountry were limited by the fact that the soldiers were acting more as constables than soldiers, making arrests rather than engaging in combat. With the soldiers' lack of experience in the backcountry, the poachers had the upper hand. As one military superintendent noted, even scouts could be hard-pressed since "it is so easy to

Mud Volcano cabin, circa 1913. Cabins such as these provided shelter for patrolling soldiers and scouts during the winter months. (Yellowstone National Park Museum Collection)

place poison or set traps where the eye of the most expert scout cannot find them; it is so easy to pack the pelts out of the Park without detection, that it has seemed to me one of the most difficult problems I have been called upon to handle."[26]

The hunters would try to have the inexperienced soldiers reveal their locations and avoid capture by hiding in the woods and firing shots into the air, waiting to see if soldiers would arrive. Scout George Whittaker claimed that on a patrol in 1898 "two shots were fired just to draw us out of our camp and to find out if we were still camped here." The poachers were also keenly aware of the soldiers' presence through simple observation. In 1898 Sgt. M. J. Wall came upon a poacher's cabin that had been recently occupied since "a fire [was] burning inside, but no one [was] at home." He noticed mink and fox skins all around the cabin. Hoping to catch the occupant, he hid and "waited to see if anyone would show up, but none did." If the poachers were not captured near their shelters, the soldiers would burn the cabin and confiscate the equipment but to little effect as poachers would simply renew their efforts after the patrols had gone.[27]

A few soldiers, like Sergeant Wall, seem to have really taken to their job of patrolling the park for poachers. Lieutenant Frank Amos, a recent West Point graduate on his first posting, took to the work immediately and impressed his superiors. On just one patrol along the main roads in the park,

The first Tower Falls Soldier Station, circa 1905. Soldiers at isolated stations such as this one were tempted to hunt the park's game. Archaeology at this station indicates that wild game constituted a substantial part of the soldiers' diet, perhaps as indicated by the numerous elk skulls and antlers in this photograph. (Yellowstone National Park Museum Collection)

he discovered two separate groups of poachers posing as tourists, while smuggling hunting dogs into the park. Amos became so familiar with the park, its topography, and its wildlife as well as the poachers' tactics that his transfer was seen as a deterrent to the army's mission in Yellowstone. Yet, not all soldiers took to their new job with such enthusiasm. Many appeared "indifferent" according to Superintendent Col. S. M. B. Young, especially since the work could hardly be described as a soldier's work. At the soldier stations, regular patrols were required, but without the watchful eye of the commissioned officers, they could be neglected and the records easily falsified. In 1912 the soldiers at the Sylvan Pass Soldier Station likely did not make as many patrols as the station log suggested, and they openly discussed it among themselves. One of the soldiers there also reported that the sergeant in command even told him he wanted to kill a beaver for its skin if he could find one.[28]

The soldier stations, with their lax discipline and minimal oversight by officers, allowed the soldiers themselves opportunities to poach, almost openly. Sgt. Edward Offley wrote his brother about the "fine dinners" of local elk and deer as he visited soldier stations throughout the park. Sgt. Clearance Brittain at the Sylvan Pass Station brought in a deer so that the men of his station could have fresh meat to supplement their rations. Archaeological evidence at the Fountain Flats, Tower, and Soda Butte soldiers' stations deep in the park suggest that the soldiers were regularly supplementing their rations with the park's game. They appear to have engaged in a type of poaching that Karl Jacoby termed "moral ecology," the harvesting or use of natural resources in a way believed responsible for one's survival, even if it broke the law. Besides, hunting was emotionally connected with the idea of independence, self-sufficiency, masculinity, and republican ideals, all of which were perceived as threatened with the growing industrial economy. This subsistence poaching was more common among working class and rural people, a population from which the ordinary enlisted men were drawn and one likely more sympathetic than the more elite officer class. In addition, even though the soldiers were charged with enforcing the law against hunting, the idea that they were feeding themselves and that there was "no harm" in hunting the occasional animal from an abundant population would allow them to keep their conscience clear.[29] Yet, despite the hostility from many locals around the park, numerous soldiers may have had a more similar outlook than some residents might have suspected. Still, the soldiers did their duty and enforced the rules as directed.

At least some officers enjoyed the mental challenge of chasing poachers and thought of the pursuit in military terms, thinking strategically and tactically. An organized and cooperative group of poachers lived just west of the park at Henry's Lake, Idaho. Second Lt. Elmer Lindsley and Capt. George L. Scott undertook a winter mission to capture that "gang of hardy mountain pirates who make a scanty living by hunting, trapping, and fishing." Thinking in military terms, Lindsley and Scott wanted to "make a sort of turning movement against them—to get them in the rear." Making such a flanking maneuver would be difficult. That area was so remote in winter that the officers had to head north by train to Livingston, west to Butte, and then south to Market Lake, Idaho. Lindsley described the settlement as "a dismal little place, lost in the alkali valley of the Snake River, with only a post office, a store, a saloon, and two livery stables, but no market or lake—hence the name." After hiring a local guide, they took off into the southwestern portion of the park. Even though he claimed not to be a poacher, their guide, "Old Shep," was familiar with the poachers and their tactics. He "knew of a cached [poacher] cabin near the ford of Belcher

River, built by a poacher in the palmy days when poaching in that part of the Park was uninterrupted."[30]

The terrain was difficult at best and deadly in winter. The search for the cabin did not go well and Old Shep became confused on its actual location. As the day wore on, the men "had a brief council of war" and came to a "unanimity of opinion that we could not reach the cabin before dark and could not find it after dark," so they made camp. Again Lindsley used the military terminology to describe the ordeal, though there were no enlisted men, only Captain Scott, the guide Old Shep, and himself. The lack of enlisted men on the expedition is noteworthy. The next day the small group pressed on. They finally discovered the unimpressive cabin almost entirely buried under the snow. "The cabin was simply a big crib of logs with a roof over it, and a hole about three by four feet where a door should have been. The snow bank on which we stood was level with the eaves and we took off our skis and slid into the cabin like so many beavers." Snow covered the interior, and the small party had to bring in boughs to sleep on, "but our beds were quite comfortable, and by taking turns in keeping the fire, we each got considerable sleep," Lindsley claimed. The cabin had no supplies and without signs of the poachers, the next morning they started the long journey back to Fort Yellowstone.[31]

If the flanking maneuver that Lindsley and Scott undertook provided no results, the superintendents hoped more covert methods might be more productive. In 1895 Acting Supt. Capt. George Anderson described the people of the area around Henry's Lake as a "merciless and persistent lot of head and skin hunters." Anderson could not hide his disdain for "the worst and most daring and desperate gang of poachers who ever defied the park law." He added that "in most civilized countries the occupation of such vandals as these is held in merited contempt, but it is not so in the region of which I have made mention." The group was so efficient in their activities that Anderson feared that "that this last remaining herd [of bison] is in danger of extinction by these people of whom I have made mention." The next year Anderson received $2,000 to fight the poachers and used the money to covertly infiltrate the "merciless freebooters" at Henry's Lake. He organized three groups. One group of hired men acted as covert "detectives among the suspected element," while the other two operated independently of the traditional outpost garrisons and patrols along the western and southern borders of the park.[32] The scouts and soldiers would also periodically leave the park and arrive in Henry's Lake unannounced to intimidate the poachers.

The use of undercover "detectives" was unusual and against traditional military thinking in the late nineteenth-century army. Most military and naval officers believed that intelligence gathering was incompatible with the country's military practice despite a long tradition of engaging in it as early as the Revolutionary War. Even during the Civil War, Union officers generally preferred to gather information from other sources rather than direct the activities themselves. In the 1880s Congress passed several reform acts for the military that, on paper at least, created the first peacetime military intelligence bureaus. As historian Roy Talbert notes, in reality, neither the army nor the navy actually utilized them because of the scorn for intelligence gathering, keeping only minimal staff and conducting virtually no training or activities. Despite the growing threat to the United States and its military as the country became an imperial power in the late 1880s, the resistance by the military to intelligence operations was not overcome until the Philippine insurrection at the turn of the century and more completely during World War I.[33]

The federal government's use of private detectives in other areas was not entirely unheard of in the late nineteenth century, but it was unusual and not at all popular. The most famous detective agency, the Pinkerton National Detective Agency, amounted to a private covert intelligence agency, and a private army often used to keep tabs on labor unions and break strikes. The government had periodically hired Pinkerton "dicks" in the 1870s and 1880s, but the unpopularity of doing so led to the passage of the Anti-Pinkerton Act of 1893, specifically forbidding government employment of Pinkertons.[34] Anderson's hiring of detectives to gather intelligence in and around Henry's Lake in 1895 violated the spirit of the 1893 act, even if it did not technically violate it by keeping clear of the Pinkerton Agency directly.

The use of detectives to conduct domestic surveillance by the army was a murky legal area in other ways as well since the Posse Comitatus Act prohibited the army from performing law enforcement duties where functioning legal structures existed. The act was passed in 1878 when the Southern states were readmitted to the Union after Reconstruction and northern Democrats resented the participation of the army in the Great Railway Strike of 1877. Army officers almost universally approved of the act as it kept their duties more martial in nature and delineated a clear chain of command that limited interference by local politicians.[35] Of course, the president, as commander-in-chief, could order the military to perform such duties, as was done in Yellowstone Park where no functioning law enforcement existed, but moving beyond the park's boundaries into the Henry's Lake region to gather intelligence, intimidate, and apprehend wrongdoers could easily have been considered overreach even if the ends justified the means. Captain Anderson's covert actions in and around Henry's Lake, while arguably necessary to combat such organized poaching, was outside the traditional military thought of the time and stretched the mission of the army in Yellowstone into potentially perilous legal waters. At the same time, it is a demonstration of the seriousness with which at least the military superintendents and officers undertook their mission.

The group of poachers at Henry's Lake was organized around the Courtenay family and operated in near mafia-like ways through intimidation. Brothers James and Al Courtenay, James's father-in-law, Silas McMinn, and his stepson Jay Whitman were the core of the group. Al Courtenay was a particularly dangerous man; he had killed a companion in a minor disagreement, creating an aura of fear and intimidation. Silas McMinn's neighbor Dick Rock joined the faction and provided suitable cover for selling the group's poached meat as he owned a herd of domesticated elk. The poached meat was packed and sold to mining camps as "beef" or "domesticated elk," and Rock's herd provided a plausible shield for selling the fruits of their poaching efforts. However, these efforts were only a thinly veiled attempt to create plausible deniability for the consumer as it was readily reported to Captain Anderson that "a man who had just come [to Butte, Montana] from Henry's Lake, packing on a horse, two buffalo calves that he had caught in the Park, and the local people were checking that the hardy frontiersman had got the best of Uncle Sam."[36]

The group's primary territory was the southwest corner of the park along the Belcher and Madison Rivers. They would travel along stream beds, cache supplies, and even occasionally drive game out of the park to kill it. Lieutenant Lindsley claimed they were "natural poachers. They are banded together and work in concert, completely dominating the sparsely settled section adjoining the park in which they live. Such skilled robbers are they and so minute their knowledge of the country that it is impossible to convict them." Buffalo heads were sold to the local taxidermists for handsome prices, and the group often drove bison out of the park in the spring to capture calves and let them grow to adulthood, again to provide a cover for their poaching efforts. Despite these pains to conceal their hunting in the park, locals admitted that "there is no secret made about these hunting expeditions" by the group into the park to harvest game.[37]

As Lindsley noted, the group thoroughly intimidated the small population of Henry's Lake. One local wrote to Captain Anderson with information regarding their activities but pleaded to "keep this perfectly secret" since "if they should find out that I have given you any information [I] would be in danger of my life." One of the detective-scouts reported that he thought the town's storekeeper "will give up any information he gets but only in secret, as he claims—I think truly—that they would burn his store and sawmill if they knew he informed on them." As their poaching became more precarious given the information gathered by the army, a local warned Lieutenant Lindsley that the group "tried very hard to find out where you got your information, and even warned some locals to 'be very carefull [*sic*] don't let yor [*sic*] best friend no [*sic*] our business.'" Given their reputation, when Pvt. David Mathews became lost on patrol from the Riverside Soldier Station in 1894, it was erroneously believed by local Charles "Buckskin Charley" Marble that the Courtenay group had killed him and claimed that his being "shot through the back" was proof.[38]

The increased patrols, the use of covert detectives, and the scouts' unannounced visits to the settlement paid off. Finding poaching no longer profitable, the Courtenay brothers left Henry's Lake around 1900, and Jay Whitman moved to the new settlement of Yellowstone (later named West Yellowstone) and opened a tourist campground. The pressure from the army was compounded by the willingness of other residents of Henry's Lake to covertly and anonymously inform the military superintendents about the group's activities. It is not clear whether they provided information because of a growing appreciation of the park and its wildlife or whether they had merely grown tired of the intimidation of the group of poachers. Whatever the motive, it must have become clear to the outlaws that it was time for them to move on. The final member of the group, Dick Rock, did not have the luxury of that decision as he was ultimately gored to death by one of the buffalo captured in the park.[39]

The covert efforts to infiltrate Henry's Lake for information about poaching was successful enough that commanders expanded the practice to other border communities. Like the working-class laborers in the factories of the time period who came to despise the Pinkertons, locals around the park disliked the scout-detectives gathering information surreptitiously. The military, lamented the editor of the *Livingston Enterprise*, had "spies at every turn."[40] However, by the turn of the century, the detectives had become "so well known" that residents were able to "surround themselves with such safeguards that it is impossible to secure evidence against them."[41] Yet, it should be noted that these efforts against the poachers around the park were directed almost entirely by the officers and the hired civilian scouts. Even Lieutenant Lindsley's expedition consisted of two officers and a civilian. The enlisted men were noticeably absent. They patrolled areas in the park from their soldier stations, and they often accompanied scouts on random backcountry patrols. However, the efforts against the poachers appear to have been primarily driven by the officer class and the scouts.

Perhaps the most common and mundane duty of enlisted men was monitoring the standard tourist areas and routes. Using soldiers as a constabulary force was not unheard of before 1886, but it was unusual and typically of only short duration, especially when compared to the thirty-year history of the army in Yellowstone. Occasionally in the West garrisons had been called out in exceptional circumstances to support the local law officers. Using soldiers as primary enforcement officers of the law over civilians is legally considered martial law, something considered suspicious by most Americans and unpopular when it had been used. The imposition of martial law by the British under the Massachusetts Government Act was one of the "Intolerable Acts" that led to the Revolutionary War. The United States did impose martial law briefly in New Orleans during the War of 1812 and for only a few days after the Great Chicago Fire of 1871.[42]

Perhaps the most prolonged and most controversial use of the military as law enforcement happened during the Civil War and later Reconstruction. Imposing martial law to stifle dissent in areas of Ohio and Indiana during the war resulted in military commissions and civil courts operating independently in the same area. The conflict led to the case *of Ex Parte Milligan*, in which the Supreme Court declared that military courts could not operate where functioning civil authority existed. After the collapse of the Confederacy, the Union's troops assumed all the functions of government in the occupied states. During the first few weeks after the war, they were responsible for everything from issuing marriage licenses to arresting and trying suspected criminals. President Andrew Johnson began establishing provisional governments though the jurisdictional boundaries were not clear and conflicts existed between these governments and the military commanders. Congressional Republicans distrusted Johnson's provisional governments and provided for military oversight of them by the end of 1865. But the conflicts only increased.

Further strengthening the military's role, the first Reconstruction Act of

Soldier standing on a horse at an unknown date but, based on the uniform, likely after the turn of the twentieth century. British author Rudyard Kipling was unimpressed by the behavior of the soldiers in Yellowstone. However, he felt sympathy for their being snubbed by his fellow travelers, with whom he was even more unimpressed. (National Park Service photo)

1867 demanded that states draft new constitutions and elect new officials, all under direct military supervision. Soldiers provided the bulk of law enforcement personnel, and even where new officials were elected, the soldiers supported them. It was an uncomfortable situation for everyone. Officers disliked the political wrangling and the conflicting chain of command while Southerners resented the army's presence and interference. As the newly readmitted Southern states exercised their political power in Congress, they joined with Northern Democrats who disliked the army's interference in recent labor disputes and limited the army's authority to enforce civil law through the passage of the Posse Comitatus Act of 1878.[43] Internally the military did not even have its own police force since "military police" units were not organized or trained until near the end of World War I, although the army had experimented with paramilitary police organizations with the creation of the Philippine Constabulary in 1902.[44]

From the twenty-first-century perspective, the use of the military in reestablishing and enforcing civilian law, similar to modern "national building," is commonly perceived as part of the military's broader mission, having been effectively done in Germany and Japan after World War II, in Panama and Grenada in the 1980s, and more recently during the wars in Iraq and Afghanistan. However, when the US Cavalry entered Yellowstone in 1886, such a mentality was neither natural nor necessarily thought of as a proper military duty, especially after the disagreeableness of Reconstruction. No training manual on law enforcement existed for soldiers in the late nineteenth and early twentieth century. Nor did the soldiers see themselves as police, but rather as soldiers. Despite the rather unpleasant experience of Reconstruction, using soldiers as law enforcement officers was quite surprising. Other than being a highly organized and armed force, what skills did the soldiers actually possess that would lead people to assume that the army would effectively enforce the law in the park? Lack of training and experience were only some of the difficulties the enlisted men encountered. They also faced a hostile social class environment and wrestled with their own sense of mission in performing duties they neither fully embraced nor were trained for.

Placing soldiers in a new environment with an alien mission, often in small groups in isolated outposts throughout the park, required them to adapt themselves in ways for which their training had not prepared them. As a general rule, when the military encounters a situation with no preexisting norms, it relies on leadership in the decision-making process. Yet, the unique situation of isolated groups of enlisted men visited only infrequently by officers gave the soldiers room to continuously negotiate their own norms relative to the group's values and ideals. The soldiers developed new norms that combined their military experience, their own preconceived concept of law enforcement, and the social values and expectations of society. Given the unique forces behind the process, some new norms might have been considered "deviant" to others in society as not conforming to more well-established modes of behavior. However, the soldiers could accept them if the ultimate outcome supported their own values.[45] For example, hunting the park's game for food at the stations would be acceptable since it supported the soldiers' own ideas of conservation and benefited the group. Likewise, given their new police duties, their treatment of tourists might run against the general norms of society since they could exercise legal power over their perceived social superiors almost mercilessly.

Acting as lawmen, the soldiers also were forced to reshape, at least temporarily, their self-identity to embrace both soldier and policeman. Unlike more established and trained police forces, the soldiers had to establish their own norms and procedures. Sociological studies have shown how the police mentality is nearly ubiquitous and very resilient despite place and time. Full of contradictions, they are adversarial to the public that they serve; they are esteemed by society, while often being alienated from much of it because they are denigrated by social elites and hated by the poor; and they are given and develop a sense of authority that is detested by the society that gave it to them. Such contradictions create a solidarity and a closed group identity that is distrustful of the public and often does not adhere to the expected social rules when out of sight.[46]

People who perform law enforcement shape their actions based on their prescribed mission, location, and internal motivators. The situational context, with its social and community structure as well as internal group norms and traditions, will often determine the quality of implementation and the level of corruption. Direct daily contact with the public can cause conflicting social pressures when the community and the policing force have an asymmetrical social relationship. The soldiers enforcing park rules and regulations were very much aware of their unbalanced social relationship with the tourists. The social class system of the late Victorian era was very much still in place, and soldiers fell near the bottom of the scale. While democratic societies like to minimize social class inequalities, the reality is much more complicated, and the Victorians had an obsession with imposing order on everything, including groups of people based on various elements such as wealth, behavior, occupation, ethnicity, and race. The late Victorian American social class was nonetheless in flux as the old New England aristocracy, which emphasized accumulated family wealth, service, and education, was giving way to the new industrial middle class as the driver of social influence and power. The middle class emphasized behavior as a method of promoting social mobility by emulating gentility through strict codes of conduct to obscure the disadvantages of birth. The obsession with appropriate behavior and self-control provided a polished image of gentility, thereby creating order in the perceived chaos of the industrial revolution's social upheaval. While easterners perceived that the West had greater social mobility and less defined social classes, the truth was very different: many westerners strove to emulate Eastern civilized society.[47]

The unique milieu of Yellowstone Park thrust together different elements of Victorian American society, including people of different perceived social classes. The hotel guests were usually wealthy and convinced of their own superiority. The camping company patrons were generally from the more middle-class set of teachers, lawyers, clerks, and the like. "Sage brushers" were usually the more impoverished tourists who came through the park. Soldiers, despite their own positive self-identity, had to navigate through an occupational/social environment in which they were legally more powerful than their perceived social superiors, especially the hotel set. Following orders, paramount to military service, allowed the soldiers to monitor the park, and some assumed that only the military could bring order and stability. However, the mission and the orders given the soldiers challenged the existing social norms, leading to rigid enforcement of the rules and regulations but in an environment that increased the hostility between soldiers and civilians.

Those who came to Yellowstone Park from the East, courted and catered to by the powerful railroads and park hotels, brought their perceived social expectations with them like luggage. "Civilized society," in their bourgeois minds, was imbued with values and a lifestyle that differentiated classes of people. This was bolstered by the new idea of Social Darwinism, which suggested these differences were not only natural but that one class had no obligation to the other. Separation was, in fact, desirable in a competitive social environment. The separation of individuals into their classes accorded them both their proper and appropriate privileges and limitations. Just as in America at large, separation of the social classes did not have legal precedent, but in Yellowstone Park it came perilously close. Within the park there existed unofficial, and sometimes official, regulations that structured the interactions of social class.[48]

From the Civil War to World War I, enlisted men were generally stereotyped by the upper and middle class as men of the "dangerous classes," those who had character flaws that would prevent them from succeeding elsewhere in American society. The social tension between the soldiers and the hotel class of tourist was evident in the word used to describe the soldiers: "swaddies." This was a term interchangeable with "soldier" both in and out of the park. However, the *Oxford English Dictionary* suggests that the etymology of the term "swaddy," as applied to a soldier, originates from "swad," a slang term for "country bumpkin; clodhopper, a loutish or clownish fellow" and that it was "a common term of abuse." Used in contempt, it added to a feeling of "disrespect for the uniform" felt by many soldiers as late as 1908. The alienation of the soldiers from the tourist class was evident, especially to foreign visitors. Even the snobbish Rudyard Kipling, when touring Yellowstone,

A group of tourists climbing a thermal feature in the park, circa 1903. Tourists before and even after the military era in the park would do things prohibited today, including climbing and carving names on features and taking "specimens." Army officials would compare new names on features to hotel registries and determine the itinerary of the guest. They often were met at one of the exits, detained, and marched back to remove the vandalism. (Library of Congress)

A soldier talking with tourists about one of the park's features, circa 1903. Even though they were prohibited from providing interpretation like modern NPS rangers, soldiers often interacted with tourists and shared what they knew about the park's unique geology in some of the more pleasant interactions between soldiers and tourists. (Library of Congress)

was surprised and noted that "America is a free country, but the citizens look down on the soldier." Soldiers were so shunned by Yellowstone's hotel tourists that Kipling took it upon himself to talk with and "entertain that trooper" as nobody else from his party would. In short, he noted, the tourists wanted "nothing to do with them."[49]

While the public viewed the enlisted men as suspect because they were soldiers, the social understanding of police officers also contributed to the unique situation in the park. Soldiers, tourists, and locals around the park brought with them their concepts of what police officers were and how they fit into Gilded Age society. In the West the police were often the heads of criminal rings, such as the notorious Sheriff Henry Plumber of Virginia City, Montana. In the cities they had become tools of patronage for the political machines and open to corruption. Police jobs were given to people who supported the machine, often poor immigrants, and in return the police became susceptible to political influence and exploitation.[50] As the soldiers adjusted their own identity from soldier to soldier-constable, they had to contend with their own perception of what a law enforcement officer was and the public's perception of them. Unlike traditional police forces where older colleagues would help indoctrinate new recruits into the organization's cultural norms, the soldiers had to discover these norms on their own each time the command rotated. Merely understanding the rules and regulations and how they were to be enforced was problematic enough that by 1908, twenty-two years into the military administration, all soldiers were finally required to know them and take an exam on them at the beginning of their deployment.[51]

Ironically, while the common soldier was perceived to be of a lower social class, he had legal authority over his assumed social superiors. Even his mere presence at one of the park's features caused tourists to "instinctively put their hands behind their backs or guiltily move in the opposite direction." The soldiers' having to establish their own methods for enforcing rules and regulations on their assumed social superiors seems to have led to an overly adversarial demeanor. The constant and vigilant eyes of the soldiers made some tourists uncomfortable. One tourist noted that "it depresses one to be constantly under the watchful eye of the soldiers." The soldiers treated people "courteously enough," but the tourists could also expect "little mercy from these vigilant guardians." Even in the army's first years in the park, Captain Harris reminded his soldiers that they were "not to use abusive language to, or otherwise maltreat, the visitors to the Park." Several changes of troops later, Maj. John Pitcher, the acting superintendent in 1902, attempted to curb the rigid deportment of his uncompromising troops. He informed his command that "a majority of the people who visit the Park during the summer are law-abiding citizens and as a rule, it will be quite sufficient to courteously call their attention to the Rules and Regulations of which they may be ignorant, in order to have them enforced." Even in the waning years of the military administration, Col. Lloyd M. Brett had to instruct his command that "tourists will be cautioned of dangerous places on the formations by the guards. If tourists ignore the caution, they do so at their own peril. The guard will not try to restrain them."[52]

Courteous treatment was not just limited to the tourists. Lieutenant Colonel Brett also wrote to all hotel managers, "When [soldiers] do come to your hotels, please see that they are treated with due respect [and] shown the same courtesy that you would extend to a guest." This reminder stemmed from the fact that the upper-class hotel tourists traditionally found refuge in the hotels from the lower-class soldiers; if the soldiers entered their domain, the social-legal paradox was removed. The park regulations clearly stated,

"Under no circumstances will any noncommissioned officer in charge of a station permit any of his men to go upon the premises or to enter any hotel in the park for the purpose of enforcing any rule or regulation." Without soldiers in the hotels, or at least stripped of their power when there, the managers and tourists were largely free of unwanted regulations and their enforcers. The directive was reinforced periodically with orders such as Park Order No. 12, dated June 1, 1914, which stated: "Enlisted men are forbidden to enter the hotels." Some limited exceptions existed, such as an "invitation of hotel guests to visit them and to attend 'Formation Dances,' or other entertainments by invitation of the managers." But the soldiers were warned "not [to] loiter about the porches or entrances of the hotels." In those rare exceptions when they entered hotels upon invitation, they were required to put their best appearance forward and could only "wear their dress uniform."[53] Even those limited visits must have been problematic since the commanding officers also felt compelled to remind the hotel management to treat the soldiers with respect. Such reminders would not have been needed if it had not been a problem. Spheres of power were established. Outside the hotels, the perceived lowly soldier had legal authority over tourists, contrary to the norms of society, but within the hotels, the guests had their own superiority reestablished and protected.

The tension in the social-legal paradox of Yellowstone likely centered on the expectations of deference by each group. The majority of encounters revolved around an exchange of deference and the maintenance of a proper demeanor in speech and behavior. Soldiers, acting as constables outside the hotels, held certain beliefs about how tourists should behave in any given encounter, as do police everywhere. Levels of respect and deference should be shown that acknowledged their asymmetrical power at that moment. Cloaked with legal authority, there was an expectation of courteousness and even a level of submissiveness. When this behavior was not displayed, the soldiers may have acted uncompromisingly, leading to warnings by their commander to treat tourists considerately. The hotel tourists, at the same time, expected that the socially inferior soldiers would treat them with the appropriate deference due to their social position. This created a conflict of expectations. The legal authority of soldier was stronger and usually won out but temporarily inverted the social rules that would have existed outside the park. Those tourists confronted by soldiers for violations were naturally unwilling and reluctant participants. Emotions governed their interactions; feeling embarrassed or guilty, or temporarily reduced in social status before

Tourists watching bears feeding at the Canyon Hotel dump, circa 1910. Watching bears feed on hotel garbage was one of the favorite pastimes in the park well before and after the military era. Soldiers were often present to ensure the safety of the tourists, lessening the conflict with the bears but increasing the conflict with the park visitors. (National Park Service photo)

their perceived social inferior drove their actions. Therefore, they would often demonstrate a lack of poise, act distracted, or be confrontational in an attempt to reestablish their position.[54]

A clear example of this clash occurred at Canyon Hotel in 1914. Mr. F. W. Trible wrote the commanding officer, Col. Lloyd M. Brett, about the soldier monitoring the "bear show" at the hotel dump. At around dusk, "a large party of guests of the Hotel, including some friends of mine, went up to see the bears feeding at the garbage heap. After some few minutes, a young man clad in khaki, whom I thought was a boy scout, or some visitor to the Park, walked out from the crowd and around the bears on the far side, chased a black bear up a tree, scattered all the bears but one, whistling and displaying considerable bravado all the time and finally stopped on the other side of the garbage with the bear between him and the crowd, who were looking on." It is interesting to note that Mr. Trible claimed he did not even recognize the man as a soldier at first, demeaning him as a juvenile Boy Scout, thus justifying his own behavior in the incident.

Trible feared that the soldier would "start that bear in the direction of the crowd, I called out to him to desist, and that he was pretty fresh to make

Bears at the Lake Hotel garbage dump, circa 1913. Note the soldier partially visible on the right. (Library of Congress)

such a disturbance." The lack of deference shown by Trible offended the soldier, who decided to directly and openly confront him. "He came up to me," continued Trible, "and wanted to know whom I was calling fresh." The soldier, attempting to exert his situational power flatly told Trible that "he would 'take me down' and that he would show me who he was" in a show of masculine bravado. The confrontation continued, but even after discovering he was a soldier, Trible still did not feel compelled to respect the soldier's authority or display any deference. Rather, he told the soldier "that he had spoiled the pleasure of everyone who had gone up to see the bears feeding." He closed his account by explicitly telling Colonel Brett that this soldier had expressly defied the social rules of deference as he "continued his impertinence and was most insulting." The tension and lack of deference between the working-class soldier and the upper-class hotel tourists were clearly evident and not, according to Trible, just his own personal impression. Trible claimed that "a number of the guests of the Hotel came to me afterwards, and said that I should report the matter. . . . In view of the many stories that I was told of the conduct of soldiers in the park, and the impression made by this incident . . . I feel that the matter should be brought to your attention."[55]

Local newspapers were also more than willing to sensationalize encounters

Visitors on Mammoth Terraces, date unknown but likely late 1880s or early 1890s. The tradition of allowing tourists to be so close to the park's features only increased the temptation to purposely damage and vandalize them. (National Service Photo)

between soldiers and tourists. If they are to be believed, differing perspectives and expectations of deference are likewise evident. In 1887 the *Livingston Enterprise* published a letter penned under the pseudonym "Albion," which protested the "despotism [of the] military rules and regulations." The writer complained that when a person entered the park, he was "watched as if he were guilty of some crime," and the soldiers were ready "to pounce upon the victims and inform them they are under arrest, and that they must leave the Park at once under a military escort." It seemed wrong to Albion that the soldiers became "sheriff, judge, and escort, without giving the person the least right of defending himself." He then recounted a recent event in which a soldier approached his party, which was viewing the geysers, and arrested three of them "because some young lady wrote her autograph on the formations and they were gallant and brave enough not to reveal her name." As they were marched to the soldier outpost, one of "the prisoners did not walk fast enough to suit his captor and he was ordered to 'quicken the pace,' which he evidently was not inclined to do." Note how the soldier expected deference from the violators and reluctance by the tourists to give it. "This aroused the ire of the soldier and he clutched him," accused Albion. "This caused the prisoner to show a spirit of decided resentment." To extract the expected deference he felt due, the soldier informed the prisoner that "unless orders were obeyed he would knock him, at the same time flourishing the butt of the pistol near the victim's head," again with the threat of masculine bravado. Even if exaggerated, the incident certainly demonstrates the different levels of expectations of deference in soldier-civilian relations.

The editor of the *Livingston Enterprise* also lamented the lack of deference traditionally shown and claimed that "Cpt. Harris is the despot of the Park and his lieutenants, sergeants, corporals, and privates are his aids." He recounted the story of a man named "Nock" (but reported in the superintendent's annual report as "John Noack") who was with several people at the Upper Geyser Basin. "Nock espied a number of names penciled in the formation in one of the numerous little pools around the geysers. Some of the names he knew to be those of friends in Butte, and, in a spirit of recognition of old acquaintances, he started to add his name to the list." A soldier promptly arrested him. Even though Nock was admittedly guilty, "a parley ensued," but the soldier would not yield.

The right to protest the arrest is somewhat surprising to the modern eye, but class privilege had its own level of expectations, one that hoped social deference would allow the incident to pass without punishment. When that failed, "one of the party offered the soldier money," hoping to use the class resources of wealth to reestablish social dominance and extract their comrade from his predicament. But the soldier "indignantly refused to accept the bribe" of ten dollars. Nock then handed the soldier a smaller fifty-cent piece, which the soldier ironically accepted but only to give it to "Capt. Harris as a proof that an effort had been made to bribe him." Nock was ordered to leave the park, and he complied since "the bayonets of a company of soldiers were handy." The wealthy elite, usually accorded privilege and social power, were at the mercy of the lower-class soldier, and when the tools of status could not extricate him, he had to comply. The editor admitted that "this is only one side of the story" but that it nonetheless "furnishes evidence of the fact that men [read here men of status] are molested, arrested and ejected from the Park without being heard in their own defense, and for trivial causes."[56]

Captain Harris reported the incident in his annual report and claimed that when "Noack came to my office, he admitted his offense" and that "the young man's speech and manner evinced a contempt for authority." The expected deference to the soldier clearly had been ignored, which explained the soldier's reaction. However, Harris did "not desire to subject [Noack]

Soldiers leaving Upper Geyser Basin in pursuit of stage robbers on August 24, 1908. Writer and photo essayist Mode Wineman was "tramping" alone through the park on the day of the famous robbery of seventeen stagecoaches on the road between Old Faithful and West Thumb. Despite the army's quick reaction to the robbery, the robber's victims were very critical of the military's response. (Yellowstone National Park Library)

to unnecessary humiliation of being escorted out of the Park by a military guard" so he was given "twenty-four hours leave."[57] In other words, the superintendent was willing to acknowledge a level of deference to Noack's social class, defusing the situation. That hardly placated the *Enterprise* editor, who added that he hoped Noack's and similar stories would "break up the present despotic and tyrannical rule that now prevails in the nation's pleasure ground."[58]

The social tension and lack of deference occurred even when the tourists were only victims of a crime and had done nothing wrong themselves. Victims are still embarrassed and temporarily reduced in status, remaining reluctant participants in such interactions with police, both during and even after the encounter. In 1908 seventeen stages were robbed on the road from Old Faithful to West Thumb. Using "vulgar, blasphemous language," the bandit stole $1,363.95 in cash and $730.25 in jewelry and watches. When the stages reached West Thumb, the army was informed, and a detachment was sent vainly in pursuit. However, already demeaned by a lower-class bandit, the victims showed no mercy toward the soldiers helping them. According to Jack Haynes, son of the famous park photographer, "All the passengers in their excitement blamed the soldiers," though Haynes defended them since "the character of the country is such that the entire Army of the United States could no[t] prevent an evilly-disposed man from entering the park with a gun."[59] Despite that, when the victims reached the Lake Hotel, they gathered and urged that "the Hon. James A. Garfield, Secretary of the Interior . . . make a suitable investigation" because, as they resolved, "the military authorities in charge of the Park have proven themselves incompetent to protect the tourists visiting the Park" and further that Congress should "provide funds with which to thoroughly police the Park."[60]

The problem of enforcing laws against the tourists in the early years of the military's tenure was the same as with poachers. Without a presiding magistrate, the army could do little more than briefly detain violators and then expel people from the park. However, being creative in doing this could amount to a punishment for lawbreakers that they would not soon forget. "The soldiers patrolled the places where vandalism was likely to occur," wrote Owen Wister of his trip in 1891. "If they found a name after the writer had gone on they rode after him and brought him back to rub it out." Wister noted that one person was already back at Mammoth ready to depart the park when he was "escorted back clean across the Park." When another man assaulted a maid at Lake Hotel, he was arrested and marched out of the park while the soldiers comfortably rode their horses at a healthy pace. The accused attacker nearly collapsed from exhaustion but was revived and forced to finish his walk out of the park. [61]

While locals and tourists resented what they saw as the soldiers' overly rigorous enforcement of the law in the park, perhaps it was what the park needed at that time. The combining of the military mindset with law enforcement duties in the context of Victorian American class expectations allowed the soldiers to exercise a power they were traditionally denied over their perceived social superiors, possibly more harshly than a more established police force would. Yet, the transient and elitist tourists had shown little or no will in stopping their transgressions within the park. The park was established for the benefit of the people and perhaps as one of the greatest testaments to American democracy, well ahead of its time as regards the country's developing social-class system. By the end of the army era in Yellowstone, that class system had changed and the rule of law in the park had become more firmly established than ever. That is not to say that tensions eased over time. To the contrary: as late as 1908 the situation had become critical. Soldiers deserted the Yellowstone garrison in unusually high numbers, partially because they disliked the duty and the "disrespect to the uniform" shown by the tourists. Still, the army brought a significant level of stability, even if its job was not strictly a "military duty."

CHAPTER TWO

# "Peculiar, Perplexing and Severe Duties"

## Life at Fort Yellowstone

As Capt. George "Gory" Goode came out of his quarters on officers' row at Fort Yellowstone on the cool and windy day of May 24, 1901, he must have had mixed emotions. He and his wife of under two years, Susie, had moved out of the commanding officer's quarters at Fort Yellowstone only a few weeks before. A telegram from the headquarters of the Department of Dakota, dated April 27, informed him that he would be removed from command of Fort Yellowstone and his duties as acting superintendent of Yellowstone National Park.[1] Nevertheless, he was to stay in the park and remain in command of Troop G, First US Cavalry, but under the new commander and acting superintendent, who had arrived on May 8.

His new position, clearly a demotion, must have been surprising to Goode. He had a distinguished record. Born in St. Louis, Missouri, in 1856, he was appointed to the US Military Academy in 1875. For reasons that were not clear, but probably due to the hazing of new cadets, he was held back a year in 1879. Despite this, his classmates stated that "he had a kind heart and not a mean streak in his makeup. Hazing was the thing to do at the time in the Corps of Cadets in leisure moments." Even though "it was not a thing in the Cadet world," if the administration found out, punishments could be severe. Goode immediately stood out among the cadets because of his bright red hair, which gained him the nickname of "Gory," a moniker he kept even after he retired in 1918. However, at Fort Yellowstone, his men often affectionately called him "Reddy" for the same reason. His skills were exemplary, especially in horsemanship, and after he met Frederic Remington, the famed artist stated, "He is my ideal of a Cavalryman." In 1887 Goode had been a second lieutenant at Camp Sheridan for a year under Capt. Moses

Harris, gaining familiarity with the park. After bouncing around western commands, he was appointed professor of military science and tactics at the Missouri Military Academy in 1896. During the war with Spain, he led a regiment in the Santiago Campaign and won a Silver Star for his gallantry in the taking of San Juan Hill on July 1, 1898. In the summer of 1900, he returned to Yellowstone National Park as the acting superintendent and commanding officer of Fort Yellowstone.[2]

In those positions he had received a favorable review during the post's inspection. Lieutenant Colonel Theo J. Wint noted that

> Captain George Good was subaltern in Troop M 1st Cavalry, and on duty when Captain Moses Harris 1st Cavalry was on duty in the Yellowstone National Park. He became practically familiar with the needs, workings and merits of the military system as applied to the protection and preservation and legal duties of an army officer charged with the arduous and essential responsibilities of the Acting Superintendent. In consequence, when detailed as Acting Superintendent of the Yellowstone National Park last July, he was equipped for the duties of the position much better than an officer unacquainted with the peculiar, perplexing and severe duties involved. He impresses me as the right man in the right place.[3]

Like most acting superintendents, Captain Goode enforced the rules and regulations of the park, at least as he understood them, with military efficiency, often frustrating important people. Goode even alienated the post surgeon, a contract civilian named Dr. Gilliam, whom he accused but did not charge with poaching. The surgeon took serious offense at what he described as a trip to merely photograph wildlife and the scenic beauty of the Rocky Mountains. The angry Gilliam told Sgt. Edward M. Offley that "he is a personal friend of General [Nelson] Miles and of Col. Wm. F. Cody [Buffalo Bill] and he is going to use his influence with both those gentlemen to have Captain Goode relieved from duty in the Park." While entertained by the gossip, Offley noted that "nearly everyone around here is doing his best to get rid of Captain G . . . [but] Reddy (Goode) doesn't care and neither do any of the men." Lieutenant Colonel Wint noted in 1900 that some were unhappy with Goode but determined that "the complaints regarding him that have come to my attention have been voiced by those who have been aggrieved by Captain Goode's official action in such matters as taking up loose stock, trespass, poaching, driving through the Park at night, and like matters."[4] In other words, commanders made few friends while administering the park.

Major John Pitcher (on the left) with naturalist John Burroughs in a photo taken during the presidential visit of Theodore Roosevelt, 1903. (National Park Service photo)

Despite being replaced as the post commander and acting superintendent, Captain Goode was still in military command of the troops and had a better working knowledge of the post and the park than the new commanding officer and acting superintendent, Capt. John Pitcher. Pitcher had arrived at Fort Yellowstone on May 8, 1901, a mere two weeks before the inspector general was to arrive. Like Goode, Pitcher was a graduate of West Point but had a deeper military pedigree. His father was Gen. Thomas G. Pitcher, the seventeenth superintendent of the US Military Academy. In fact, John's father ended his tenure at the academy just weeks before his son was appointed as a cadet at large by President Grant in 1872. The younger Pitcher had participated in the Nez Perce war of 1877 and other smaller campaigns in the Pacific Northwest where he gained a reputation as an accomplished marksman and wrote informative pamphlets on the topic. Like Goode, Pitcher had served in Yellowstone under Captain Harris in 1886 as a first lieutenant. In 1898 he broke his leg and could not participate in the Spanish American War, "which was a great disappointment to him." He made his way to Fort Yellowstone in 1901 after a brief tour of duty in the Philippine War.[5]

As the inspection approached, Pitcher would naturally lean heavily on

Goode to help get the command ready for the inspector general's arrival. It was customary for commanders to want to have the command put its best foot forward, so he spent time preparing for the inspection by directing troops to make needed repairs, reminding them of the importance of following proper procedures, and presenting an exceptionally clean or policed environment.[6] Pitcher met daily with the officers of the post when they were not in the park, and this day with the arrival of the inspector general would be no different. How to conduct the inspection would be of particular interest to the subalterns, who had not experienced as many inspections as their superiors. There were two lieutenants attached to the command. First Lt. Charles B. Drake, known as "Ducksie," was an 1896 graduate of West Point from Scranton, Pennsylvania. Popular among cadets at the academy, he was also a good student who excelled in math. He was first stationed in Texas and then Puerto Rico before coming to Fort Yellowstone. Captain Goode stated that he was "an exceptionally good paper man."[7]

The other lieutenant was the fresh-faced, 1900 graduate of West Point, Second Lt. Frank Porter Amos. Despite being a lower rank than Drake, Amos was "a promising young officer, especially good at fieldwork." Amos was born in Racine, Wisconsin, but his family moved to western Nebraska when he was young. He attended Iowa State College for two years before receiving an appointment to the US Military Academy in 1896. He graduated in 1900, and his first posting was to Yellowstone Park. His tour in the park "was one of the happiest memories of his Army career as it opened his active service in a country that was familiar and gave him great opportunity for much outdoor life filled with hunting and fishing of which he was very fond."[8]

Even though Pitcher had been there only two weeks, the park (not to mention the post) had changed considerably since he was posted there as a young lieutenant fourteen years before. He must have been relieved that the officers of his command were well rounded, competent in both the fieldwork in the park and the necessary paperwork that accompanied it, and that the previous commander remained on station and was known as one who "does not delegate any of his duties to subordinates and makes monthly inspections of post regularly." They could ably prepare the post and lead the inspector through the command. Besides, there was a congressional delegation from Ohio and Indiana that Pitcher would be obliged to attend to as the acting superintendent, forcing him to delegate to his subordinates.[9] There was little to fear from the inspection, even from a tough inspector.

And the inspector general assigned to the Department of Dakota that

Lieutenant Frank Porter Amos as a West Point cadet in 1900. Amos's first posting after West Point was Yellowstone Park. He was a natural at his park duties, particularly in the field. He recalled later in life that his time in Yellowstone "was one of the happiest" of his life. (From the United States Military Academy class album of 1900, United States Military Academy Library.)

year was as tough as they came. Lieutenant Colonel Philip H. Reade tried to join the army during the Civil War, when he was underage. Despite being rejected, he nonetheless merely assigned himself to the signal service and performed with such distinction he gained the notice of Maj. Gen. Benjamin Butler, who commissioned him. His service during the war earned him an at-large appointment to the US Military Academy, from which he graduated in 1867. He was stationed throughout the West, and Maj. Gen. John Pope characterized the diligence of his duties "as beyond praise." During the Spanish American War he was shot in the head at the Battle of San Juan Hill and left for dead, even being listed on the mortality report. He was found alive three hours later, lying entangled in a bed of barbed wire under the hot Cuban sun. He recovered, and the head wound did not diminish his mental abilities. One of his later contemporaries noted that he had exceptional "mental and physical activities, versatilities, and observances. Whatever he speaks about, he speaks with such breadth of knowledge as to carry the conviction that he has made a study of the subject."[10]

Lieutenant Colonel Reade arrived on a chilly day in the end of May. After

A stereographic print of troops drilling near Mammoth Hot Spring, circa 1903. (Library of Congress)

the usual pleasantries and a dinner with the officers, the inspection of the command would commence the next morning. Reade would be looking for deficiencies in the command, both regarding the physical condition of the post and the performance of the troop. First would be a review of the troops with attention to their appearance and ability to perform specific military drills. As they gathered that morning, he noted that the new recruits coming from the recruiting depots were "mostly American born and of good moral, physical and intellectual character" and had received between one and six weeks of instruction in drill, regulations, and the articles of war before being assigned to the troop. Troop M's performance during the previous year's inspection had clearly left room for improvement. They garnered only a "fair" ranking in the mounted inspection, saber drill, dismounted drill, troop drill, and troop drill with mounted carbine. Since both Goode and Amos had led

Troops of the First United States Cavalry, led by Second Lt. Johnathan Wainwright (future general of World War II fame), drilling on the parade ground of Fort Yellowstone, circa 1912. Despite their unique duties, the soldiers had to maintain military discipline. (Yellowstone National Park Museum Collection)

the troops in drill during the 1900 inspection, they were motivated enough to improve the performance so Reade would find no deficiencies. Lieutenant Colonel Reade needed to pay special attention to the military readiness of the command, who split their time between park duties and soldiering. He gathered troops and ran them through various drills. "The Cossack drill of 1st squad by about a dozen troopers . . . under command of 2d Lt. F. P. Amos . . . was very credible. It included Greco-Roman riding; taking the hurdle, dismounting before and after jumping the hurdle; mounting from ground, horse being in motion; circling right, left and rear, both at rest when in motion."[11] Captain Goode must have felt particular pride in Reade's positive review as he was directly responsible for their improved performance.

After inspection of the troop, Reade was escorted around the post by Captain Goode and Lieutenant Amos. A new, larger, and more permanent fort had been constructed in 1891 after the small buildings of Camp Sheridan had become inadequate. Fort Yellowstone had not taken its final form as the stone buildings would not be built until 1908 and the old buildings from Camp Sheridan were still used for many purposes. Previous inspections noted the lack of a suitable parade ground. Since the last inspection Captain Goode had taken considerable effort to bring in dirt, manure, and seed to the area between the officers' quarters and the National Hotel. Sergeant Edward

To demonstrate their proficiency, soldiers had competitions that accentuated the monotonous drills, such as this horsemanship competition where Sgt. Henry A. McCartney clears a jump with a little help from the spectators on the ground, circa 1911. (Yellowstone National Park Museum Collection)

Offley noted the disdain for that duty. "Everybody working every day hauling dirt and scattering it over the coat of manure now on the parade ground. I am afraid it is all labor lost as far as we are concerned as we are almost bound to leave here next summer; however, some other troop will probably get the benefit of our improvements. It seems to be a characteristic of this troop to be always cleaning up after some other 'outfit' and as soon as everything is getting in fine shape and running smoothing, to be ordered away." The area was not officially part of the military reservation, and the ground was believed to be nearly hollow in many places. Captain Goode joked that when the troop put up a new flagpole, he "wouldn't be surprised if the whole thing slid China-wards." Reade noted several holes on the parade ground, and "one of these holes was made by a cavalry horse during mounted maneuvers" that cool morning in May.[12]

The geology under the new post was both something of a mystery and a point of concern. After interviewing the officers and their wives about it, Reade stated that

> Some believe that numerous subterranean caves exist and some predict that area is a mere shell that may cave in any day. Portions of the formations sound hollow. The wife of a cavalry lieutenant stationed here says that sometimes at night she can hear sounds of a geyser beneath her

A photo of Fort Yellowstone from Capitol Hill, included in the Inspection Report of 1901. The photographer is unknown but may have been Reade himself. (National Archives and Records Administration)

> husband's quarters. . . . The senses of residents of Fort Yellowstone cause them to declare that abnormal conditions prevail there, out of sight, but not out of feeling or hearing.[13]

With the curiosity of a gentleman scholar who himself delivered several lectures on military, historical, and anthropological topics, he suggested, "Perhaps a representative of the U.S. Geodetic Survey or other government specialists, would be interested in visiting this place" to investigate the geology.[14]

The officers' quarters consisted of four wood-framed buildings. While they were more than adequate, they were close enough together that Lieutenant Colonel Reade felt obliged to note that "should any one of the wooden sets of officers' quarters burn and an unfavorable wind prevail, the entire row would be at the mercy of the flames." Reade discussed the matter with the commander, Capt. John Pitcher. He went on to add, "This officer appreciated the existing situation and acted energetically," though exactly how was not mentioned.[15]

The officers' quarters were duplexes but the "demands of hospitality of the commanding officer continue to be such as to absolutely require his

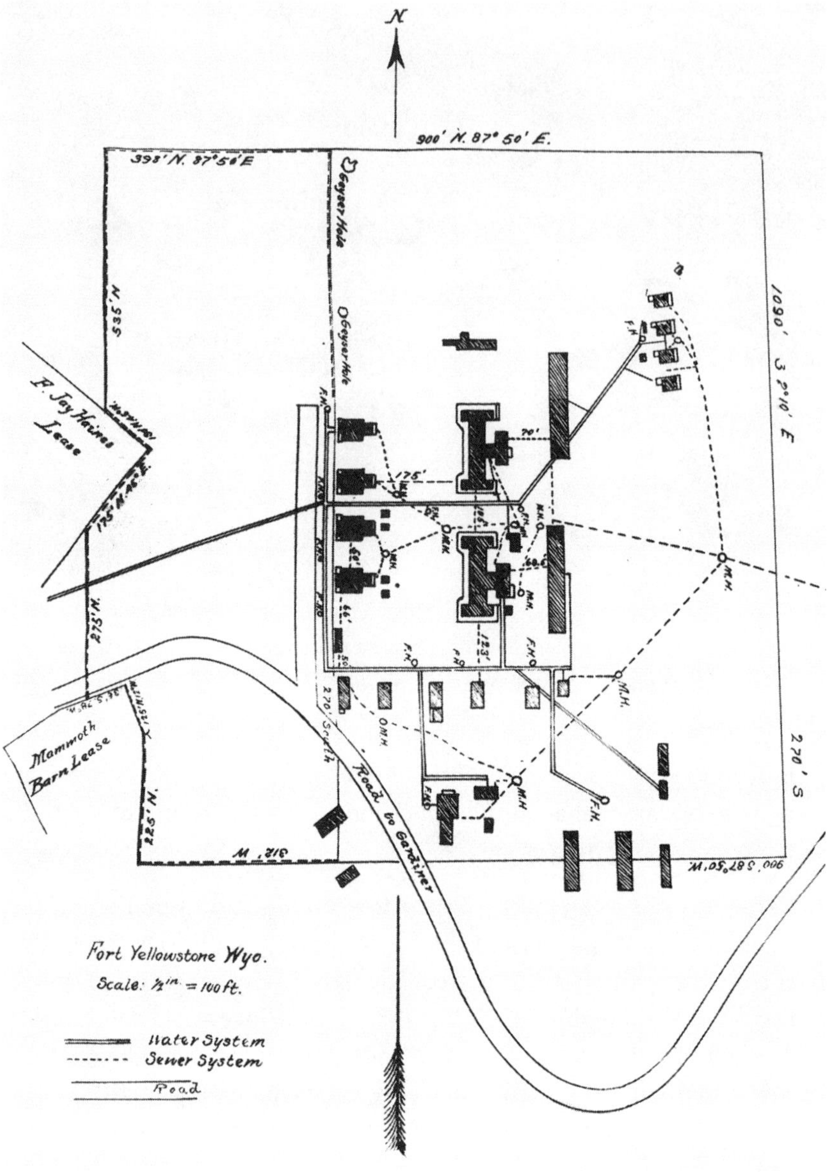


Plan of Fort Yellowstone, 1901, included in Lieutenant Colonel Reade's inspection report. (National Archives and Records Administration)

View of Fort Yellowstone from behind the National Hotel, included in the inspection report of 1900. The photographer is unknown but may have been Lt. Col. Theodore Wint. (National Archives and Records Administration)

occupying a double set of quarters." The commanding officer had a particularly burdensome social responsibility as guests and dignitaries to the park would call upon him. Captain (and then Major) Pitcher made frequent purchases from the National Hotel and its commissary to meet these social obligations. From the invoices one can only imagine the gatherings: In just May of 1903, he ordered fifty pounds of coffee, fifteen boxes of Egyptian cigarettes, fifty Arthur Panatellas cigars, a case of beer pints, a gallon of cooking sherry, and twenty-five pounds of prunes. In July of the following year he ordered 400 quarts of beer, six bottles of whiskey, sixty bottles of Riesling wine, twelve bottles of Selger liquor, and three bottles of Old Tom gin. He also ordered plenty of food, including two sixteen-pound hams, a seventeen-pound ham, three pounds of bacon, two cans of tomatoes, and six boxes of sardines in a single purchase.[16]

Even the other officers' quarters were the scenes of significant social activity, especially among the officers' families. Bessie Haynes remembered that "entertaining was informal," though it could be frequent. "Sometimes there would be a progressive dinner, with dancing afterwards, a few children's parties, bridge or playing rummy." The genteel ritual of "calling" was important as well; it included formally visiting another of equal social standing as a way of permitting entry into a group of acquaintances. A person might first drop a calling card with servants, indicating that they wished to meet. The card would often have the person's name; for officers, it would also have their rank and contact information. Once deposited, another calling card would be returned indicating that a more formal visit was welcome. In other situations, cards could be exchanged person to person, much like more modern business cards, as a form of introduction and to arrange future visits. According to Haynes, "There was a great deal of calling always among army people, calling on newcomers, calling if anyone had a house guest, and people always called when they were leaving for another post."[17]

Calling on people of similar status visiting the park was important, especially at the hotel in Mammoth, which catered to the wealthy, upper-class visitors. The stagecoaches usually "arrived at the hotel about five o'clock," remembered young George Tutherly, whose father, First Lt. Herbert E. Tutherly, was stationed at the park with the First US Cavalry when the army first arrived in 1886. As the stages arrived, his father would tutor his son in the ritual of calling since "Paddy and I would be there to meet them."[18] Officers were accorded this privilege of calling based on their social position, but enlisted men were explicitly forbidden from visiting the hotels without an express invitation, clearly defining the unique social atmosphere of Fort Yellowstone and the park.

While the enlisted men were largely forbidden from entering hotels, officers faced no such restrictions. In fact, they would often saunter over to the hotel daily when the new tourists arrived. While the enlisted men were looked down upon by the hotel tourist class, the visitors welcomed officers as members of upper social strata. Officers may have lacked the financial affluence of the hotel class of visitors, but their education and their genteel customs, beliefs, and habits gave them recognition as members of the upper class. Calling and even possibly dining with the hotel guests allowed officers to assert their membership in and commonality with the genteel class of the upper elite.[19] Enlisted men stationed at the main post—less than three hundred yards from the hotel at Mammoth Hot Springs—and even at some of the more isolated posts near other hotels, could see this lifestyle and these rituals but were excluded. Yellowstone Park, with its semi-institutionalized class structure, made this divide more evident than at other posts, where civilians were kept at a distance off the military reservation. However, officers and their families could cross that divide and maintained the appropriate social ambiance.

Not all officers or their wives were always comfortable with the social atmosphere of the post. Lieutenant Henry L. Watson and his wife "hated society-stiff, formal functions," remembered Bessie Haynes. Rather, "they love out-of-door things and informal functions." Other times the officers' families simply did not get along. As noted in chapter 1, Captain Harris, the first military commander in the park, was considered "a most disagreeable man." This disposition limited the social interactions between the officers' families as young George Tutherly's father Herbert and Captain Harris "never spoke except official." This relationship bled over to their wives. "Mother and Mrs. Harris never spoke at all, after she found out Mrs. Harris had gone through our quarters one time [when] we were away," wrote George.[20]

Of course, all of this unofficial activity was beyond Lieutenant Colonel Reade's inspection, as was the presence of children and the society they created. Several officers brought their children with them to whichever stations they were assigned, and in Yellowstone there often could be several civilian children around the post, or very few. In the early years George Tutherly remembered that "I had no school or playmates, but did not feel badly for lack of either." He was quite able to entertain himself learning to ski on the hills around the post.[21] Bessie Haynes, daughter of park photographer F. J. Haynes, remembered the children sledding in the winter as well. Once the post exchange was built, children would also roller-skate in its gymnasium. "I had fine luck skating, didn't fall once and got so I could go around the hall several times alone," she wrote in her diary. The post surgeon was not as lucky. "Dr. Sparrenberger had a bad tumble, and from his height it was quite a distance to the floor!"[22]

Within socially acceptable limits the children and enlisted men would interact and sometimes cause mischief with one another. To entertain himself, Bessie's brother Jack used a trap gun to fling small rocks from Capitol Hill onto the tin roof of the guardhouse. When the soldiers on duty came out, he hid in the sagebrush. Eventually, the soldiers got wise to the prank, and one day he was "taken from the rear" and brought before the post commander. The good-natured ribbing could go both ways. One soldier asked George Tutherly if he knew "it is wrong to say 'dollar bill?'" The puzzled Tutherly hesitated and the soldier quickly answered, "You should always say 'Dollar William.'"[23]

After inspecting the officers' quarters, Lieutenant Colonel Reade's

The interior of the barracks at Fort Yellowstone, date unknown. (National Park Service photo)

inspection moved to the enlisted men's living quarters, which were naturally more austere than the officers'. The barracks were in two buildings behind the officers' quarters. In 1901 men lived in one-story wood-framed buildings as the later two-story stone barracks had not yet been constructed. They held all of the enlisted men from Troop G, numbering eighty-five in total; the married noncommissioned officers, hospital stewards, and cooks had quarters elsewhere. During the inspection thirty-four men were on detached service and stationed at the park's various outposts so that the buildings would have been about half full.[24] Soldiers would sleep in a common room with an additional room off the side for the noncommissioned officers.

Reade noted that the barracks were generally in a clean state and good condition, though soon they would probably need a new coat of paint. The more northerly barracks had four porcelain bathtubs, three urinals, six washbasins, five stools and sinks with both hot and cold running water. The other building had three iron bathtubs, two urinals, and seven washbasins with hot and cold running water. The buildings' plumbing was not insulated enough for the harsh winters as faucets needed to be left running and windows near the plumbing fixtures kept tightly closed to prevent the pipes from freezing. The washroom in the building had been expanded in 1899

Troop F of the First US Cavalry in front of the stone double barracks, circa 1913. The stone two-story double barracks, still seen today and the background of this photo, were built in 1909 and not present when Reade made his inspection. (Yellowstone National Park Museum Collection)

at a cost of $930, but the southern building was small and needed a similar expansion. In addition, given the propensity of soldiers to visit the "sporting women" in Gardiner, the post surgeon in later years ordered that "each troop lavatory, one shower bath, and one water closet" were to be "set aside for the use of men with venereal disease, and plainly marked to show the purposes for which intended." One of the barracks—it was not stated which one—also had a barber shop and two pool tables for the soldiers to enjoy themselves at a nominal price of five cents a game. If civilians played, they paid an additional five cents to rent a pool cue. The troop had been provided gymnastic equipment to promote physical activity, but since the gymnasium would not be built for several more years, the equipment was stored in the barracks and not used.[25]

Some civilians also lived in the barracks. Captain Goode allowed two Chinese men to live there and do laundry. Sergeant Offley resented their presence in remarkably racist ways. "Do you think Captain G has acted wisely in allowing the two Chinamen to start a laundry in the quarters?" he asked his brother in a letter. The soldiers harassed the poor immigrants mercilessly. "I don't think they will last very long here in the post." The next week he was even more annoyed. "Those Chinamen are getting to be a perfect nuisance already. They want everything they see and want all the troop to be 'dog-robbing' for them all the time." The soldiers' frustration was growing, and Offley thought that "the boys will be taking matters into their own hands pretty soon and will be running the Chinamen out of here, minus a pig-tail or so."[26]

In the evenings social gatherings were common in the barracks. Sergeant Offley, who was diligently studying for an examination to become a commissioned officer, found it impossible to concentrate because "the boys are amusing themselves with an accordion out in the quarters, so it [is] impossible to try and study in here for a while." As typical with garrison duty, particularly at Fort Yellowstone after the tourist season ended and the harsh winter set in, there was not much to do. He added that "they have little enough to do to amuse themselves in these long, winter evenings, and on the whole, I would rather have the noise than have them off somewhere to gamble away all their money, and even their clothes." Soldiers were instructed to keep the barracks clean, and orders stated that the soldiers were "responsible for the police of grounds and walks about their quarters," before the officer of the day would check up on them and report any deficiencies. Some noncommissioned officers, like Offley, took particular pride in the appearance of their troop's quarters. In January 1901 he noted that "quarters were looking very nice and the Captain even remarked on it. It was very pleasing indeed to me, too." However, the men's appearance often left something to be desired, especially when off duty. Commanding officers often reminded the troopers that "men off-duty will, when outside of the barracks, wear the prescribed uniform for the garrison. Campaign hats and leggings will be worn off duty only when on mounted pass. The blouse will be kept buttoned. The blouse may be dispensed with while engaged in athletic sports, provided a uniform blue flannel shirt and belt are worn. Either the blouse or the blue flannel shirt and belt will be worn at meals." In a rather extreme case of being caught out of uniform, one soldier "dressed like a clown and somehow got down to the hotel just as stagecoaches with tourists were coming in. There he danced about and performed until a soldier was sent for him." For the embarrassment he caused the command—and more importantly, the post commander—he was arrested, "tried, declared insane and discharged."[27]

Like the clown some soldiers were forced to reside at least temporarily in the guardhouse. The building was "a small one" but the year before Reade arrived there were several deficiencies. The bathroom was in particularly poor shape. The "wooden seat of the stool is broken; fecal matter is deposited on the side of the basin which does not flush contents when the trap is

Guardhouse at Fort Yellowstone, circa 1900. The building was originally built in 1891 and housed both military and civilian prisoners. In addition, all people coming into the park had to check in there. (National Park Service Photo)

pulled. The wash basin is not kept clean." In addition, the "brick arch of the fireplace in the guard room is partially fallen in; needs to be repaired." One of the lieutenants was in charge, but he delegated almost all responsibilities to a noncommissioned officer who was posted at the guardhouse with four privates. "Men go on guard every fifth day." Inspector Reade found they were "well instructed" and "the reports properly kept."[28]

Both civilians and soldiers whose violations were severe enough to warrant confinement were kept in the guardhouse. Life for those under guard was, as would be expected, generally unpleasant.

> Prisoners will not be allowed to go to their troop quarters or elsewhere, except to work, without the authority of, or by the direction of the Prison Officer. While at work, they work under the direction of the police officer and Provost sergeant. The Officer of the Day is responsible that the regulations relative to the number of prisoners under one or more sentries is enforced. When prisoners are sent out for other purposes than for work, the time of their departure, purpose for which sent, and time of return, and name of sentinel, will be entered on the book kept by the Provost Sergeant for record of work. . . . At no time will singing, loud talking, or other notice be permitted among the prisoners, nor will they be allowed any books, smoking materials, playing cards or other means of diversion.

. . . Garrison prisoners, when confined, will bring much of the foregoing articles as they possess. . . . Bedding will be aired every Monday morning. . . . Military convicts will not be allowed to wear any part of the military uniform, but will wear the uniform prescribed for convicts.[29]

Even Reade found little to criticize during the day of his inspection, but at other times the guards could be less than diligent. Private William Fitzgerald and later George Collins were convicted of not making the prisoners work. Corporal Achilles Taitt let the prisoners play cards and read magazines. Private James Todd and Sgt. William Shook allowed their prisoners to become drunk. The sirens of alcohol could even enchant the guards. Privates Henry Herton and John O'Mara were convicted of being drunk while on duty in the guardhouse.[30]

Perhaps the center of the soldiers' world lay at the post exchange, where several recreational opportunities existed. Prior to 1886 military posts had a civilian contractor, known as a sutler, who provided a store and social facility for soldiers. However, they were phased out, and by 1890 the army had moved entirely to the post-exchange model run in a type of co-op fashion by the soldiers themselves. Physically, the Fort Yellowstone exchange building had been a problem for several years before Lieutenant Colonel Reade's arrival in 1901. In 1899 the inspector noted that it was "in an old building which is not suitable for the purpose," the exact words that Reade would use in 1901. The exchange had a "saloon," sometimes called a canteen, staffed by a civilian bartender who earned $50 per month. The rules of order were "prescribed and enforced" including "no gambling allowed." It is interesting to note that officially there were to be no saloons in Yellowstone Park, though they were known to exist to both military commanders and the park's chief magistrate, Judge Meldrum, who once met an incoming military superintendent at the barroom at the Fountain Hotel. In fact, the barroom at the hotel in Mammoth was directly across the hall from Meldrum's office and was often frequented by him and the army officers.[31]

The sale of liquor to soldiers by hotel staff could gain the ire of more temperance-minded park visitors. One such tourist complained to the secretary of the interior that at the Cottage Hotel in Mammoth "liquor was also sold to the soldiers," which he noted "was another violation" of the park's rules and regulations. He went so far as to say, "Whiskey was sold at $2.50 per quart, beer at 40 cents per quart." The accusation also implicated the post's commanders. "The several Park officials who have had charge of park affairs

The interior of the old Fort Yellowstone post exchange at an unknown date but probably circa 1901. The post exchange was the best place for soldiers to relax off duty and served as the primary social center for the garrison. Despite the regulations expressly forbidding saloons in the park, this photo and Lieutenant Colonel Reade's description make it clear that the exchange functioned as one. (Yellowstone National Park Museum Collection)

have allowed wagon loads of liquor to be hauled to Mammoth and in plain sight of the Acting Superintendent's office."[32] While a complaining tourist's charges may be suspect, the mention of the saloon at the post exchange in as official a document as an annual inspection suggests that the prohibition of barrooms was perhaps the most neglected regulation in the park.

That is not to say that commanders acknowledged such. In 1910, in response to a tourist complaint, Acting Superintendent Maj. Henry C. Benson wrote to the secretary of the interior and stated categorically, "No saloons are maintained in the park." Clearly, that was not accurate, but he could finesse his statement with the clarification that "the concession is made that wine and other beverages may be furnished to bona fide guests of hotels, at their meals." Since the soldiers were forbidden from entering hotels to enforce the rules and regulations, the hotel managers would dispense alcohol freely with plausible deniability to the commanders. Not that the soldiers would likely have had a problem other than that they too might patronize the establishments. Benson seemed to acknowledge that, as he continued, "Liquor is not knowingly sold to soldiers—or at least if it has been in the past, it has now ceased, and the Yellowstone Park Association has been cautioned not to exceed the limits of the above mentioned privilege, and it is not believed that either the letter or the spirit of the law will be violated." However, Benson did have to admit that "when I first took up the duties of superintendent, I found that liquor was being sold generally, without any restrictions, to whoever desired to purchase it." He added that "in fact, barrooms were maintained freely and openly." Even after he gave orders to the concessionaires to stop, he nevertheless "found that bottled liquor was still being sold, through trickery."[33]

Political pressure had been mounting to prohibit the sale of alcohol on all military posts, effectively closing the canteens. Needless to say, when Congress outlawed the sale of alcohol at all post exchanges in 1900, it was hugely unpopular with the troops. The January before Lt. Col. Reade arrived, Sergeant Offley wrote home about the unfortunate situation. "So I see by the papers that the Senate has passed a bill to abolish the Canteen. That is evidently the work of the WCTU [Women's Christian Temperance Union], one of the most meddling organizations that ever existed. They have succeeded in dealing the Army a blow that will have a very demoralizing effect upon it. I believe they have always done much more harm than good. They certainly have in this instance."[34]

The 1901 inspection had the special charge of interviewing soldiers to get their feedback regarding the changes imposed on the canteen. Inspector generals were asked to interview several soldiers about the effect this would have on the morale of the troops. Even though no move had been made to actually close the canteen at that point, it was imminent and everyone knew it. Lieutenant Colonel Reade asked the following question of troop commanders: "State, in general, how, in your opinion, recent legislation abolishing the canteen feature of the post exchange has affected, or will affect, the discipline, morals, or habits of the enlisted men?" Capt. George Goode replied that "evil effects are already noticeable and morale and discipline of command at this post will suffer as long as men are deprived of beer in the canteen."[35] Clearly, the officers and men were not wholeheartedly embracing the temperance movement.

The exchange also had a "general merchandise and lunch counter. The lunchroom contains tables, chairs, and an oil stove for cooking." A private who received $20 per month extra compensation manned the counter. The menu was undoubtedly better than the usual army mess. "Ginger ale, lemonade, bottled orange soda, sarsaparilla, lemon soda, soda water, cream of various flavors" were the nonalcoholic beverages. Soldiers had a choice of sandwiches. Cheese sandwiches cost five cents; pork, beefsteak, or sausage sandwiches would put them back fifteen cents. Reade noted that "men spend the most money on fruits, tobacco, then sweets." Soldiers were extended a small line of credit. All the privates in the troop could have $4 credit, corporals $6, and sergeants $7. Reade estimated that the merchandise at the store and counter was worth approximately $1,500. Profits from the sales varied according to the product but had been consistent since 1899. The profit on beer was noted at 100 percent, cigars at 35 percent, eatables at 5 percent, and everything else at approximately 33 percent. The store also sold select books and some newspapers from around the country. Most of the merchandise was purchased from Marshall, Field & Company in Chicago, but the beer was specially ordered from Anheuser Busch Brewing Company in St. Louis, Missouri. Since it operated a type of co-op among the enlisted men, the profits were shared, but they had not recently been regularly distributed back to the troop.[36]

In off-duty moments, soldiers would congregate at the exchange; it was the center of the soldiers' social world. In fact, the next year's inspection noted that "at present, the enlisted men have no place for amusement except in the exchange." That being said, it was not very well suited for the central place it held in the lives of the men. It was "very dingy," and one inspector noted that it "should be brightened up by kalsomine or paper." Reade noted the next year that "the room in the exchange is so limited that the men cannot assemble there in mass for balls or other amusements, save the use of one billiard table. Papers and periodicals are kept there, but it is so inconvenient that a suitable place should be built, to be used as a library and reading room. Such a room could be utilized for other gatherings." Since Fort Yellowstone was extremely isolated, particularly in the winter, Reade emphasized the importance of fixing the exchange. "This, I regarded as important, because these troops are thrown entirely on their own resources for amusement the greater part of the year. There is no place they can go to outside of the post."[37]

Ideal or not, the exchange was all the soldiers had, and it had to suffice for their social center. Jokes were told, gossip exchanged, and rumors overheard. Private Hugey Hollins said that he was "in the canteen one evening, and I was passing a group of men and I heard someone making the statement somewhere about" another member of the troop who had a predilection for certain "immoral" acts. He shared his juicy tidbit of an overheard rumor with other soldiers, which led to a series of courts-martial.[38]

The soldiers could also go to the small town of Gardiner and visit the saloons or "sporting women," but they might also engage in the healthier amusements of being on one of the fort's sporting teams. Naturally, as long as sports did not interfere with their military duties, the post commander encouraged participation. The emphasis on athletics grew significantly in the late nineteenth century in schools, colleges, and the military to promote manly qualities and provide models of ideal masculine paradigms. In the heavily masculine society of the army, sports were highly promoted. In later years the soldiers competed against each other in fencing, boxing, gymnastics, sprinting, and weightlifting, among other things, as individuals and companies. These competitions were used to measure one's masculinity and in at least one case were explicitly stated as such.[39]

The post also had baseball and football teams. The teams competed against nearby communities and even against the employees of the hotel at Mammoth. Baseball games against the Livingston town team could be "evenly matched" and "snappy," or "the game lost interest . . . when the score stood at 15 to 5" in favor of Livingston. Jack Haynes remembered that the rivalry with the hotel employees could be particularly sharp. One July 4 baseball game "went along without violence until the fourth inning when an altercation developed in the vicinity of second base." The hotel's second baseman, a drummer in the band, was also a prize boxer from Chicago named Jesse "Kid" Liponati. He and a soldier exchanged words and "three soldier players in succession set upon him with dire results. The game was stopped promptly by order of the commandant, but small group battles continued the rest of the afternoon and evening." The commander ate that evening at the Haynes house and "remarked that the guardhouse wasn't big enough to hold a fraction of the civilians—to say nothing of the soldiers—who should have been arrested."[40]

Ironically, the football games could be more genteel, at least when the fort's team played the high school from Billings, Montana. The Billings team played a game against the Livingston high school and then traveled south to play the fort's team. When the team left Billings, some people were concerned that "the soldiers would treat them roughly and brutally, if necessary, to win." They were "reminded of the great differences in their own weights and sizes compared to those of the troops." Once the game started, "the game was too one-sided to be interesting." However, as far as the students

This real photo postcard shows the Fort Yellowstone baseball team playing the Gardiner team in 1910. (Yellowstone National Park Museum Collection)

were concerned, "it took only a few minutes . . . to cause them to overcome all fears and misgivings, for the soldiers were gentleness itself and several times ceased playing when they believed one of the visitors had been hurt." The sportsmanship did not end when the soldiers won 22–0. "After the game, the soldiers allowed themselves to be jolly good fellows and entertainers. They took the Billings men into their quarters at Fort Yellowstone and fairly swamped them with attention and courtesies. The visitors were arrayed in uniforms . . . and given a ride of about 15 miles into the park and shown the sights." The revelry continued into the evening as the players were "again entertained in the barracks and spent a hilariously happy night with their hosts." When they returned to Billings, "all wore yellow cords, crossed sabers and other emblems and devices indicative of the cavalry branch of the army." When the students disembarked from the train, "they looked more like a detachment of cavalrymen returning from campaign than schoolboys coming home from a visit."[41]

Had any of the players from Billings been seriously injured, they would have gone to the post hospital. The army hospital staff also served the tourists and hotel civilians. When Lieutenant Colonel Reade visited in 1901, it had one ward with eight beds, staffed by the contracted civilian surgeon, a hospital corps consisting of between three and four privates who acted as hospital stewards, and one hospital matron. Reade interviewed the surgeon,

The Fort Yellowstone hospital, date unknown, but based on the soldier's uniform, it was likely taken before 1901. The building was completed in 1893 and renovated several times. (National Park Service Photo)

Dr. James B. Ferguson, and found him to be "excellent in conduct and efficiency." Ferguson had assumed his post on June 22, 1898, and made daily "inspection of the hospital every morning and of the corps every Saturday." The corps, Reade noted, "were not required to perform any military duty," and they were "reported as being of temperate habits." They had received "instruction in litter drill, first aid to the wounded in addition to lectures and are proficient." Other men at the post had training by the hospital corps in addition to their regular duties, particularly at the remote outposts distant from the only official hospital in the park. In the year before Reade's visit, Ferguson had visited the Norris, Canyon, Lake, Thumb, Snake River, Lower Geyser Basin, Riverside, and Soda Butte Stations to "extend instruction in first aid to the men." The previous year the inspector noted that "no instruction in first aid [has been] given company officers. Samuel McCormick, Hospital Corps, is not proficient in this duty. All men in the troop on duty at the post are not instructed as required." Reade made no note of it in his inspection, but the instruction had been taking place though it was not necessarily appreciated. Sgt. Edward Offley noted his disdain for "that miserable, sickening Hospital Corps drill every Saturday morning. It is the most useless waste of time imaginable."[42]

The medicines were carefully controlled and inventoried so the exact amount used each year could be measured. In 1899, for instance, the post issued two quarts of whiskey for medicinal use, along with one-quarter ounce of chloral, forty-five ounces of chloroform, 1.2 ounces of cocaine, 7.5 pints of glycerin, one ounce of morphine, ten ounces of quinine, three pints of opium, and two quarts of brandy. Losing some of this inventory could result in being court-martialed. In 1914 Pvt. Robert Normal left some opium accessible when he left his station temporarily to chat on the telephone. Several courts-martial focus on the hospital staff and patients regarding alcohol and drugs. Private Emil Simminger of the hospital corps not only let one of his patients get drunk but also imbibed enough himself to be unfit for duty. Private Clyde Rhodes was so drunk when he was on duty at the hospital that he started fighting with anyone nearby. The staff did not sufficiently watch Pvt. Blaine Werr, a patient, who left the hospital specifically to get some liquor.[43]

Overall, though, Lieutenant Colonel Reade's reports on the hospital and its staff were very positive. "The police of the hospital and its premises was excellent. The instruments and supplies were in excellent condition." Despite being very clean and well maintained, the building had some deficiencies. "The operating room is accessible by a narrow stairway with two turns, very difficult and awkward for moving patients. It is recommended that an operating room be built as an addition to the ground floor. The present operating room could be utilized as a bacteriological laboratory." Reade noted that when there were only two troops stationed in the park, there was "sufficient capacity for the post," but when the number of troops increased to four in 1902, Reade noted that it was "too small," even without counting the civilian demand in the increasingly popular, but dangerous, park.[44]

The annual inspections usually made a note about the "health of the command." Reade noted that it was excellent, with "no diseases particularly prevalent during the past year according to the surgeon who also reports command thoroughly vaccinated." He noted there were "four cases of smallpox in Gardiner," just six miles away. The veracity of his observations is a bit suspect. Only four months before the inspection, Sgt. Edward Offley noted, "I have just gotten over the grip myself. There has been quite an epidemic of it in the post and it came near being the cause of trouble between the Post Surgeon and myself, but it has all blown over now, I am glad to say."[45]

The health of the command was important. This included both preventive care and treating problems once they arose. In 1900 and 1901 the army had provided gymnastic equipment including "a vaulting horse, horizontal and parallel bars, a ladder, chest eights, boxing gloves, dumbbells and

Indian clubs" as well as instruction "by noncommissioned officers" in how to use them.[46] One of the more common ailments was venereal disease. If an infected soldier failed to report his condition to the doctor, he could be court-martialed. This was so important that an official order explicitly stated that "men who expose themselves to the danger of contracting venereal disease shall at once upon their return to the camp or garrison report to the hospital or dispensary for the application of such cleaning and prophylaxis as may be prescribed by the Surgeon." The order added that "anyone who fails to comply with such instructions, if found to be suffering from venereal affliction shall be brought to trial." The post surgeon also could warn soldiers to avoid certain areas in Gardiner. In 1910 Capt. Wallace DeWitt suggested to the commander that "enlisted men of the command be warned that one of the inmates (name unknown) of the brothel in Gardiner, known as the 'Big Four,' is infected with venereal disease" and they should act accordingly. Practicing unsafe hygiene that endangered the troop was also a court-martial offense as when Pvt. James Severns cleaned the syringe he used to treat his venereal disease in a washbowl of the troop lavatory.[47]

To keep the command healthy, the post surgeon made himself available for preventive care, but often the commanders had to coerce the soldiers to attend. For example, in 1910 the commander offered the following declaration: "The Surgeon will examine the teeth of the enlisted men of the command, at the reading room at the Post Exchange, commencing at 1 pm today in the following order—Troop E, F, G, and H. Troops will be reported to the Surgeon by First Sergeants, who will have listed all members of their troops. Absentees will be sent to the Hospital at Sick Call tomorrow." The soldiers complied, even if it might interfere with their duty, such as when Pvt. Ernest Freeman skipped guard duty and went to the dentist even though he was intoxicated.[48] The hospital corps also had to make themselves available for troops and civilians in the park. Stewards and surgeons were ordered to take station periodically throughout the park at the soldier stations.[49]

In the wintertime, when the soldier stations were more isolated, medical attention was harder to provide. In 1912 Private Cunningham and Private Carroll were shot at the snowed-in Sylvian Pass Soldier Station, and a doctor had to be summoned from Cody. The doctor only agreed to come to the soldiers' aid once he was assured that "the government will pay for it." At the Upper Geyser Basin Soldier Station the same year, civilian Howard O'Connor, the Old Faithful Inn winter caretaker, had been on the roof of the inn, knocking off the heavy load of snow and ice when it gave way and he slid to the ground and severely broke his leg between the ankle and knee. He managed to crawl into the inn and phone the soldiers, who came to his aid. They, in turn, called the post surgeon, explaining how the break looked. The doctor told them they would have to set the bone and walked them through the excruciating process. According to the corporal in charge of the post, "The leg seemed to stretch a foot or more. . . . We succeeded in resetting the leg although the yelling of the patient must have been heard in Salt Lake City. He accused us of attempting to murder him and every time we came near him he would let out a yell." Despite the pain, O'Connor had no hard feelings and later sent a check to the men as a "little reward for the tender care and consideration" the soldiers had given him.[50]

The health of the command also depended upon the food they consumed. Soldiers have a long tradition of griping about military food, and a service-wide investigation in 1903 determined that the poor quality of food was a key contributor to the high desertion rate.[51] Perishable goods were important. The post had a baker who could produce between 200 and 240 rations daily. The baker was a private from the command who earned twenty-five cents a day for extra duty. To provide fresh produce, the command had a three-acre garden approximately two and a half miles from the post. Since the altitude limited what could grow during the short season, items such as lettuce, radishes, peas, beans, onions, beets, and carrots were all that could be produced. Even then, some noted that the garden "produced so little . . . as to make it impossible to give detail." Buying fresh produce on the open market was difficult. Thus, Reade noted that "fresh fruits and garden vegetables are high-priced at Fort Yellowstone." Echoing previous years' reports, he concluded that the "lands cultivated at present are not entirely suitable and that a better site for a garden can be found on the first level below the post," where there might be better soil and irrigation.[52]

Great care was taken by many noncommissioned officers to provide good food when they could, particularly on special occasions. Sgt. Edward Offley proudly wrote to his brother that "I managed to give the troop a very good Thanksgiving dinner. Oyster stew, roast turkey, roast beef, cranberry sauce, mashed potatoes, bread and butter, pies, cakes and hot chocolate, and a plenty of everything." However, he added that such a feast came at a price. Each troop had a budget, and special events could stretch it thin. The cost was not insubstantial as the food had to be purchased from the post exchange or the markets in Gardiner. He claimed that "after Christmas, we will have to live but poorly until the troop is out of debt for the Post Exchange."[53]

In late December Offley was reassigned to other duties, and a Corporal Schols began procuring the food. He turned out to be less than diligent, and Offley was put back in charge of rationing this company in February. Just after he was reassigned to the duty, "the Captain called me into the Office . . . and showed me a meat bill for $112.90. That nearly took my breath away. Thank goodness, I didn't have a thing to do with making it. Last month I was in charge of the mess I paid $16 on beef." He noted that for the troop to make their way out of debt, the "boys you all will live on slum and bacon for a few months I thought. Corporal Schols knew what he was doing when I put [him] in charge of the mess, but another month like that and he would have the troop bankrupt."[54]

The men tried to acquire additional foodstuffs quietly and off the record by trading with local civilians. Offley noted that at least once he "went to Gardiner, Cinnabar, and Hoar today to see what I could do in the way of trading some rations," but he "did not have much success." He continued his efforts a week later as he and a Corporal Bryan went to Bear Gulch, the mining settlement north of the park, to "see if I could dispose of some surplus rations." Again, he "did not have much success in a business sense, but enjoyed my ride very much and went all through the big Jardine gold-mine up there. Quite an experience and very interesting indeed."[55]

Another important element in the health of the command was water. For several years before Reade's first visit, previous inspections had raised concerns about the lack of water to the post. In 1901 "Army officers do not feel justified in using any water save for household purposes. . . . Likewise, of the 27 cottonwood trees, 17 are dead from lack of water." Not everyone felt the spirit of self-deprivation in the face of a short water supply, however. "[Park Commissioner] John Meldrum resides near the post and has a lawn and flower garden maintained by water" from the same water source as the fort. Part of the problem was the supply. The hotel, only 300 yards from the fort, drew from the abundant Sepulcher Creek while the soldiers took their water from the smaller Clematis Creek, which filled a small reservoir. "Attempts made to divert Sepulcher Creek to the post [were] stopped by the Yellowstone Park Association hotels."[56] The generally cordial relationship between the military officers and concessionaire management apparently had its limits.

The previous year's inspection report noted that "stress is strongly laid upon the fact that a water famine may exist at Fort Yellowstone if forced to rely upon Clematis Creek for supplies."[57] Therefore, Lieutenant Colonel

Reade and the new post commander, Captain Pitcher, looked for and found a potential solution to the water problem. Reade suspected that the reservoir leaked, as it had only three inches of water in it, and he recommended the construction of a new one. Reade had Lieutenant Amos and Captain Pitcher help him locate a place for a new reservoir in consultation with the head of the Army Corps of Engineers in the park, Capt. H. M. Crittenden. They concluded that a new one could be built near the quartermaster's corral, but that solved only one part of the problem. Clematis Creek would still be insufficient, and they believed that to alleviate the problem they would have to pipe water from Sepulcher Creek. Reade noted that, after some arm-twisting, "Captain Pitcher succeeded in obtaining the consent of Messer's Childs, Bach, and Huntley [of] the Yellowstone Park Association, to borrow enough water to fill" the new reservoir.[58]

Besides their duties in protecting the park and maintaining military readiness, the soldiers had to drill for potential emergencies, such as building fires. Lieutenant Colonel Reade and other inspectors looked at the equipment and the soldiers' demonstrated abilities to note efficiencies and deficiencies. Commanders had taken the threat of fires at the post seriously and structured the emergency response accordingly. Special Order 95 in 1899 described it this way:

> In case of fire:
>
> 1. 1st Lt. Wm Yates, 1st Cav, is designated as Fire Marshal. Upon the breaking out of fire, he will proceed to it without delay and assume general control.
> 2. The non-commissioned officer of the guard with all members of the guard not on post will report at the location of the fire to the Fire Marshal.
> 3. The following details from Troop M will upon alarm of fire proceed rapidly to its location with their respective appliances and report to the Fire Marshal,
>
>    1st—2 noncommissioned officers and 8 privates in charge of hose cart,
>    2nd—2 noncommissioned officers and 14 privates as ladder men.
>    3rd—1 noncommissioned officer and 10 privates as bucket men.
>    4th—all remaining members of troop formed and marched to location and report to the fire marshal.
>
>    Members of these details will report to the fire marshal at such times as he may designate for thorough instruction.

Until further orders there will be Fire Drill every Tuesday morning, beginning at 10 o'clock.[59]

The training was not just an academic exercise. Fires were genuine threats. Reade had pointed out that the wood-built officers' quarters with their unwatered lawns were particularly susceptible to catastrophic fire. But other buildings were as well, at a time when wood or coal fires produced the standard heat. In 1910 the old Cottage Hotel, then used as an employee dormitory for the larger National Hotel at Mammoth, caught fire. The soldiers' response probably did not unfold precisely as they drilled and delineated above, though it may have been close. As the soldiers tried to actively suppress the fire in the attic, they were carrying mattresses down the stairs when the commotion woke a young female employee, who rushed out of the building. She was not fully dressed, drawing the attention of the soldiers. Gallantly they offered her one of their blankets and resumed their duties. In 1910 the new, two-story barracks caught fire as well. Though the fire was extinguished and the building saved, there was substantial damage and at least one soldier fighting the fire was seriously injured when the floor gave and he fell three stories.[60]

Hospital and fire drills were not the only training that soldiers were required to do. The military still required regular drills of marksmanship, saber, horsemanship, and small-unit tactics. However, balancing those duties with patrolling and protecting the park was difficult. In 1889 Captain Harris, the first of the military acting superintendents, stated that "the present status of . . . a military force for the protection of the Park is in a very unsatisfactory condition." He went on to detail that using soldiers to patrol the park was an "impairment of military efficacy in the force so employed." That tension between duties was never alleviated throughout the military tenure. In 1899 the inspector found that "practically all drills within the last two months have been conducted without an officer, there being only a detachment for drill, with two and sometimes only one officer at post." Therefore "a number of men . . . need more individual drill. There are some good horsemen in the troop, but the majority . . . are not well-instructed cavalrymen . . . [because of] limited time for instruction with the duty assigned." The following year the inspector general found there was "no riding school for mounted troops at the post." The inspector added that "practical instruction in minor tactics are not practicable" because of the duties required in the park. Reade pointed out this was not the typical army protocol but necessitated by the unique duties performed in the park.

The 1910 fire in the Cottage Hotel. By the time the fire took place, the Cottage Hotel was being used as an employee dormitory. According to some accounts, as the fire spread and the soldiers responded, some of the female employees were taken by surprise and did not have time to fully clothe themselves as the young woman in the foreground suggests. (Yellowstone National Park Museum Collection)

> The division of duty at Fort Yellowstone requires that the junior lieutenants should be ready for detached service in the park at any and all hours. Lt. Amos does not perform, is not required to perform, all of the troop duties that customarily devolve upon the junior subaltern, but he is ranging about the Park a good deal, and the captain of the troop take nearly all of the stable and troop duty. The first lieutenant is the paperwork man and does not perform much troop or any detached duty. The captain thus becomes the drill master and is more directly responsible for the appearance and condition of horses, etc., than either of the subalterns.[61]

This was even true at the most basic of training, target practice. The main target range was about one mile to the northwest of the post on rolling ground. A larger and more open target range for practicing skirmishing was located approximately four miles away. A third gallery range was in the old stables at Camp Sheridan. Usually, the commander oversaw only the initial exercises and relied heavily on the noncommissioned officers to improve trooper performance. That is not to say these men did their job with full diligence. The summary court-martial records are replete with instances where

When incidents such as the Cottage Hotel fire occurred in 1910, the soldiers' firefighting training paid off. The duty was hazardous given the questionable construction of some buildings and the steep nature of the roofs as this photo suggests. (Yellowstone National Park Museum Collection)

range officers were drunk on duty, particularly in the pulling pit, limiting not only their effectiveness but the safety of the range.[62] Given its location closer to the saloons at Gardiner than the fort in Mammoth, the temptation for drinking was all too real.

Though Maj. John Pitcher had only recently been placed in command when Reade conducted his inspection, he would come to appreciate the extraordinary difficulty in balancing the park duties and proper but unrelated military training. In 1903 Pitcher wrote to the adjutant general, "Owing to the peculiar nature of the duties required of Troops in the Park, it is, simply impracticable to give the officers and enlisted men of this post all of the drill and instruction which they should have during the Drill Season from April 1st to Oct. 31st." He noted that at least some military duties were being attended to, particularly with regard to new technology. "[A] detachment has been detailed and drilled in the manual of the machine gun and one thousand rounds have been fired from it at target practice."[63]

The education of the troop was only partially fulfilled by drills. The officers participated in an officers' lyceum—a type of study group. The lyceum was not particularly well organized and seemed to occur irregularly and only in an ad hoc manner. In addition, "no room is available except the

Even the fort's buildings were not immune to fire as this 1910 photograph of the stone double barracks demonstrates. The last additions to the fort, completed in 1909, were of sandstone, but the wood interior was combustible nonetheless. (National Park Service photo)

Commanding Officer's office, which is too small and not satisfactory." In 1899 the inspector even listed the books read that year, which included works on the Civil War including the battles of Spotsylvania and the Wilderness, and on the Santiago campaign in the recently concluded Spanish-American War. The post surgeon, Dr. Ferguson, led a discussion on first aid, military hygiene, and camp sanitation.[64]

Junior subaltern officers who wished to advance in rank also had a school during the months of December, January, February, and March led by the commanding officer. This was the most practical time given the isolation and lessening of duties during the off-tourist season. The courses included studying administration, drill regulations, and small-arms firing regulations. Reade noted that "owing to the insufficient number of officers at the post, a board of officers to examine" the successful candidates and the examination date had to be rescheduled. The two candidates, "being under orders for the Philippine Islands . . . preferred to be examined at a later date when settled in a more permanent station."[65]

The enlisted men had their schools and instructions too. The noncommissioned officers had a more regular schedule of classes. They met three times a week for "recitations" on practical military skills such as drill regulations,

Soldiers at the rifle range, date unknown. Maintaining their marksmanship was important for the soldiers. The rifle range was approximately three miles from the post and one mile from Gardiner. (National Park Service photo)

cavalry school of the soldier, troop deployment of cavalry, stables and care of horses, and firing regulations. For many enlisted men, particularly those who were recent immigrants with limited English skills, basic literacy was the goal of their education. The children of the post and civilian employees at Mammoth Hot Springs also attended the schools. The enlisted men went to school from 1:30 to 3:00 p.m. and the children from 3:00 to 4:30 p.m. An officer was put in charge, but "one enlisted man is detailed as a teacher who gives instruction in the following subjects: arithmetic, geography, history, reading, spelling and writing." In 1899 the average daily attendance was ten enlisted men and four children from military families and two with civilian parents. While "progress on most subjects was good, in some excellent, and others only fair," the building was "not suitable." The old carpenter shop at Camp Sheridan housed the school, but "the requirements of the post-school under existing order will demand more room . . . than can probably be provided."[66]

In the years immediately before Lieutenant Colonel Reade's inspection, the reading material at the post was noted as inadequate. In 1899 the

Members of the machine-gun platoon, circa 1915. Since machine guns would be of dubious help in enforcing park rules, this photo shows that the garrison maintained their identities as soldiers. Their dual role of protecting the park and maintaining military preparedness was problematic from the start, as noted by the first military superintendent, Capt. Moses Harris. (National Park Service photo)

inspector reported: "There is no post library except of 39 volumes of fiction, all the [other] books are either government publications or tactical works and none are ever read by the enlisted men. [There is] no suitable room for a library and reading room. There are 247 books on hand, kept in cases in adjutant's and CO office." Half a year before Reade made his visit, railroad heiress Helen Gould (later Helen Shaw), who had visited the park the previous summer and been escorted by some of the men, sent what Sgt. Edward Offley called "one of the finest collections of books I have seen for a good while. All the latest and best books published and beautifully bound." He was very grateful and noted that "she is certainly the friend of the solider."[67]

Miss Gould's donations aside, Reade noted that the official books were "not accessible to or used by the enlisted men. It is made up almost entirely of official publications. Books are kept in the adjutant's office." He did note that Miss Gould's donation consisted of "50 volumes." Troops had their own

The remains of the pulling pit at the Fort Yellowstone rifle range in 2019. Soldiers would raise targets on the metal frames, some of which are still visible, while safely shielded in this long trench. The pits were wide enough to have horses in them so they could become used to the sound of live rounds of ammunition. Court-martial records indicate that, with the rifle range's proximity to Gardiner, several soldiers manning the pits succumbed to the temptations of the saloons and were sometimes drunk while performing their duties. (Author's collection)

collection of books as well. "Troop G has a library of 275 volumes comprising, chiefly, the standard novels. The books are well cared for [and] kept in bookcases. The Troop uses the post-reading room which is open from 9 am to 10:30 pm daily." However, in 1902 Reade suggested that the current places where books were accessed "is so inconvenient that a suitable place should be built, to be used as library and reading room. Such a room could be utilized for other gatherings."[68]

Reade took eight days to complete the inspection of Fort Yellowstone, during which he noted several other deficiencies. The cemetery needed a fence, the magazine's foundation was unstable, there were not any hand grenades in the munition stores, a new quartermaster's storehouse and wagon shed needed to be built, and an ice house should be built near the proposed

The buildings from old Camp Sheridan, circa 1900. These buildings were still used for various purposes throughout the history of Fort Yellowstone. (National Park Service photo)

reservoir. Reade did not mention many things in the final report. The inspection naturally focused on things typically military, but, unlike other posts he inspected, the unique duties and obligations of the command were already evident. A distinct social climate existed at the post because the soldiers were in close contact with people who considered themselves the soldiers' social superiors. Social rules, expectations, and behaviors created a set of social obligations not present at other posts. Where and how those rules applied to the soldiers stationed in the park affected not only the experience of the soldiers there but also their ability to perform their duties. Even if Reade only hinted at it, the division of duties between military and civil were becoming clearly inadequate for both the army and the park. In fact, as Capt. Hiram Chittenden, commanding the Army Corps of Engineers in Yellowstone, stated in his *Yellowstone National Park: Historical and Descriptive* published in 1900, with the arrival of the army "an entirely new order was obtained. It was to be seen how much could be accomplished, even in the absences of laws, toward a vigorous and healthful administration. . . . Real authority was made manifest." However, he did add that the military was also inadequate and "some provision, of course, should be made for an adequate police force . . .

Every day at sunset for over thirty years, soldiers fired a cannon from the top of Capitol Hill as seen in the 1916 photograph. (Yellowstone National Park Museum Collection)

designed solely to preserve it unimpaired, as its founders intended, for the 'benefit and enjoyment' of succeeding generations."[69]

CHAPTER THREE

# "Conditions . . . Resemble Those Existing 30-Odd Years Ago"

## Life in the Park's Interior

The extreme uniqueness of the duties required by the troops in Yellowstone would only become more evident the next day when Lieutenant Colonel Reade began his tour of the remote stations throughout the park. As he prepared, he must have reflected on the responsibilities of the park's garrison spread across remote stations, possibly reminiscing about his own lengthy and distinguished career. The army had changed significantly since he enlisted during the Civil War, served on the frontier, fought in Cuba and the Philippines; it now stood as the guardian of American's burgeoning empire. Yellowstone's troopers were a throwback to a bygone era. In his final report he noted that the "conditions at Fort Yellowstone resemble those existing 30 odd years ago when the commands at military posts were split up by such detached service as guarding stage stations, escorting mail coaches, protecting surveying and construction parties, etc., along proposed transcontinental lines of railroad."[1] He had personally experienced that era, as would have many of the higher-ranking officers at Fort Yellowstone. However, few men or junior officers, a generation removed from such service, would have similar experiences on which to rely. His inspections would provide valuable insights on how to effectively garrison small detachments away from the main post.

On the "pleasant and mild" morning of June 2, 1901, Lieutenant Colonel Reade headed north out of Fort Yellowstone on the road toward the Norris Geyser Basin. He would tour most of the remote outposts throughout the park where soldiers were stationed to patrol and protect the park. The guide on his tour was First Lt. Frank Amos. Along the trail Lieutenant Amos greatly impressed the inspector general, who described the young lieutenant as "a trained hunter and keen sportsman . . . a natural cavalryman" who "loves range work." Unlike many of the soldiers stationed in the park, Amos was motivated and skilled at backcountry patrolling. Normally the soldiers' skills were limited in that regard, and they relied on the backcountry scouts to effectively patrol the area for poachers. Amos was an exception. "Lt. Amos' functions are those of a ranger. He ably performs these functions. His vision and instincts enable him more than once during our trip about the park to discern herds of elk, bunches of deer or antelope at long distances."[2]

Lieutenant Amos also had a keen eye for poachers. During the inspection tour he ably demonstrated those skills for Lieutenant Colonel Reade. Reade claimed that "poachers smuggle hounds, or other dogs, into the Park by concealing them in covered wagons. Mr. Amos detected two cases of this kind whilst we were journeying or camping together." The backcountry was Amos's home, and his talents were a perfect match for the park. He had recently been promoted to first lieutenant and would soon be transferred to the 11th Cavalry stationed in Virginia, though his love for the work and his exceptional talents for Yellowstone made it desirable for him to stay. Reade suggested that since Amos was "so familiar with the topography of the park and the methods of trespassers and depredators that it is recommended he be retained at his present station of arduous and useful service." Reade added that even the new acting superintendent, Capt. John Pitcher, "desires this."[3]

The outposts that Reade and Amos were inspecting had their roots in the final years of the civilian administration. Before the arrival of the army, six small buildings were scattered around the park for the "assistant superintendents," who were in charge of protecting the park. They were located at Soda Butte on the road to Cooke City, near the Grand Canyon, Norris Geyser Basin, on the Madison River near the west entrance, by Old Faithful, and at Lower Geyser Basin. The army would steadily increase the number to sixteen though several were only occupied during the summer.[4] As the summer tourist season grew in popularity, the small crews—typically one noncommissioned officer in charge of four men—proved inadequate. Extra troops from other posts in Montana or the Dakotas would erect tents and supplement the tiny garrisons during peak periods.

Naturally, the army tried to keep things at the outposts as systematic as possible, and orders were issued regarding the standards that commanders expected. The primary concern was that soldiers' discipline would become lax away from the watchful eyes of commissioned officers, who only could inspect the posts every few weeks. A slovenly appearance, especially

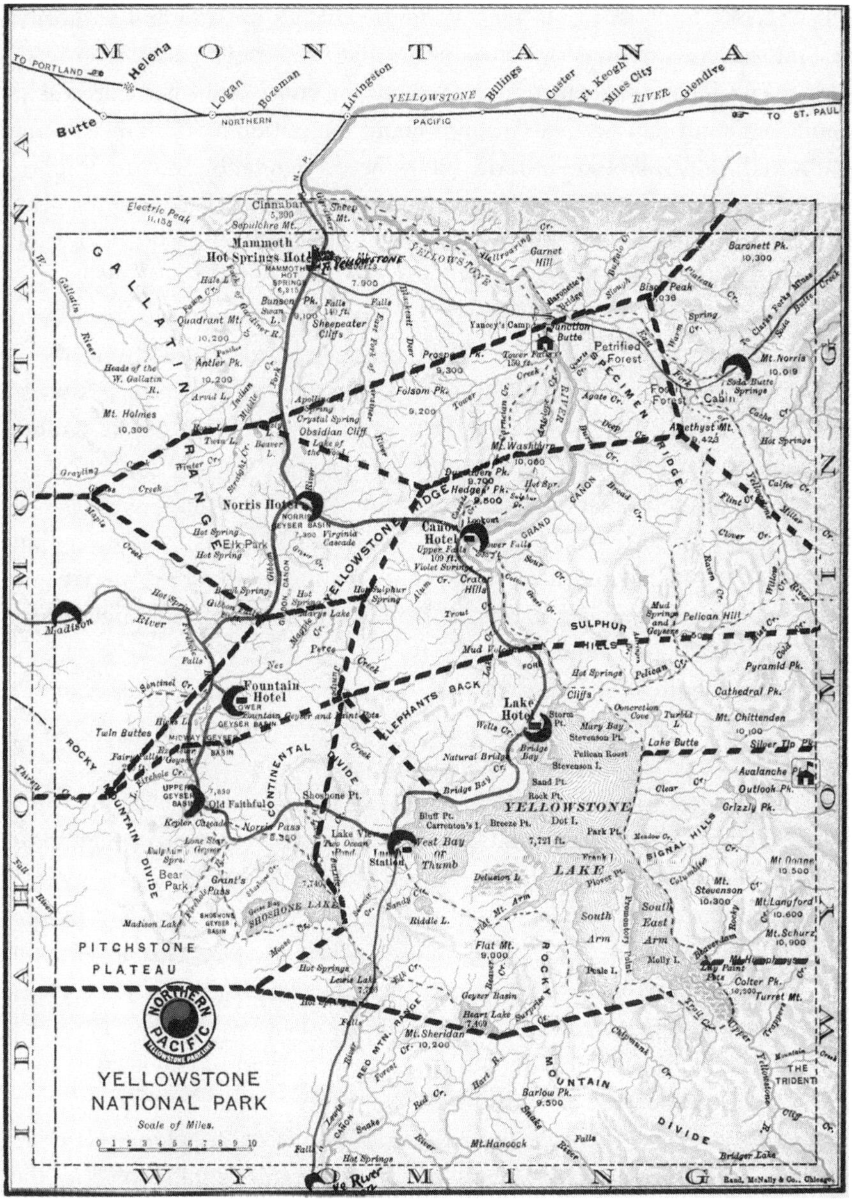


Map of the soldier stations visited by Lieutenant Colonel Reade on his inspection tour in 1901, as included in his final report. It is interesting to note that he used a tourist map made by the Northern Pacific Railroad. Military superintendents often did the same for their annual reports. (National Archives and Records Administration)

to traveling tourists, would undermine the army's mission and authority. Commanders consequently issued orders that "the strict regulations governing the uniform arrangement of bunks and the police of the barracks will be enforced at all stations. . . . Grounds about the station to a distance of one hundred yards will be kept thoroughly policed." Sanitation was also important. Regulations stated that "the manure in the corral will be kept spread-out and exposed until ready for removal. . . . Garbage will be kept in covered galvanized iron cans, not too near the station. The can will be hauled to the dump and the garbage removed every evening after supper, the can cleaned and stored inside for the night, or the can may be suspended from trees." As noted by the suggestion to suspend garbage cans in trees, bear safety was paramount. The dump "will be as far away as practicable from the station. . . . For the bears, the refuse must be frequently raked together and burned." No detail was too small to escape regulation, even the latrines. "At least two seats and a covered urinal with pipe connection will be provided each year. The covers to the seats will be hinged and so adjusted that they will fall and cover the holes when not in use. . . . The closet must be fly and light proof and the rear fly and almost light proof."[5]

Every station was supposed to keep the same hours of duty and service to the public. The soldiers fed their horses at 6:00 a.m. and 4:30 p.m. They ate breakfast promptly at 6:30 a.m., dinner at 12:00 noon, and supper at 5:00 p.m. "Immediately after breakfast, beds will be made up, the station thoroughly policed, and made ready for inspection." The stations could allow tourists to enter and even eat in them "between the hours of 4:00 o'clock p.m. and 6:00 p.m.," though they would have to pay for the food. The money would be kept in a lockbox at the station and used to purchase supplement rations for those consumed. However, "no women will be permitted to enter any station, at any time."[6]

Despite their isolation deep in the park, the outposts could keep in contact with headquarters at Fort Yellowstone through a telephone network maintained by the Yellowstone Park Association. The "telephones used are licensed for the use of the Signal Service only" and "rental is paid by the Signal Service" to the hotel concessionaire, the Yellowstone Park Association.[7] In 1901 Reade noted that "the cost of maintaining the lines is in excess of receipts and communication is made precarious by falling trees and further made uncertain by the temporary repair done by the occasional lineman." Winter also created its own problems as avalanches could regularly cut some stations' lines. The Sylvan Pass Station regularly had this problem,

The third incarnation of the Norris Hotel or Norris Lunch Station, date unknown. Two previous versions of the hotel burned down, the first just after construction in 1887 and a second in 1892. After that, the area was serviced by a complex of tents run by the famously jovial Larry Matthews. When Lieutenant Colonel Reade made his visit in 1901, the third version of the hotel, with twenty-five rooms, had just opened and would remain in use until 1916. (Yellowstone National Park Museum Collection)

something the soldiers annually anticipated. The telephones alleviated the isolation of the outposts but were prone to abuse, and commanders had to order that "on account of the gross and scandalous abuse of the privilege by enlisted men on station, the practice of visiting over the park telephones is withdrawn" and that "the lines will be used for official purposes only by enlisted men. . . . It is the duty of the noncommissioned officers of the station to see that this order is rigidly enforced and they will be held responsible for any disobedience of the same."[8]

As Amos and Reade traveled into the park, they headed south out of Mammoth, through the Golden Gate, the Swan Lake Basin, past Obsidian Cliff and down into the "remarkable geyser region . . . formerly called 'Gibbon Geyser Basin'" but later changed to Norris Geyser Basin. The basin contained many natural features including large boiling pools, geysers, and the Gibbon River. The Yellowstone Park Association maintained a lunch station there as well, known over the years as the Norris Lunch Station, Norris Hotel, and Larry's Lunch Station. Lieutenant Colonel Reade commented that

"'Larry' Matthews, the voluble famous human steam radiator of Irish wit, keeps the lunch station nearby" the soldier station.[9]

The establishment had several incarnations. First built in 1886 in the woods across from the soldier station, it burned down in 1887. A second, more temporary establishment was built with limited overnight accommodations, but it too burned down, in 1892. After that, the Yellowstone Park Association temporarily used the soldier station "as a waiting room for stage passengers" on the condition that they would make some temporary "arrangement for shelter and workplace for the two soldiers stationed there." A more permanent tent lunch station was erected the following year until a new hotel opened in 1901 overlooking the geyser basin. These lunch stations were the scene of significant activity during the summer as the stages coming from the Canyon Hotel arrived daily at 10:30 a.m. to tour the formations and those from Mammoth arrived shortly after lunch.[10]

As Reade and Amos approached the area, just to the east of the main road, they would find the Norris Soldier Station, in approximately the same location where a later incarnation of the soldier station, built in 1903, still stands today as the Museum of the National Park Ranger. Like the civilian lunch station and hotel, the soldier station had several incarnations. The original station, predating the military's tenure, was substantially remodeled in 1897 and was the building Reade inspected. He described it as

> two stories high and about 25 ft. deep and an area built on [the] rear. Built of logs with wooden shingles on the roof. Two rooms upstairs and three downstairs. [The] House is built a little above ground and banked up on sides. Ceiling of laths, no plaster; newspapers are pasted on the wall. Brick fireplace. One heating stove, Rock Island Wood Heater No. 1. Range in kitchen was made in 1885 by Wm Muller and Co.

The post was "equipped with telephone, connected with Fort Yellowstone, Cinnabar, Canyon, Fountain, Lake, and Norris," and he noted that "blacksmithing [is] done at Fort Yellowstone." Improvements were always needed. Previous inspections noted that the Norris Station's "water closet is not kept in good sanitary condition. They were directed by me to correct this with free use of lime and dry earth" and that "the interior of the station at Norris would be . . . improved by papering the rooms with surplus target paper."[11]

A detachment of three privates and one noncommissioned officer typically manned the station, but at the time of Lieutenant Colonel Reade's inspection, Norris only had two privates with Private Kirschke being listed as the man

The Norris Soldier Station, circa 1905. This is the version of the soldier station that Lieutenant Colonel Reade visited. It was replaced in 1908 with the current building still standing today and used as the Museum of the National Park Ranger. (Yellowstone National Park Museum Collection)

in charge. All soldier stations in the park were required to "see that all the Rules and Regulations and the 'Instructions to be Observed by All Persons in the Park' are complied with by all persons." But each station also had its own designated territory to patrol for poachers and a unique set of duties and obligations. The region that the Norris crew was responsible for "started at Beaver Lake, runs west to Mount Holmes, thence southwest to the junction of Maple and Cougar creeks, thence easterly to Gibbon River at the mouth of Canyon Creek, thence northeast to the point on main road midway between Norris and Canyon, thence northwest to Beaver Lake." During the summer the soldiers were also charged with "the protection of Norris Basin, and daily from the time the first coach arrives until the last one leaves, one man must remain on the formation" to enforce the rules. They made three daily patrols along the roads. The first was north to Apollinaris Spring and back to the station, the second was south to the Wylie camp on the Gibbon River, and the third east on the Canyon Road to the Wedded Trees. During the winter, "immediately after the discountenance of the summer road patrols, the winter duty of scouting and patrolling the interior of the district for the special protection of the game will be taken up." The soldiers were to take particular note of the number of beaver, moose, and sheep in the district and keep "a sharp lookout . . . for bear trappers and other poachers, and for forest fires." During unusually dry years these soldiers would make "special fire patrols, in addition to the regular patrols, except in cases where they coincide [with regular patrols] . . . unless weather conditions are such as to preclude any possibility of forest fires."[12]

For all stations, fighting fires was difficult and dangerous, especially for a small detachment of men. "It has been found in the past," wrote Acting Superintendent Maj. John Pitcher, "that it is almost useless to send a small detachment to handle a forest fire after it has once gotten well started." The best way to prevent them was for soldiers to educate tourists in fire safety. Pitcher noted that "their warnings to tourists and campers seem to have resulted in the gradual education of the traveler as to the importance of care in the use of fires." It was not always to good effect. In 1900 soldiers from Norris came upon a camper named John Beagle who was "tramping," or camping independently, along the side of the road. A bear came near and frightened him, and he built three large fires near his camp. "These he was compelled to extinguish some time during the night from the patrol from Norris, and he was cautioned about the danger of forest fires, but he rebuilt the fire after the patrol left him and the next morning failed to properly extinguish them, and as a result about noon these fires started up again and soon spread into a serious forest fire."[13]

Fighting fires was often beyond the ability of the small garrison to handle on its own. In 1902 soldiers stationed at Norris spotted smoke in the backcountry north of Norris. "We went to it but had quite a time getting there," reported one of the soldiers. After assessing the situation, they "went to Wyllie [*sic*] Camp for pails but we could do nothing much with the fire so the Corporal went on to the post [i.e., Fort Yellowstone] for help." While the fire grew, the management of the camp, presumably the one at Swan Lake Flats, became concerned. "He asked me about the fire. I told him the Corporal had gone for help and that we had it so it would not spread until the troops got there." As a sign of gratitude, the camp manager let the soldier "go in and eat dinner. The girl waitress asked me if I wanted coffee or milk. I took milk. The first I had had for several months."[14]

Keeping order in the park extended beyond simply protecting the features and patrolling for poachers and forest fires. Since most soldier stations, like Norris, were near hotels or lunch stations, the behavior of disorderly tourists often led to confrontations between management and visitors. In 1894, for example, a tourist named C. S. Bannerman, accompanied by three ladies, stopped at the Norris Lunch Station and asked for milk. The gregarious Irish manager, Larry Matthews, told them all he had was beer at twenty-five cents a glass, a price that Bannerman refused to pay. Matthews told him that "no pricks were allowed in his house" and that he would have the soldiers escort him out. Taking the initiative, Bannerman went to the sergeant at the soldier station and reported his side of the affair first, but Matthews came rushing in and told the sergeant that Bannerman was a thief and had stolen a glass and broken it. The soldiers had to muddle through accusations and counteraccusations as best they could.[15]

The soldiers' hospitality could be generous and warm for those who behaved and were willing to forgo the class distinctions. A solitary tourist traveling alone by the name of Mode Wineman came to a soldier station during a rainstorm, and the soldiers invited him in. As he recounted, "A short distance beyond was the Norris Geyser Lunch Station (Hotel), but I stayed to supper with the soldiers who had the meal ready spread on clean oilcloth. The fragrance of bacon, freshly baked bread, jam, fried potatoes, and coffee made me as hungry as a wolf. The food they gave cheerfully and urged the storm bound stranger to remain for the night, longer if he chose." He stayed for a bit, "smoking on the veranda" and "gave meager news of the outside world" until the rain passed. He then checked into the hotel and visited the steamy geyser basin.[16]

Wineman's interaction with the Norris soldiers did not end there. That evening, while walking in the basin after the sunset, he walked to a place where the ground was unsafe, and a soldier cried, "You'll sink! Follow quick!" The soldier led him to more solid ground. He explained that "had the crust really broken under my weight I should have been scalded to the knee." The soldier added, "It is pretty lucky I chased after you." The soldier led him back to the Lunch Station Hotel in silence until they came upon an evening social of the hotel employees around a campfire. "Cooks, maids, stablemen, and porters were dancing in quadrille to the music of a mouth-organ played by a fat, young Irish lad. . . . The dancers with their ruddy, healthy faces, their hearty laughter and their gay raiment made a merry scene." Noticeably absent were the hotel guests, other than the "tramping" Wineman. However, the hotel workers showed a level of comradery with the working-class soldiers. "Here [at the dance] the soldier found friends and joined in the dance."[17] These interactions were common. As one soldier stationed at Norris put it, "The girls from the hotel come down nearly every night to go horseback riding or play games."[18] Undoubtedly, there was also some flirting among the soldiers and hotel girls. Why else would the hotel stewards and stablemen be missing from such an observation?

As feared, in their leisure time at Norris Soldier Station, away from the watchful eye of officers, the soldiers often misbehaved. From 1909 to 1913, the years that the garrison court-martial records are available, alcohol accounted for eight of the fourteen offenses at the Norris Station. Most cases resulted in insubordination while intoxicated, but in at least one case drunkenness and poor behavior were displayed in front of tourists. Privates Frank Bedell, Joe Sattler, and Louis Bradshaw of Company F, First US Cavalry became drunk at the station in August of 1913 and "did disgrace the uniform of the United States by using profanity in the presence of ladies." They also neglected their duty of patrolling the geyser formation "by behaving in such a manner as to cause unfavorable comment by tourists that [they] be taken away . . . to the scandal and disgrace of the service near Norris Soldier Station."[19] In the milieu where middle- and upper-class Victorian tourists encountered soldiers enforcing the rules and regulations, a natural tension already existed. The sight of the enlisted men's openly drunk and disruptive behaviors only reinforced the social differences between the soldiers and at least the hotel class of tourists, straining the paradox between their social and legal relationships.

Alcohol also interfered with the Norris Station soldier's official duty four years before Lieutenant Colonel Reade performed his inspection. On August 14, 1897, a line of stages left Canyon heading west on the road to Norris. The line included a military ambulance taking Maj. Gen. Hamilton Smith Hawkins, other officers, and their wives on a sightseeing tour of the park. General Hawkins was probably visiting his son, a second lieutenant assigned to Company D, Fourth US Cavalry, stationed at the Lower Geyser Basin.[20] Two armed men wearing masks stopped the stagecoaches, had the passengers disembark, and proceeded to rob them at gunpoint. The incident was reported to the soldiers when they reached Norris, and Sgt. Dennis Driscole, of Troop H, Fourth US Cavalry quickly marshaled his men and went in pursuit over Canyon Road. It is not clear whether he had been drinking when he left Norris, but when he arrived at the Canyon area, he was intoxicated and acted belligerently, making several "unwarranted arrests," and was disruptive to the soldiers at the Canyon Soldier Station. Its commander, Sgt. Max Welch, reported that in his opinion, Driscole was "so far under the influence of liquor as to place him beyond the use of any judgment in the actions he took."[21]

The Riverside Soldier Station, circa 1905. (Yellowstone National Park Museum Collection)

The employees of the lunch station and hotel often exacerbated the problem. At the end of the tourist season in 1912, the winter keepers of the civilian lunch station were apparently on such good terms with the soldiers that they made the hostel's excess liquor freely available to them. As four enlisted men drank heavily and played cards at the lunch station, a Private Peters caught another soldier cheating. A fight ensued; Peters went back to the soldier station, retrieved a pistol, and returned with the intent of shooting his opponent. Fortunately, the corporal in charge of the station stopped him. The incident was so alarming to the commanding officer that he ordered the Yellowstone Park Association's management to remove both the winter keeper from the park and the stock of liquor.[22]

At the time of the inspection, Lieutenant Colonel Reade noted that the only deficiencies he found were that "1 Army range, 2 carbines, and 2 holsters" were deemed "unserviceable property on hand at this station."[23] Lieutenant Amos and Reade then left the station, following the winding road along the Gibbon River, then down the Madison to the Riverside Soldier Station near the west entrance to the park. The station was on the Monida-Yellowstone Stage Line road and monitored traffic into and out of the park's west entrance. A small seasonal hotel named the Dwelle Hotel was close to the park's boundary, near where the town of West Yellowstone, Montana, is today. But until the Union Pacific Railroad extended its line to the edge of the park, the town did not exist. Traffic along the road, however, was not insignificant as it was a major entry point for people traveling to the park from Utah, Butte, or the Henry's Lake area.

The small cabin that served as the soldier station housed three privates under the command of Corporal Campbell. The soldiers were responsible for the area from the mouth of Canyon Creek on the Gibbon River to the western boundary of the park, south to the north end of the meadows of the Little Firehole River, northeast to the falls of the Firehole River and then back to the mouth of Canyon Creek. Their summer duties were "principally the enforcement of the park rules, regulations, and instruction, and the thorough performance of patrol duty." They were also to keep an "accurate registration in the registration book of all visitors to the park passing the station, except those carried by the Monida-Yellowstone Stage Line and the Wylie Permanent Camping Company" as well as "special instructions concerning opening and closing of [the] gate at [the] western entrance to [the] park."[24] Their daily summer patrols consisted of traveling up the Madison River to its headwaters at the junction of the Firehole and Gibbon Rivers and returning the same day.

Riverside's location made it one of the army's vanguards against the "merciless freebooters" and "head and skin hunters" from the Henry's Lake organized gang of poachers. Special field operations originated from Riverside to catch them in the act—but to limited success. In 1896 an army patrol ran across some of the gang near dusk, "but they escaped by flight in the darkness" and the "pursuit had to be soon discontinued." Capt. George Anderson, the commander and acting superintendent, lamented that "in Idaho, nothing has as yet been done [to stop the gang], and the authorities seem inclined to encourage this form of lawlessness rather than to aid in its repression." The operations against the Henry's Lake gang led to an early "park legend" of the time. Private David Mathews, stationed at Riverside, was reportedly shot by poachers in the winter of 1894. Charles "Buckskin Charley" Marble, a longtime local civilian, recounted that the private had left the station in February on patrol and to exchange mail when he disappeared. Despite efforts to find him, his body was not discovered until May, "lying face down on his skis, as he fell forward, shot through the back." Despite the vivid account and its believability because of the ruthlessness of the Henry's Lake gang, when they found his body, the commanding officer instead concluded that "it was evident [Mathews] became lost, and while in that condition became crazed and perished from the cold."[25]

While the soldiers at the Riverside Station may have followed the orders to suppress the poachers, they may have had more sympathy for them than suspected. The high-minded debates of the conservationist movement from the likes of John Muir or Gifford Pinchot might have resonated with the administrators and politicians in Washington, DC, perhaps even with the officers at Fort Yellowstone, but the enlisted men may have had quite a different view. Working-class people, especially those in rural areas, embraced a view of "moral ecology," where the breaking of conservation laws was justified under certain circumstances, in order to feed one's family, display masculinity through the traditional frontier pursuits, or engage in one of America's favorite traditional pastimes. Though they were knowingly breaking the law, these people did not seek to destroy nature as much as they simply held different ideas and morals regarding the environment from the progressive-minded conservationists; while it was justifiable in their own minds to break the laws, they actually self-regulated their use of the environment.[26]

The enlisted men stationed at outposts had ample opportunity themselves to poach for subsistence or at least as a relief from drab military rations. In the October before Lieutenant Colonel Reade inspected Riverside, Sgt. Edward M. Offley visited the station as the soldiers were preparing for the long winter season. He wrote to his brother that it was "a nice, warm, one story log building. In charge is Corporal Campbell with three men, and one of them is the best cook in the troop, and then it is almost the border of the Park, so all they have to do is slip across the line and hunt all they want to. They won't starve all this winter." He added that "supper was simply dinner repeated, but I was ready for it when it came, and I wish you could have had some of it with me."[27] Even though Offley suggested that the soldiers would hunt just outside the park, doing so out of season would still be considered poaching. He found no negative moral implications in doing so to provide food and to eat well.

Riverside's location next to the boundary of the park also made it a common avenue for deserters. This created problems for the soldier who had knowledge of or even abetted his comrades' escape from military service. In 1916 Pvt. George Miller was stationed at the Upper Geyser Station but left without permission around 1 p.m. on July 23. He made his way down the road along the Firehole and Madison Rivers toward the west boundary of the park. At the Riverside Station, he met up with Pvt. Frederick Moses. Miller gave his equipment—a saddle, saddle blanket, bridle, his .30-caliber rifle, and his .45-caliber pistol—to Moses, who helped conceal them. The two also tied up Miller's horse some distance behind the station so as not to attract the attention of the station's commander, Sgt. Howard Higginbotham. Aiding in the escape earned Private Moses a court-martial after Miller was arrested in Butte, Montana, the following day.[28]

As at Norris and other stations in the park, alcohol led to disciplinary actions, and at Riverside, the station's commander was complicit in at least one case in which the whole garrison became intoxicated. Cpl. George Derosier "introduced whiskey into the station" in July of 1913 and shared it with his comrades. Sgt. Richard J. Bohen, "being on duty in charge of Riverside Soldier Station, did knowingly and willfully permit" the men to drink despite "it being his duty as [commander] to prevent liquor from being brought into the station."[29] Since Sergeant Bohen was brought up on charges, the men must have been intoxicated enough to draw the attention of tourists who in turn reported it to military officials. Despite the rules against alcohol at the stations, one wonders how many incidents went unreported without the watchful eyes of the commissioned officers.

Of course, everyone had put their best foot forward for the inspection by Lieutenant Colonel Reade. The only deficiency he noted was that "there is no connection by wire with this station. There should be." The previous year the inspector noted that the soldiers "desire some benevolent person or society to furnish a supply of reading matter," but Reade made no note as to whether that had been remedied.[30] After their stay, Lieutenant Amos and Lieutenant Colonel Reade headed back up the Madison River, up the Firehole River, and then south to the Fountain (or Lower Geyser) Soldier Station on the banks of Nez Perce Creek, not far from the Fountain Hotel. Though Reade made few notes about the station other than its unserviceable equipment, the previous year's inspection described the building as having "one story; peaked roof; ceilings of rooms 9 feet high." An enclosed floor plan notes that the building was twenty-eight and a half feet by twenty-six and a half feet and had four rooms: a kitchen, office, sleeping room, and dining room. There was both a front and rear porch. The detached stables measured twenty-eight and a half feet by twenty and a half feet with "7 stalls; peaked roof, with loft or upstairs."[31] Photographs of the station in 1908, 1912, and 1915 show the station and outbuildings surrounded by a fence of elk antlers.

When Reade and Amos arrived, the garrison consisted of four privates under the command of Sergeant Busser. The district of the Fountain Station extended from the mouth of Canyon Creek on the Gibbon River west to the falls of the Firehole River, south to the north end of the Little Firehole River meadows, east to the head of Juniper Creek, north to the head of Magpie

The Fountain Soldier Station, circa 1905. The small building to the right was quarters used by officers so they would not have to quarter with the enlisted men as they made their rounds through the park. (Yellowstone National Park Museum Collection)

Creek, and back to the mouth of Canyon Creek. The daily patrol north traveled along the road all the way to the Wylie camp on the Gibbon River over a dozen miles away from where the soldiers were to meet the patrol coming from the Norris Station at 11:00 a.m. The daily southern patrol was to travel along the road to the crossroads near the much closer Excelsior Geyser five miles away. In addition, there were weekly patrols. On alternate Thursdays the soldiers went to either Upper Geyser Basin ten miles away or Riverside Soldier Station seventeen miles away.[32]

Special duties existed for this garrison given the high tourist traffic around the geyser basin and the large, first-class, 350-room Fountain Hotel run by the Yellowstone Park Association only two miles away. The hotel had been constructed in 1891 on a small hill close to the Fountain Paint Pots and remained one of the busiest hotels in the park into the early years of the twentieth century. Guests typically stayed two nights at the hotel to visit both the Lower and Upper Geyser Basins before the construction of the Old Faithful Inn in 1904. The hotel was luxurious by turn-of-the-century park standards: it had electric lights and hot baths with water from a hot spring.[33] Consequently, there were many tourists in the area on any given day.

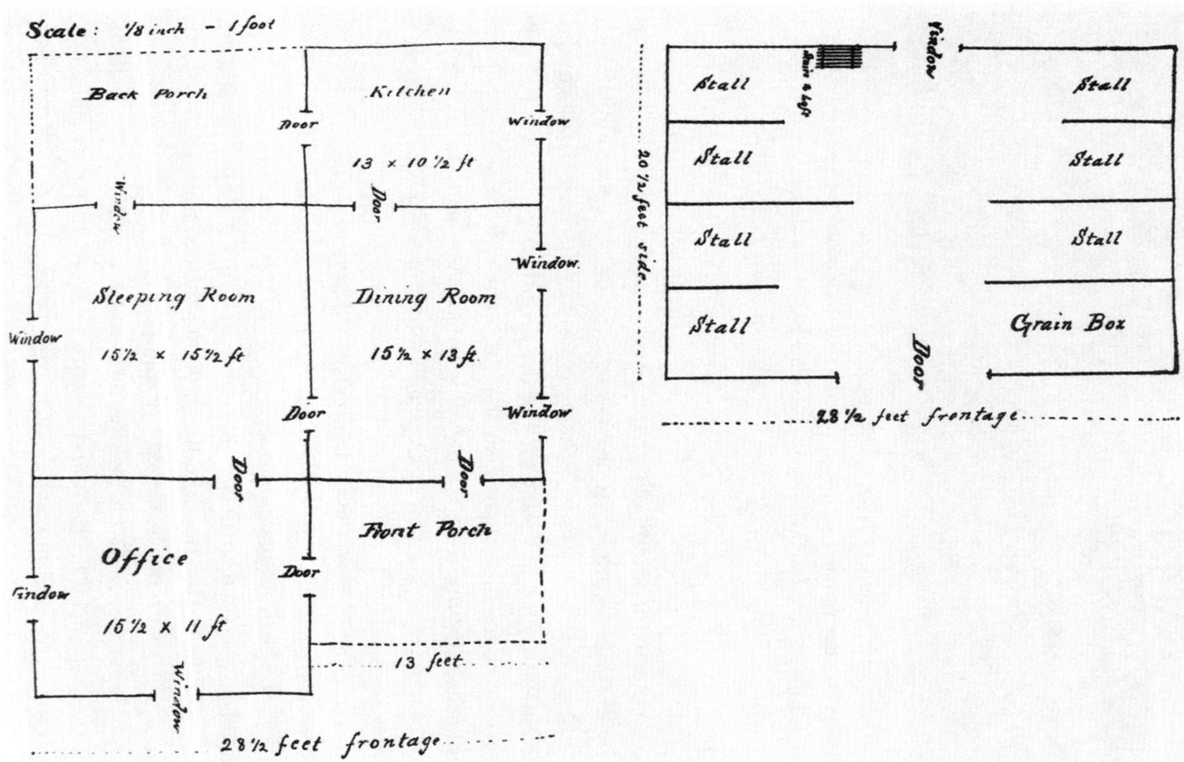


A plan of the Fountain Soldier Station in 1900, presumably drawn by Lt. Col. Theo J. Wint and included in his inspection report. (National Archives and Records Administration)

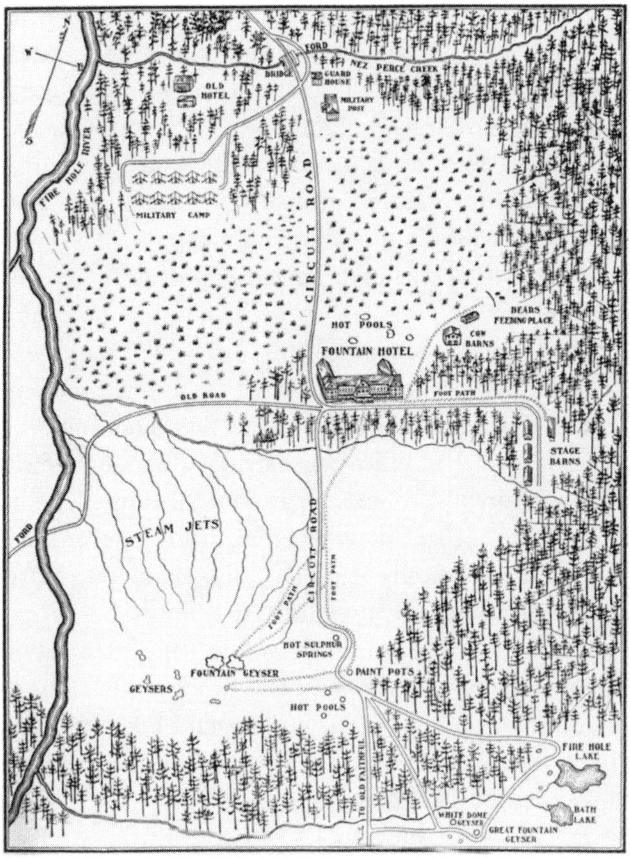


Map of the Lower Geyser Basin from the 1909 edition of *Campbell's New Revised Complete Guide and Descriptive Book of the Yellowstone Park*. Note that the map includes both a "military post" and a "military camp." In some years the army brought in additional troops during the tourist season. The "camp" is referring to one of those deployments of additional troops, similar to that described by Pvt. Herbert Angelo.

The soldiers at the station were busy. In addition to the regular patrols, all except regular coaches were to stop and register at the soldier station, and two men were "kept on the [geyser] formation during visiting hours, 6:30 am to 9:30 pm." The soldiers were also charged to keep the hotel tourists safe during one of the favorite early Yellowstone activities, watching the "bear shows" at the hotel dump. Every evening a guard was sent to "the hotel garbage dump to enforce orders in regard to bears," and he was to "remain on duty as long as there are visitors in the vicinity, not later than 9 o'clock p.m. and will allow no one to approach the bears inside the barrier, or nearer than 100 yards." There was also a blacksmith stationed with the garrison at Fountain who performed blacksmithing services for patrol horses and other government animals deep inside the park, but he was "discharged without honor by reason of misconduct" in 1900, which resulted in a station that "now has a sort of blacksmith shop, but no blacksmith."[34]

The Fountain Hotel and all of its amenities provided a unique social atmosphere not present at Riverside, where there was no hotel, or at Norris, with its tiny hotel. The well-appointed hotel had regular dances for its guests. Provided they behaved properly and dressed accordingly, soldiers might be invited to attend. The regulations clearly stated that "under no circumstances will any non-commissioned officer in charge of a station permit any of his men to go upon the premises or to enter any hotel in the park for the purpose of enforcing any rule or regulation pertaining to any hotel or transportation company." Orders periodically reinforced and clarified these regulations. Even off duty, "enlisted men are forbidden to enter the hotels" except upon "invitation of hotel guests to visit them, and to attend 'Formation Dances,' or other entertainments" unless it was only "by invitation of the managers." If given such permission, "enlisted men visiting the hotels to see friends that are guests of the hotel, or to attend the entertainments on an invitation of the managers, will wear the dress uniform."[35]

The concern of soldier misconduct was real. Private Archie Lane was "drunk and disorderly at the Fountain Hotel" and subsequently court-martialed. Despite a case such as that, the manager of the Fountain Hotel was apparently open to soldiers regularly attending the dances. Perhaps soldiers in dress uniform added an air of sophistication and civilization in the heart of the wilderness. The soldiers were very appreciative, and one noted that "We have dances at the hotel and on a platform near the camp two or three times a week and those that dance have a good time, they always have good order." These opportunities to socialize, particularly with women visitors or, more likely, with those employed at the hotel, led to flirting and attempts at romance. Private Clarence William of the First US Cavalry, "without authority and contrary to existing orders and regulations" took a woman named Emma Coleman "riding" on a horse "assigned to Private Carl Martz . . . for use in military service." The indiscretion cost Private Williams ten dollars a month for three months. Archaeology at the site suggests that women may have come into the station itself as well. Several pieces of jewelry, including a lady's lace pin made of brass, a brass locket, and four porcelain buttons typically associated with women's clothing have been found, but it is very possible that a soldier may have used them in a time before sexual identities became firmly established in the public's consciousness.[36]

As expected, drinking by the soldiers at the station was somewhat common. Interestingly enough, only two cases in the surviving summary courts-martial are from the Fountain Flats Station, those of Pvt. Archie Lane and Pvt. Amil Moravek, who "did introduce into his camp at Fountain Station, one bottle of intoxicating liquor . . . and did become drunk and disorderly in his quarters . . . and did fire his revolver, loaded with ball cartridge in the quarters of his detachment at Fountain Soldier Station." Despite the low number of courts-martial, other evidence suggests that drinking was much more common. Away from the vigilant eye of officers, men might break the rules without repercussions more easily than at the main post in Mammoth. Archaeology done in the 1990s at the site of the soldier station found significant evidence of alcohol consumption. At least thirty-five beer, gin, whiskey, brandy, and wine bottles were identified in just the footprint of the building itself. Ken Karsmizki, the principal investigator at the site, speculated that more would have been found in the trash pit if it had been excavated.[37]

Gunplay such as that of Private Moravek may have been frequent at Fountain Flats as well. Archaeologists found 274 spent cartridges at the station with a very large concentration, over 200, around the front porch, the social center of the outpost. Perhaps the soldiers were shooting game that came close to the station, maybe even in self-defense, as one evening a soldier was "going back to the cabin" and "was chased by a bear. The bear came up on the porch at night and they have great times [to] keep him away."[38] However, given the excessively large number of cartridges it seems more likely that while socializing on the porch, soldiers may have taken it upon themselves to have informal target practice. The irony of soldiers engaging in such activity was that civilians who brought firearms into the park were expressly forbidden from discharging their weapons. Each gun was to be turned into a soldier station at the entrance and retrieved upon exit, or soldiers would "seal" it at the entrance. Soldiers at each station would inspect the sealed weapon and stamp an endorsement on the owner's permit to indicate that it had remained sealed throughout the journey. The soldiers clearly did not see that the prohibition on guns applied to themselves.

Soldiers at Fountain Flats, like those at Riverside, were also eating wild game even though they were not near the border of the park to "slip across the line" and hunt as Sergeant Offley noted at Riverside. Each station was given army rations; nonetheless, they seemed more than willing to supplement their mess in multiple ways. Some even kept a small amount of livestock such as young pigs purchased with troop funds and fattened at the stations, and the archaeology suggests that at Fountain Flats, there was also a chicken coop. Even with the known presence of domesticated animals at the soldier station, the archaeology found that the largest group of identifiable bones were from large wild animals such as bison and elk. However, it also included small animals such as ground squirrel, rabbit, fish, grouse, geese, and ducks.[39] Again, despite being stationed in the park to prevent poaching, the soldiers themselves appear to have poached and accepted poaching in certain circumstances, mainly for their own benefit and subsistence. While soldiers enforced the park rules on tourists, such as the prohibitions on hunting, guns, and drinking, the same rules appear not to have applied to themselves.

General discipline could often be lacking at the isolated post as well. In 1902 Cpl. Frank Notruba, Troop B of the Third US Cavalry, in charge of the station wrote to the commanding officer at Fort Yellowstone, requesting that a soldier in his command be tried before a court-martial. "Sir, I had breakfast at 7 am this morning and this Pvt. Lamb talking about he would not get up at 7 am no more. I told him to get up and he started to talk back to me all the time. I ordered him to keep still. He did not do it until I put him under arrest and this man Pvt. Bohlke spoke up and I'm with you Lamb, he meant that if Pvt. Lamb would be sent to the Post that he wanted to be." The tension seemed to have been growing over time, as Corporal Notruba added that "these two men are very hard to get along with at the Station. . . . They are very troublesome at all times and they would like to do what they please. Sir, I wish . . . these men, Pvt. Lamb and Pvt. Bohlke, [be] relieved from Fountain Station."[40] The tension among soldiers was not uncommon and, in the winter of 1912, resulted in the murder of a soldier at the Sylvan Pass Soldier Station (see chapter 5).

Given the large patrolling distance and the particular duties on and around the geyser basin and the hotel, the small contingent of five soldiers would be hard-pressed to fulfill them diligently. During the heavy tourist seasons between 1889 and 1892, and again in 1902, 1903, 1907, 1908, 1912, and 1913, additional troops from around the West were brought in and assigned to various soldier stations seasonally. Fountain Station was one such station, needing additional troops because of the high traffic. For example, the year

Herbert Angelo, Thirteenth US Cavalry, circa 1902. (National Park Service photo)

after Amos's and Reade's visit, Troops A and C of the Thirteenth US Cavalry, approximately 150 men, marched from Fort Assiniboine in northern Montana for summer duty in Yellowstone. Private Herbert Angelo of Company C wrote that "we were half starved on the march to Fort Yellowstone." The contingent left on May 12 but did not arrive in the park until June 3. Upon their arrival Company A, under the command of Capt. R. C. Williams, was stationed seven miles from Mammoth "patrolling between Yancey's and 10 miles toward Norris" while Company C, under the command of Capt. P. S. Sockridge, was stationed at Lower Geyser Basin "performing the patrolling and garrisoning necessary for the care and preservation of that region of the park." Upon their arrival at the Fountain Flats Soldier Station, Private Angelo stated, "We are in a good camp and glad to be here after marching through rain, mud, and clouds of dust. We marched 460 miles" though they had "to sleep on our blankets" as there were "no mattresses or canvass bunks yet." The discomfort of the spartan accommodations was compounded by waking up to a surprise "two inches of snow on the ground" on the Fourth of July.[41]

The camp for the additional troops was set along military lines. The rows of Sibley tents were nice and orderly. "We sure have a good camp here," claimed Private Angelo. "[There is] plenty of wood and water near, both warm and cold. . . . There is a grassy plane [*sic*] near where we can drill." Even though they were patrolling the park, they still had to maintain military readiness. Angelo added that "there is a boiling spring not far off where we boil and wash our clothes," which they called "the Irish Washerwoman." However, in August the little geyser "blew up or Played as it is called" sending the clothes up along with it. It took a while "before it was clear again" and they could gather their clothes. There was even a hospital tent where Angelo reported that "four or five boys have the measles." He also took ill and had to spend time in the tent and "had to stay in quarantine." Not all the troops stayed at the camp. Some twenty-two soldiers were detailed to put up telephone lines. The work was intensive as they "made poles, strung wire, and dug holes" for two months.[42]

The summer troops were allowed the luxury of traveling through the park to see the sights on their government mounts. When his turn came, Angelo and his friends packed up some "three days of ration in the saddlebags and started out," heading first to West Thumb, where they fished. Then they traveled through the Hayden Valley to Canyon, a sight so grand that Angelo said, "I can't describe it." In their camp near the Canyon Soldier Station, the bear that frequented the area regularly harassed them. Then they traveled to Norris and back to the Fountain Flats camp. After the pleasure trip it was back to the business of patrolling and "lots of hard riding but as drill." At the end of August, Angelo's company prepared to depart for Fort Meade, South Dakota. The summer sojourn was generally pleasant as the young private reflected that "we have had such a good time" and that "it was with regret that we saddled our horse and rode away with the troop from this station."[43]

After finishing their inspection of the Fountain Flats Soldier Station, Reade and Amos moved on to the Upper Geyser Soldier Station near Old Faithful. Though the area received heavy day traffic, the Upper Geyser Basin did not have substantial overnight visitors until Old Faithful Inn was constructed in 1904. Before that, a lunch station served the day trips from Fountain Hotel, but the only overnight accommodation was at the Wylie Camp. The garrison at Upper Geyser Basin consisted of one corporal and four privates. Lieutenant Colonel Reade was not impressed by the station and noted several serious deficiencies. "The stable is not shingled on the east side. Hay used as bedding for horses is rotten; about six bales spoiled by rain

The Upper Basin Soldier Station, circa 1917. (Yellowstone National Park Museum Collection)

and snow. . . . The quarters need plastering and shingling. The Army range [is] in bad condition; subject for condemnation."[44]

Reade's harsh report is in contrast to a previous year's internal inspection report by Lieutenant Traub, who "found everything in excellent condition" except that the garrison complained "about the contractor's meat" in their official government rations. The meat was of poor quality and often rotten "and on one occasion had to be thrown away after inspection by [Acting Assistant Surgeon] Dr. [Carroll] Buck." The men had tried to bring attention to the poor quality of meat in vain. "These [complaints] had also been made with the contractor and the Commissary but without avail."[45] Perhaps this complaint was more widespread and the poor meat was delivered to the other stations as well. Since the soldiers had access to wild game and had little compunction about breaking the regulations about hunting to supplement their rations, perhaps the other troops simply failed to register such complaints.

The patrol area of the Upper Geyser Basin garrison was extensive. It started at Excelsior Geyser and went west to Fairy Falls and Twin Buttes, north to the end of the meadows of the Little Firehole River to the west boundary of the park, south to the end of the Madison Plateau, east to Moose Creek, to the southeastern point of Shoshone Lake, along De Lacy Creek to the headwaters of Juniper Creek, and back to Excelsior Geyser. The soldiers were to patrol the roads to the west toward Excelsior Geyser and east toward Thumb Station. Two men were on duty as "formation guards" in the geyser basins. Once the Old Faithful Inn was constructed in 1904, the

Soldiers by one of the park's thermal features. Date is unknown, but based on the uniforms, it is probably after 1902. (Yellowstone National Park Museum Collection)

social atmosphere was likely similar to that at Fountain Flats. This also seems to have tempted soldiers to act more inappropriately, and one soldier was court-martialed for wearing civilian clothes against the regulations.[46] However, fewer courts-martial survive from Upper Geyser Basin than from other outposts, though that may not necessarily indicate that things were any different from the other stations, but only that those breaking the regulations were not caught and tried.

After noting the deficiencies at Upper Geyser Basin, Lieutenant Amos and Lieutenant Colonel Reade rode over the mountains to the Thumb Soldier Station on the shores of Yellowstone Lake. Unlike the stations they had visited before, Thumb Station was only a summer encampment of three privates commanded by Corporal Ness. They "were sheltered in one conical wall tent" but also had "one common tent and a shack" that they used "for a kitchen and dining room." At nearly eight thousand feet above sea level, the Sibley tent provided only minimal protection against the high-altitude summer storms that frequent Yellowstone Lake, and by late summer and early fall the station could be quite miserable. Second Lt. F. J. Arnold wrote to the commanding officer, Capt. James Erwin, in September of 1898 that

> Cpl. Holte reported to me yesterday . . . [that] Thumb [Station] is becoming very uncomfortable on account of the cold day's weather and that a couple of the recruits are suffering from rheumatism on that account. They have no stoves for the tents at all. The corporal says that tourist

This Detroit Photographic Co. postcard is entitled "Summer Camp on Yellowstone Lake." However, the military Sibley tent and the fact that it corresponds to the description of Lieutenant Colonel Reade suggest that it is actually the soldier's outpost. The photographer may have chosen it for the subject matter because of the docked steamer *Zillah* in the background. The tent station was occupied only in the summer and by late fall was very uncomfortable. (Library of Congress)

> travel is very light and since the station was not established till the 16th of July could it not be relieved a little early, on or about the first of October.[47]

Regardless of their accommodations, the soldiers' duties remained the same: they were to protect the natural features of the park and patrol for violations. They patrolled fourteen miles south along the Snake River Road two or three times a week and nine miles north along the Lake Road and posted a formation guard. The area assigned to the Thumb Station garrison started at Arnica Creek and ran northwesterly to the headwaters of Juniper Creek, south along Delacy Creek, along the eastern shore of Shoshone Lake to the headwaters of Moose Creek, east to the mouth of the Upper Yellowstone River, and then along the southern and western shore back to the Arnica Creek. To some visitors the army's patrol of this region was disappointing. Mr. Edwin Ingalls of Chicago wrote an editorial in the *New York Sun* that "the 'supervision' by Federal troops is a joke!" He added that his party traveled "twenty miles . . . and not a soldier in view! We did see one soldier between Old Faithful and Thumb Station. And when the soldiers were seen, what were they doing? Sitting on piazzas or walking along with a mess of fish."[48]

By 1904 the army had built sturdier soldier quarters at the station, as seen here around 1905. (Yellowstone National Park Museum Collection)

As at other posts, food was supplemented locally. When Sergeant Offley visited in the fall before Lieutenant Colonel Reade's visit, he "tried a little fishing but even though I could see swarms of fish, I could not get a bite." The summer after Reade visited, Herbert Angelo had better luck. He and "the boys caught some big fish here on the lake and we have all we want." As at other stations, land animals also supplemented the government rations. Offley noted that "though I nearly shivered my head off while I eat [*sic*] it, I greatly enjoyed a supper of venison, potatoes, sliced tomatoes, bread, butter pickles, pie, [and] coffee."[49] Like Fountain Station, which was also deep in the park and far from the boundary, the only way to procure venison would be to hunt it locally, which would technically constitute poaching by the soldiers.

Civilian amenities consisted of only a lunch station and the dock for the steamers of the Yellowstone Lake Boat Company, run by Mr. E. C. Waters. The boat company ran steam-driven boats from Thumb to the Lake Hotel. Road-weary travelers were often encouraged by their drivers to take the boat trip for an extra $2.50 by which they could forgo the dusty road along the lake and even see animals that Waters had stranded on Dot Island. The drivers, likely happy for a respite from the travelers, also received a kickback of fifty cents for each passenger who took the boat trip. The boat company provided an opportunity for the soldiers to earn some extra money by "spooning" as security. However, on one occasion a drunk soldier "conducted himself in a disgusting manner," much to the distaste of the hotel tourists on board.[50]

The steamer *Zillah* circa 1904, operated by the notorious E. C. Waters. Waters offered a cruise from West Thumb to the Lake Hotel. Soldiers had the opportunity to moonlight or "spoon" for extra money by providing security on the ship. Army administrators fielded numerous complaints about Waters, and he was expelled from the park in 1907. (Library of Congress)

The army had long-standing troubles with the boat company, and particularly its owner, Mr. E. C. Waters. The most substantial number of complaints by tourists and other concessionaires in the park were centered on his operation. When Waters refused to pay kickbacks to the stage drivers, they began to discourage the trip by suggesting the boats were unseaworthy. Even some of the local soldiers may have conspired against Waters and his boats. When he received word of it, Waters's representative complained that the enlisted men at Thumb were "talking to tourists in such a way as to discourage them in taking the Lake trip on his boat" because the "boat was a farce" and that Waters "abused tourists after he had contained them on his boat." One soldier replied, "I wish to state that I have never said anything detrimental to the Captain's business to any tourist as I do not consider it part of my duty."[51]

Drinking was as common at Thumb as it was at other stations. Officers discovered that Sgt. Charles Leach had two suitcases full of whiskey. All the men posted at the station lied about the veracity of the report, but it was eventually discovered and the men court-martialed regardless. Soldiers would often cooperate with the civilian employees in finding drink. At the end of the 1909 season, the hotel companies were cleaning up their properties and several men passing through the area "secured liquor from the soldiers at the Thumb." Where they got the whiskey was something of a mystery, but Mr. Henry Childs, manager of the hotels, speculated that some of his other "men, or the soldiers, or both broke into the hotel" to acquire it.[52] Since there was no hotel at Thumb, it is not clear which hotel Childs was referring to, but he blamed the soldiers as much as his own men.

From the Thumb Station, Amos and Reade headed south along the Snake River to the outpost most distant from the headquarters at Mammoth—the Snake River Soldier Station. Four privates, overseen by a Sergeant Knapp, manned the station. It was located at the southern entrance to the park and consisted of a "small shack where the detachment is sheltered and is very inconvenient and in bad condition." Reade also noted that the station "has no connection by wire" to the main post though he added that "there should be."[53] The post's isolation was such that in the winter the easiest way to return to the main post at Mammoth was to travel south to Jackson Hole, then west across Targhee Pass, north around the outside of the park to Butte, Montana, then by rail to Livingston and south to the park.

Like the Riverside Station, Snake River had the typical duties of registering incoming parties as well as collecting or sealing any incoming firearms, in addition to patrolling for violations of regulations or poachers. The post's patrol area consisted of the entire southern portion of the park not covered by the other soldier stations. The area included "all that part of the park laying south of a line running from Eagle Peak on the east boundary . . . west by the mouth of the Upper Yellowstone River and south of Heart Lake and Lewis Lake and across the north end of Pitchstone Plateau to the west boundary of the park."[54] Given the vast area, "snowshoe cabins, nineteen (19) in number, are scattered about and are occupied during the winter by civilian scouts who are thus able to sleep in localities during the winter season when poachers are at work."[55]

Like the other stations, the men at Snake River supplemented their rations with locally procured wild meat. Since they were located on the border, they may have "slipped across the line" or found animals within the park; it apparently would not matter to the troops. When Sergeant Offley visited in 1900, he mentioned that a "Private Pixton, cooking for the detachment, soon had us a fine dinner of elk chops, tomato soup, his own bread and butter, coffee and milk." The station also had the typical discipline problems.

Snake River Soldier Station, circa 1905. (Yellowstone National Park Museum Collection)

In August of 1899, Corporal Travis wrote to the commanding officer that he "sent Pvt. Sifort to the Post for giving back talk and telling me I didn't know my business. I respectfully request you to relieve him from duty at this station. He seems to think he was sent here on a sporting trip, and in my opinion, if I don't send him in now I will have to do so later."[56]

The shoddy construction of the station led to an unfortunate incident when it burned down. On August 7, 1914, Sgt. James Webb with three members of the detachment were working about twenty-five yards from the building. The thick forest obstructed "all but a lower view of the building." Suddenly Webb "discovered a large volume of smoke rising from the roof." "I gave the alarm," Webb recounted, and "ran to the station and made an attempt to enter, but was unable to do so as I found the whole interior in flames." He added that "this station was heavily papered and the fire must have spread very rapidly as I was in the station about 15 minutes before discovering the smoke."[57] The building, all its contents, and its records were lost.

The complete loss of the building and the claims that followed provide a unique glimpse of the number of tourists who deposited their firearms at the station. Eight tourists, three from Rock Springs, Wyoming, one from Fort Washakie, Wyoming, one from Dubois, Wyoming, one from Bondurant, Wyoming, one from Pasadena, California, and one from Hay, Idaho, submitted claims to the government. The claimants lost five .38-caliber pistols, one Colt revolver, one Savage rifle, one Winchester Repeater, one .22-caliber automatic rifle, one 45–70 Sharps rifle, and several boxes of ammunition and holsters. The total value of all civilian items lost was $207.98. After three months the acting superintendent, Col. Lloyd Brett, had to regretfully inform the claimants that after consulting with the comptroller of the US Treasury, "there is no authority for the government to pay for the property destroyed in said fire." He added, "In view of this decision it would seem that your only way of securing remuneration would be by a special act of Congress, which you have to take up through your member of Congress."[58]

Reade and Amos moved north to inspect the Lake Soldier Station next to the Lake Hotel on the northwestern shore of Lake Yellowstone. If Reade found the other stations merely satisfactory, he was most impressed with the Lake Station and its detachment, particularly its noncommissioned officer. "Corporal Frank Ayers still remains in charge of this station with three men Troop G 1st Cav. The station is noticeably neat; has painted the interior of the station and outside of window sashes; also put up two tons of ice and stored in the root house." He also noted that the garrison has "started a garden, is about to build a new corral," and that the station "has tasty appearances, such as a weather vane and water wheel constructed, a refrigerator in a stream close by . . . built five upright lockers, also cupboard and ration boxes. The grounds are neatly kept and all belongings well cared for. The station would be improved in appearance if window curtains were supplied. It is located about thirty feet from a public road." Lieutenant Colonel Reade was impressed with the garrison, and he recommended "that the three privates on duty here, as being men of good character, all deserve to remain here." He even wrote a personal recommendation to the post commander and acting superintendent that Corporal Ayers "is a neat, soldierly young man, age 26. . . . I particularly commend [him] for his soldierly bearing and general intelligence. This station is neatly kept. He appears to be a tactful disciplinarian."[59] Clearly, Reade thought the men at Lake were exceptional when compared to those of the other garrisons, about whom he made little note.

The Lake Soldier Station had a district that encompassed an area starting at Mary Lake and ran east by Mud Geyser to the eastern boundary of the park, south to Crow Creek, then to Lake Butte, along the northern shore of the lake to Arnica Creek, and northwest to the headwaters of Juniper Creek, then back to Mary Lake. Like stations located near the other hotels, "one man will be present every evening at the hotel garbage dump to prevent interference with the bears. He will allow no one to approach the bears, nearer than 100 yards or within the barrier." The daily summer patrols included traveling halfway to the Thumb Station and eight miles north toward Canyon and returning each day.[60]

Lake Soldier Station, date unknown. (Yellowstone National Park Museum Collection)

The hotel was located approximately 300 yards to the west of the soldier station. Even though the Lake Hotel had not yet taken on the elegant appearance it had after its 1903–1904 renovation, it was still a major hotel in the park, with eighty rooms. (After its remodel, it numbered 210 rooms.) To the west of the soldier station, the Wylie Permanent Camping Company had one of its famous camps on the site of the current Lake Lodge. Though not as densely populated as the area around Fountain Hotel, it was a significant stop on the "Grand Tour," and it had more people there any given night than most places in the park.

Given the significant number of both tourists and employees, the off-duty atmosphere was rich for the soldiers. Dances were held at the hotel every Saturday evening. Even soldiers at the distant and much more isolated Sylvan Pass Soldier Station near the east entrance would time their patrols so they could attend the dances. However, there were official limits to fraternization. Women were barred from entering the stations, but Pvts. Daniel Becker, James Gearin, James Daley, and George Collins nonetheless invited women into their quarters at the Lake Soldier Station and were court-martialed. The danger of such liaisons was not limited to the soldiers. Lake Hotel employee Emilie Kryger and another worker known only as "Hanna" would often stay out "with the soldiers until dark." However, Hanna was later "discharged for immoral conduct," possibly associated with these soldier relationships.[61]

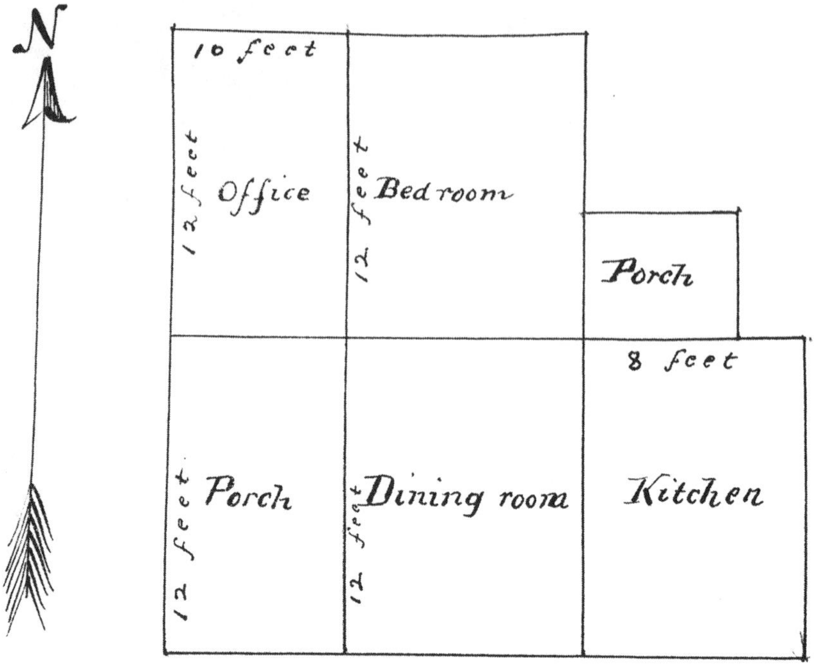


Plan of Lake Soldier Station in 1900, presumably drawn by Lt. Col. Theo J. Wint. (National Archives and Records Administration)

The soldiers at the Lake Station were also open to more than simply poaching for food. They were accused of cattle rustling from the herd of a contractor who provided food for the hotel. John Kauer of Rexburg, Idaho, owned a small number of cattle he kept near the hotel to provide fresh meat. Mr. Kauer's chief herder at Lake, Frank Starboard, provided an affidavit that "the soldiers, without knowledge and consent of the said John Kauer, Jr., killed a calf and appropriated the same to their own use, and that John Kauer, Jr. . . . would not have known of same unless they had seen the hyde [*sic*] and head of said animal at the [Lake] Station."[62]

The military investigated, and the soldiers at Lake testified that "Mr. Kauer's herd was allowed to run loose without a herder all about the station grounds." They tried to keep them off, but they were a nuisance. The men endeavored to notify the herder but "if the herder did his best to keep the cattle away from the station, he certainly was not a fit man to employ in that capacity." Finally, one day in August, "the herd broke through the roof of the root cellar and one calf fell through, breaking its leg. The calf was killed to prevent its suffering." The soldiers attempted to notify the herder, but he did not claim the carcass. Captain Sweezy, in charge of the investigation, claimed that he "was informed [the herder] also worked at Lake Hotel and spent most of his time there during the day" and that "Mr. Kauer should have well known the cause of the loss."[63]

The commanding officer, Col. Lloyd M. Brett, wrote to Kauer that "the calf at Lake Station was killed and its meat used at the station . . . after your man had been duly notified and given an opportunity to claim it." Brett also dismissed an almost identical claim made by Kauer against the soldier at the Canyon Soldier Station. However, in that case, he found that "I have been unable to secure any information that would indicate that your calf was killed by the soldiers at the Canyon Station, beyond the affidavits furnished by you which are not sufficient evidence on which to convict them."[64] While it may be true that the negligence of Kauer's employee led to killing the calf at Lake and there is no conclusive evidence of killing a calf at Canyon, the idea that soldiers were willing to break the law in order to supplement their rations had already been established. The poaching of domesticated animals fits into the pattern of poaching wild game seen at the soldier stations.

From Lake, the inspection party moved north through the Hayden Valley to the Canyon Soldier Station. It appears that Reade and Amos did not visit the Sylvan Pass Soldier Station at the east entrance as there is no mention of it in Reade's report. The Canyon Station was garrisoned with "three men including Private Smith in charge." Placing a private in charge was unusual, but Reade noted that "the paucity of the strength of the garrison at Fort Yellowstone does not admit of an increase of the detail of this station." The station's district encompassed an area starting at Mary Lake to Mud Geyser to the east boundary of the park, northwest along Mirror Plateau to the headwaters of Opal Creek, west to Grebe Lake and back to Mary Lake. The daily patrols were to go west to the Wedded Trees, south to the eight-mile post, and north to the midway point between Canyon and Tower Falls and all return in the same day.[65]

The station was near the Canyon Hotel on a hill overlooking the Grand Canyon of Yellowstone, not far from the current location of horse stables. The hotel was built in 1890 and housed 250 guests. The "bear show" at the hotel was exceptional, and the soldiers at the station took seriously their duty of protecting the visitor, sometimes to the chagrin of those they were helping thereby and exacerbating the class tensions between the soldiers and the hotel tourists. The complaint of a Mr. Trible showed how the tension between

The Canyon Soldier Station, date unknown. (National Park Service Photo)

the working-class soldier and the upper-class hotel tourist was part of the atmosphere of the park. "[A] number of the guests of the Hotel came to me afterward," Trible wrote to the commanding officer, "and said that I should report the matter. . . . In view of the many stories that I was told of the conduct of soldiers in the park, and the impression made by this incident . . . I feel that the matter should be brought to your attention."[66]

The Canyon Soldier Station was known to have severe problems with bears. Even though they were charged with protecting the tourists from bears at the hotel, the soldiers would often interact with and challenge the daring predators with masculine bravado. On his visit to Canyon, Sergeant Offley wrote

> There is a big cinnamon bear that hangs about this station all the time. After supper, I was sitting with my back to the window, when I heard a scratching at the window, and turned around to see a big wooly head with a nose sniffing at the window. I took my pistol, that was lying on a chair near me. . . . I slipped six blanks into the chambers and made a jump for the door. My bear heard me coming around the house, and just as I turned the corner, he was going away from the window. I gave him a blank and he took up the double time, and I started after him, firing him a blank at every jump until they were all fired, and then went back into the

shack. The old cinnamon was back in a few minutes. They know very well that you are not going to hurt them.[67]

Other soldiers could act rather foolishly with the bears. When Herbert Angelo stayed at the Canyon Station, he felt "the bears are getting to be a bother." He said later that "one got so cross that we had to shoot it but it ran away." However, that or another bear came back later and was very daring as it came into the tent of the sleeping soldiers and "took the shoe off of a boy who gave him a kick." Another time Angelo was "on guard one night when a bear broke in the cook shack and was getting in the bacon." When the cooks came to the tent they "went to throw shoes at him," but "about that time I came on the scene with a pitchfork but when he came at me with outstretched paws, I showed the white feather and beat it for the picket line, the bear close after me." Even more foolishly, Angelo and his comrades had a hole for garbage in the ground that the bears would visit. "One night one of the boys came in camp late and seeing a bear in the hole he went to pelting him with stones." Not surprisingly, the bear "would not stand for that so he gave chase." The apparently astonished soldier, named Bluch Estis, ran "for his tent and went in tramping on sleeping forms rolled in their blankets." The soldiers, angry about being awoken so abruptly demanded an explanation.[68] It is hard to imagine that the soldiers would have allowed tourists to provoke bears in a similar way.

From Canyon, Lieutenant Amos and Lieutenant Colonel Reade traveled north over Dunraven Pass to the final two stations for inspection. The soldier station at Tower Falls was not constructed until October of 1903. Until then, the Knowles cabin at the junction of Slough Creek and the Yellowstone River acted as "a winter station and [was] not tenanted in summer time." However, at the time of Lieutenant Colonel Reade's visit, it still had its winter garrison of one private under the command of Corporal Weston. The cabin had been built by a miner who worked the Crevice Creek before 1898, when he was expelled from the park. Once the Tower Falls Station was built, the cabin was only periodically occupied. In July 1910 Corporal Samuel Bradlor was stationed at the cabin and wrote the commanding officers, requesting "instruction in regards to patrols and where they extend, to poachers and who are allowed to fish in the Yellowstone River." Little is known about the Knowles cabin given its generally seasonal and erratic occupation. Reade could only note that "there is no unserviceable property here."[69]

Along the main road the inspection party moved to the Soda Butte Soldier Station, garrisoned by four privates under the command of Sergeant

Soldiers at the Soda Butte Soldier Station showing off their recent coyote kill, circa 1905. During the military era there was a different mentality regarding conservation and preservation. The main goal was to preserve game species and not predator species. While soldiers and visitors were forbidden from hunting game, predators could be openly killed. (Yellowstone National Park Museum Collection)

Mayhew. The station was in the Lamar Valley near the Soda Butte Cone, along the frequently traveled road from Mammoth to the mining settlement of Cooke City. The area under its jurisdiction included the area enclosed by the boundary starting at Castor Peak, north to the boundary of the park, west along the boundary to Slough Creek, south to the headwaters of Opal Creek and back to Castor Peak. The garrison patrolled halfway to Tower Falls and ten miles north toward Cooke City.[70]

The garrisons at Soda Butte were often some of the most troublesome of the outposts. In 1902 Capt. John Pitcher had to issue an order that "hunting or killing of game of any kind by this detachment or any other which may be stationed at Soda Butte Station is absolutely prohibited." Archaeology done at the site, like that of Fountain Flats and Tower Falls and the anecdotal evidence of other sites, shows that the soldiers of Soda Butte were indeed hunting and consuming wild game to supplement their rations in violation of the park regulations.[71] The irony is that the soldiers at Soda Butte apprehended some of the more notorious poachers, such as Ed Hollowell. Perhaps the Soda Butte Station encapsulates the entire experience of the army in

John F. Yancey's hotel and saloon in the Pleasant Valley circa 1900. Built in 1882, the building could accommodate approximately twenty guests. In 1884 Yancey erected a one-and-a-half-story saloon that catered to tourists, road-weary travelers to Cooke City, and soldiers. Park commanders lamented that the establishment ruined many promising careers of soldiers stationed at the nearby Tower Falls and Soda Butte. (Yellowstone National Park Museum Collection)

Yellowstone. On the one hand, there were great successes in several regards where the soldiers carried out their orders and reduced violations; on the other hand, it was clear that they did not always follow the rules themselves and often behaved in ways that were less than what they expected from the civilians whom they monitored.

Because of its location on the road to Cooke City, the Soda Butte Station was the first soldier station to be occupied year-round. The frequent traffic and easy access to the vices of the mining settlement at Cooke City, with its retinue of saloons and "sporting women," may have weakened the garrison's discipline. Moreover, if the soldiers did not want to make the trip to town, the civilians were willing to deliver the good times to the soldiers. In 1910 the commanding officer complained that "the people traveling from Gardiner to Cooke City through the park are constantly carrying liquor to the soldiers at Tower Falls and Soda Butte station." One unnamed sergeant, who was "a candidate for a commission as an officer" and who "was completely sober and trustworthy" became corrupted at Soda Butte and "within three months had to be relieved, court-martialed and reduced, due to drinking liquor he obtained from the Cooke City people."[72]

An even more pressing concern for the commanders was that a private establishment within the park was notorious for degrading the soldiers: Yancey's Pleasant Valley Hotel. Yancey's hotel was run by "Uncle" John F. Yancey until he died in 1903 and then by his nephew Dan Yancey. It was located north of the present Tower-Roosevelt junction, and John had obtained permission to run his establishment before the military's administration of the park. The hotel was primitive, even by early park standards. A visitor in 1901 described it in somber terms.

> The little hallway in which we are standing is formed by undressed boards and the doors leading from it have large numbers marked upon them in chalk from one to five. Inspection of the bedrooms proves them to be large enough for a single bedstead with a box on which are washbowl, pitcher, and part of a crash towel. Of the four window lights, at least one was broken in each room. The cracks in the wall are pasted up with strips of newspaper. No. 1, being the bridal chamber, was distinguished from the others by a four by six looking glass. The beds showed they were changed at least twice, once in the spring and once in the fall of the year. A little bribe on the side and a promise to keep the act of criminality a secret from Uncle John induces the maid to provide us with clean sheets.[73]

Even after the hotel burned down in 1907 and Dan Yancey applied to renew his lease closer to the new road being built, the memory and depravity of the saloon lived large in the military superintendent's mind. Major Benson wrote the secretary of the interior regarding Yancey's hotel and its corrupting influence. "The place known as Yancey's is . . . practically a saloon." For years the establishment was a nearly irresistible draw for the nearby soldiers. "It has caused infinite trouble due to the liquor consumed there. Every command [at the nearby outposts] . . . has been demoralized by liquor. Sergeants of twenty years standing have deserted from this place due to difficulties into which they have fallen due to drink" from Yancey's Hotel. He even provided an anecdote that one "sergeant sold the rations of the [Tower Falls] station and then deserted" for Yancey's. However, during Reade and Amos's visit, the garrison at Soda Butte put its best foot forward. Reade's only suggestions were that the station should be connected to the main post by telephone.[74]

From there, the two officers headed back to the main post at Mammoth. They arrived on a rainy June 10. As Reade correlated the information for his report, he also reflected on the overall situation of the outposts. He noted that the "unsuitableness of the buildings occupied by the detachments at outlying stations in the Yellowstone National Park remains practically unchanged" since the previous year's inspection. He advocated that the "dignity of Yellowstone National Park, as well as the comfort of the occupants of these buildings, justifies the construction of better buildings of uniform type."[75]

Reade was more concerned about the discipline of the garrisons and with good reason. Evidence available to the historian from the entire history of the garrisons and unavailable to him shows that the activities of the soldiers often were in contradiction to their official mission. Yet Reade understood the problem, and he summarized the situation with military bluntness. "There are 10 outlying stations in YNP, the circuit involved in a travel distance of 281 miles, at each of which there is a detachment of noncommissioned officer or lance noncommissioned officer and two, three, or four privates." The unique structure of the command created a problem: "the aggregate number of men permanently absent from the eye of supervision of a commissioned officer being at the date of writing forty (40) men." He even noted that the uniquely brutal Yellowstone winters compounded the problem since "these men are wholly removed from the view of any commissioned officer and, with the depleted garrison now struggling to perform the varied and unusual duties involved, these outlying stations now are seen only about four times per annum." He probably had discussed this with Lieutenant Amos and other officers stationed at the park who were aware, as Lt. Elmer Lindsley put it in 1898, that the soldiers were "absolutely unfamiliar with the country and their duties as a game warden." Indeed, the behavior of soldiers with the bears, particularly at Canyon Station, shows a significant level of "unfamiliarity." However, unfamiliarity would not fully explain the overwhelming evidence, from both written and archaeological evidence, of poaching by soldiers. Their use of wild meat would appear to be ubiquitous and evidence that they had a more working-class view of the environment and using its bounty. It would seem that the soldiers engaged in a "moral ecology," typical of the more traditional rural America, with different values, beliefs, and practices regarding the environment. While the laws might preclude hunting in the park, or cattle rustling as at the Lake Station and perhaps the Canyon Station, it was acceptable to the soldiers if what they took was used for subsistence.[76] However, as soldiers, they were caught in a paradox where they still enforced the ban on others as their duty required even if they could justify their own breaking of the same rules.

The social tensions of the park were present at the outposts just as they were at the main post, Fort Yellowstone, but without the constant supervision of commissioned officers. The tourists' view of the soldier was seen in numerous contexts such as the complaints about the "bear show" at Canyon Hotel. Despite their own private views on hunting, the soldiers were more than willing to enforce the ban on firearms and hunting on others, but they not only hunted but perhaps used their weapons as freely as they wished. They encountered strains of a social class system that marginalized them while they were legally put into the contradictory position of enforcing the park's regulations upon their perceived social superiors. Their mission, the social tensions, and the nature of their unique duties in a remote location encouraged neither the best military discipline nor the best policing practices and led to many soldiers disliking their time in the park and often deserting. The problem became so bad that in 1908 the army had to investigate why so many soldiers deserted the park garrison.

CHAPTER FOUR

# An "Undesirable Station"

## Desertion, Social Class, and the Basis for the National Park Service Ranger

Major Henry T. Allen of the Eighth US Cavalry had a problem. His command at Fort Yellowstone had an unusually high desertion rate. So high that Maj. Gen. Frederick Ainsworth, adjutant general for the whole US Army, formally requested an explanation. Allen replied that it was due to the "poor character of the recruits." This explanation disappointed Ainsworth, who ordered Maj. Samuel W. Miller, inspector general of the Department of Dakota, to travel to Fort Yellowstone to investigate and "determine how much weight, if any, be given this explanation." Ainsworth went on to add that Miller should "make minute and exhaustive investigation into the character of the recruits received at Fort Yellowstone during the past year and in case of every recruit reported of bad character, you will require the commander to make full and complete written statements describing specifically every defect of character alleged." Ainsworth instructed Miller to conduct "a thorough examination of both officers and enlisted men having knowledge concerning them . . . to ascertain the real cause of excessive desertions at this post so that proper remedy may be applied."[1]

Concurrent with Major Miller's investigation, the civilian acting superintendent of the park, Samuel Baldwin Marks Young, was writing his annual report to the secretary of the interior. Normally, the positions of acting superintendent of the park and commanding officer of the fort were held by the same person. However, in 1907 and 1908 they were separate. Though a civilian, Young had only recently retired after a distinguished forty-year military career. However, in his 1908 annual report Young fired a very articulate volley against the military's role in the park. The military's dual interest of keeping soldiers fit for duty and protecting the park was "injurious to the Army in that regimental and squadron organizations are not only disturbed, but the troop organization is largely demoralized by subdividing the men into small parties far separated for an indefinite period without the personal supervisions of an officer." He went on to add that these split duties also hurt the park since the soldiers had little sense of mission in that regard. He noted that only a few of the soldiers "have taken an interest in carrying out their instructions," and that "the majority are indifferent and appear to resent" their time in Yellowstone.[2]

Major Allen, therefore, was being questioned from multiple directions as to the quality of his troops, the execution of their duties, and perhaps even his leadership. Indeed, the whole idea of having soldiers as the guardians of the park seemed suspect. By 1908 the army had been protecting the park for twenty-two years. From the start there had been tension between the division of duties between park protection and military readiness. It was an unenviable task to serve two masters, the War Department and the Department of the Interior. It was becoming clear to the military high command that using soldiers to patrol the park was not always compatible with the new expectations of the United States as a global power. As early as 1889, the first military acting superintendent, Capt. Moses Harris, stated that soldiers suffered an "impairment of military efficiency" under the current circumstances, and he deemed it "a suitable time to urgently invite your attention to the importance of this subject." In 1894 the acting superintendent and post commander, Capt. George S. Anderson, lamented the difficulty of balancing park duties while making sure that the soldiers could still "perform all of their ordinary military duties." In 1901 the inspector general for the Department of Dakota noted that the conditions in the park were a throwback to the days of the frontier army three decades before. However, after the closure of the frontier, the army assumed a mission of a global imperial power, and the soldiers in Yellowstone were "struggling to perform the varied and unusual duties" in the park while maintaining military readiness during such duty. This was especially true at the remote outposts spread throughout the park, where soldiers were "permanently absent from the eye and supervision of a commissioned officer," and discipline could be rather slipshod.[3]

Thus, with the desertion problem in 1907 and 1908, it was becoming increasingly clear that the soldiers were imperfectly suited for the job of park management, and Major Miller's investigation brought those deficiencies to the surface. General Young's biting comments and the concurrent results of Major Miller's investigation supported other evidence demonstrating that the soldiers lacked a sense of shared mission and did not possess the required skills to patrol the increasingly popular park adequately. Soldiers faced significant challenges enforcing a mission for which they had neither enthusiasm nor training. In addition, they increasingly struggled with externally imposed expectations regarding their social standing from the class-conscious tourists of late Victorian society. They encountered strains of a social class system that marginalized them while they felt themselves in the contradictory position of enforcing the park's regulations upon their perceived social superiors. Their mission, the social tensions, and the nature of their unique duties in remote locations neither encouraged the best military discipline nor fit the expectations of military service. Taken together, these dynamics made enforcement of park regulations inefficient at best and problematic at worst. Yet, these deficiencies actually shaped the future National Park Service as much as the administrative successes of military superintendents. Ultimately, when civilian control of the park resumed in 1918, the National Park Service was able to address many of the issues with the much more successful National Park Rangers. The experience of the ordinary soldier in the unique physical and social environment of the park contributed to not only the impetus for civilian control but also shaped the conceptual development of the future National Park Service Ranger program. Through their deficiencies, soldiers demonstrated the type of person needed for the NPS rangers to be successful, the talents they required, how they needed to be invested in their mission to protect the park, and that they needed to be socially acceptable to the visiting tourists.

When Major Miller began his investigation into the desertion rate on October 10, 1908, he found the commanding officer, Major Allen, less than helpful. The post records were "packed and stored," and many captains of the troop were on leave, which "delayed the investigation." Allen's averseness was not surprising since he had provided "no written answer" to previous queries by Miller regarding the problem before Ainsworth got involved. Miller remained at the post for two weeks to conduct his investigation but quickly "found it difficult to differentiate" between the desertion of new recruits and more seasoned soldiers, so he expanded the inquiry into desertion at the post in general. "In private," he interviewed more than one hundred witnesses "from the oldest officer in commission to the latest joined recruit."[4]

Miller determined that Major Allen's claim of the "poor character" of the recruits "was not borne out by the facts of the cases" in three of the four companies stationed at the post, and it was "only in part the case" in the other. Desertion in the US Army had been such a problem that the War

Department had struggled with it since the end of the Civil War. Desertion rates reached as high as 25 percent after the war, and by 1871 almost a third of US soldiers were deserting. The rate began to decline after that and stabilized at around 5 percent until the Spanish American War. The War Department formally studied the problem in 1903 and determined that the primary reasons were the poor pay for enlisted men, "disgraceful" living conditions, a recruit's inability to adjust to military life, and abusive noncommissioned officers. Resulting reforms and greater emphasis on pursuing and apprehending deserters had lowered the rates, which is why Fort Yellowstone became such a glaring exception and prompted Miller's investigation.

Overall desertion rates for the US Army averaged 4.7 percent in the first decade and a half of the twentieth century. Fort Yellowstone, on the other hand, averaged 8.2 percent. In 1903 and 1904 and again in 1907 and 1908, the desertion rate at Fort Yellowstone spiked near 20 percent. Most surprising about the spike in 1907 and 1908 was that the army's overall desertion rate was lowering because of increased pay at a time when the nation's economy was struggling. During times of prosperity, desertions often rose as soldiers left for better-paying civilian jobs, and conversely, desertions declined when the civilian economy was not an appealing alternative. That might have been the case occasionally at Fort Yellowstone. Private Judson Conoley, of Troop F of the Third US Cavalry, "had no intention of deserting" but got on a train at the behest of a friend and went to Madison County to be employed as a miner. The opportunity for higher wages was undoubtedly appealing in some cases.[5]

Some reasons Major Miller found for desertion were perhaps surprising but were illuminated in the court-martial records. Although Yellowstone was a popular tourist attraction because of its rugged beauty and natural wonders, Miller concluded this did not always appeal to soldiers who lived permanently within its borders. Soldiers from urban areas might be less than drawn to living in the isolated wilderness of "wonderland." Winters could be particularly harsh, especially for soldiers from warmer climates. First Sgt. Edward Offley, Troop G, First US Cavalry, commented that "it seems ages since I left Old Virginia for this bleak and dreary land," adding that "I never was so tired of winter and cold and snow in my life before. It seems endless out here in this country."[6] Offley was a committed military man studying to become a commissioned officer, but his sentiments might be similar to less committed enlisted men more inclined to desert.

Several surprising factors might lead soldiers to desert. As Miller noted,

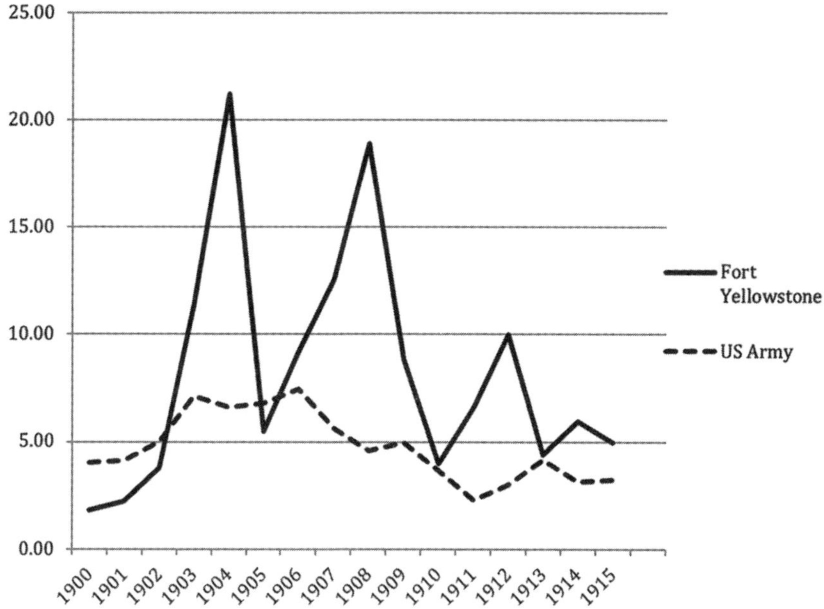


Desertion at Fort Yellowstone compared to US Army as a whole. Data for Fort Yellowstone from United States Department of War, Records of the Adjutant General's Office, Post Returns, Fort Yellowstone, WY, NARA, RG 94; US Army overall, from Robert Fantina, *Desertion and the American Soldier, 1776–2006* (New York: Algora, 2007), 205.

fear led to several unpremeditated desertions. Private Frank Anderson of Troop E of the First US Cavalry got drunk in Gardiner, fell asleep, and "was afraid to go back" because he had overstayed his pass and would face discipline. He consequently continued to drink and went to Helena, where he sobered up and then traveled to Spokane. There he reevaluated his options and ultimately decided to turn himself in to the authorities.[7]

The idea that cavalrymen would fear horses might be unexpected. Yet, eighteen-year-old Pvt. Richard Condus of Troop G, First US Cavalry had only been in the service for four months, and it was his first trip away from home. He was assigned to the cavalry at Jefferson Barracks, Missouri, and deployed to Fort Yellowstone. It did not take him long to decide he "couldn't get along riding horses," so he simply "went away."[8]

The decision to desert could be spontaneous or thoroughly planned out. In most cases the idea of deserting probably had an incubation period of days, weeks, or even months. One soldier even had time to write family members about his desire to desert and await a response. A letter found in

1967 in the attic of one of the old buildings at Fort Yellowstone was from a father to his son who had previously described plans. His father urged him to "stay and save your money" so he did not end up in prison. He cautioned him that he would "lead a dog's life if you go [desert] . . . and if you go, you will get a dishonorable discharge."[9]

Preparations could be extensive and might be quietly seen and understood by other troopers, who often understood the signs even if their comrades were silent about their intentions. This allowed them to know about desertions before officers realized the fact, and they were reluctant to let their commanders know. At the court-martial of Charlie Altvater, Sgt. Frank Maricle was questioned on that issue. The court asked him whether, when an absent soldier's property was inventoried, "Do you generally find their personal property intact?" The sergeant responded, "No, sir." The court pressed the issue. "Do not [other] soldiers sometimes take the personal property of a man who absents himself without the intention of returning but makes no statement to that effect to his comrades before going?" Clearly, the officers of the court knew that enlisted men could read the intentions of potential deserters even if they did not tell the company's officers. The sergeant was a little dodgy in his nondefinitive answer of "not that I know of." He later stated, "I have known [deserters] to go away and leave [their personal property] on their bunks and others to dispose of it." The court continued: "If other soldiers strip a bunk, or if the absentee disposes of this property, it is a pretty good sign that he does not intend to return, is it not?"[10] Clearly, the officers of the court understood that there was solidarity and silence among the soldiers regarding signs of desertion.

Something unique seemed to be happening at Fort Yellowstone that begged explanation. Desertion was such a problem that "the Commanding Officer required a member of the Gardiner Soldier Station detachment to be at each out-going train every day" to prevent desertions since "no soldier is permitted to go out on a train without a pass." Searches for deserters were also extensive. When Saddler George Collins of Troop E, First US Cavalry deserted, a contingent led by Sgt. John Cahill was ordered to search the entire town of Gardiner and find him. The court inquired if he made "a thorough search," to which Cahill replied, "Yes, sir." He claimed that he "looked in all saloons, eating houses, boarding houses, all except the lower districts that were not open" because it was before the tourist season had begun. He added that "we searched in Gardiner practically one hour and a quarter, sir." The court continued: "Do you think you could find a man in Gardiner in [that

Gardiner train station, circa 1904. Desertions were so common that a guard had to be posted there to prevent soldiers from leaving the area. (National Park Service photo)

time]?" Cahill responded, "Yes, sir." When asked how it would be possible to miss a deserted soldier after such thoroughness, the sergeant responded "providing he was hiding."[11]

The summary results of Major Miller's investigation of Fort Yellowstone only partially corresponded with the conclusions of the War Department's 1903 study of overall desertion. He listed thirty-eight reasons why men deserted Fort Yellowstone. Some were unique to the military or the particular unit, others were exclusive to the soldiers individually, and some were unique to duty in the park. Miller found that unit leadership was a problem for some companies at Fort Yellowstone but not others, and that for a few soldiers, military life was not what they expected. However, he made special note that a posting in Yellowstone Park was an "undesirable station for many enlisted men."[12] Several soldiers had a "sense of dread" or did not like being stationed in the mountains, and many felt "shut in." The rural nature of the post promoted "general discontent of young men coming from the cities."

Gardiner, the only nearby town, was also "not a desirable place to visit on pass."[13] The small town, only a few miles from the post, had the unique atmosphere of a tourist town but also a rough and isolated military town. A person known as the "Inquirer" even critiqued the town in its own newspaper, *Wonderland*:

> The people of Gardiner would like to enquire why the disorderly element are permitted to disturb the peace of the town, free from molestations. Nights are made hideous by drunken riots. Monday night there was almost continuous yelling and shooting from midnight to daylight. Women of ill-fame live in the central part of town and exhibit themselves daily on the streets in bedroom wrappers, and make a show of themselves at doors and windows on the arrival of the train, their housing being only a few yards from, and facing the station.[14]

Another individual only listed as "L.S.T." asserted that something should be done about the "drunks that stagger along the streets day and night, using vulgar and profane language in every way imaginable," causing numerous fights "which are often seen and heard in Gardiner. Respectable women of this town will not stir upon the street in the evenings for fear of being insulted by some of these characters."[15] Undoubtedly, as the only place off the military reservation for soldiers to recreate, the soldiers in the park contributed to that atmosphere.

Just like Inquirer, L.S.T. also lamented the prevalence of prostitutes. "The town is well represented with . . . women that are occupying houses of ill fame."[16] While the prostitutes catered to transient tourists, they could build relationships with their more regular clients—soldiers—particularly in the off-tourist season. In an intriguing case Adelaide Lester and Myrtle Gregg, two self-proclaimed "sporting women," were called as expert witnesses in the court-martial of a soldier at the post. Their testimony also revealed how close their relationships were with the soldiers. Both knew soldiers at the post by name and reputation. Lester and Gregg claimed a Pvt. Lawrence Moon, known by the sporting women in Gardiner as "Moony," was well mannered and "a perfect little gentleman." Gregg described one soldier, Pvt. Harvey Simpson, as "pretty rough as a rule." Even the soldiers at the post considered Simpson "dirty" and "foul." Lester claimed that he and his friend "usually get drunk every time they come down" and that Simpson was

> so disgusting to me when they are drunk that I shut the door [to the crib] and let them go. . . . They think they are real smart and I know [Simpson] came in one evening and he wanted me to go to bed with him and I told him all right and I wanted the money and he said "No, the fellow in the next room will pay you,"—I think it was George Shearer—and he said "No, he will pay you," and I said "You don't think I am going to anyone

| Factors Unique to Units | Factors Unique to Army | Factors Unique to Troopers | Factors Unique to Fort Yellowstone |
|---|---|---|---|
| • Too many new recruits at one time and confused by orders<br>• Tired of horses<br>• 1st Lt. Frank E. Davis and 2nd Lt. Talbot Smith speak harshly to troops<br>• Cpl. Rossart, and Cpl. G.L. Egbert treat troops poorly at soldier stations | • Too much fatigue<br>• Disrespect shown men in uniform<br>• Drill and other duties on Sundays and holidays<br>• Fatigue in rain<br>• Food not cooked<br>• Crowded conditions of barracks | • Enlisted just to tide over dull times<br>• Men of unsettled dispositions<br>• Become drunk and fear of returning to post<br>• Homesickness<br>• Former deserters (ie – repeaters)<br>• Life in the military not what they thought it would be<br>• Too young for service<br>• Drunkards<br>• Loneliness<br>• Domestic troubles<br>• Men grumble when required to "clean-up"<br>• Shirkers<br>• Suspected of theft or embezzlement | • Dissatisfied with post<br>• Dissatisfied with climate<br>• Don't like mountains<br>• No amusement at the post<br>• Gardiner not desirable place to visit<br>• Too much time in remote stations<br>• Winter too long<br>• Post shut in by mountains<br>• Men from cities feel too isolated<br>• Soldiers not allowed in hotels<br>• "Don't like the weather"<br>• No place except gymnasium of amusement<br>• No place to go shopping<br>• Left with girls from hotels at the end of the tourist season |

Summary of reasons for desertion at Fort Yellowstone as described by Maj. Samuel Miller, 1908.

> else to collect my bills?" So, he got pretty sore at me and never did come to see me anymore.[17]

Though the soldiers did their best to enjoy what little Gardiner had to offer, the small size of the town and its isolation did not endear it much to the soldiers who complained about it in Major Miller's investigation.

The physical location of the post did, in fact, seem to affect at least the timing of desertions. Several soldiers "left with girls from the hotels at the end of the tourist season." A review of the monthly post returns that list the strength of units and desertions indicates that soldiers were more likely to desert at the end of the tourist season. Miller noted that with the female hotel workers leaving, some soldiers were prompted to go with them. However, it is also evident that soldiers were least likely to desert during the harsh winter. Desertion patterns occurred inversely to monthly snowfall amounts. As the spring gave way to summer, both opportunity and the desire to flee presented themselves. Deserting during the harsh winters simply was not practical, and as fall approached the prospects of facing another winter, besides female attachments, may have affected the time of desertions. In short, the unique natural and social geography of Fort Yellowstone exacerbated other military problems and made the post an "undesirable station" for some.[18]

The mission of protecting the park was generally not a consideration for enlistment by soldiers stationed there. For example, in May 1901 Herbert Angelo enlisted because he "had always wanted to be a soldier. My father had kept me out of the war with Spain as I was not of age, but now when I had the chance to get in the cavalry and see the Philippine Isles, the chance was too good to lose."[19] The Philippine War that Angelo referred to lasted officially from the end of the Spanish-American War in 1899 to 1902, but with continued guerrilla resistance until 1913. Over 4,200 Americans and 20,000 Filipino combatants died in a prolonged and bloody struggle that included countless atrocities committed by both sides. The idea of America as a global power and the adventure of the military's role in promoting it, however, was appealing to many recruits such as Angelo.

A year after enlisting and after months of drill on the cold plains of northern Montana as well as a severe case of typhoid fever, Angelo's troop of the Thirteenth US Cavalry was finally deployed, but not to the Philippines. Instead, the unit marched to Yellowstone Park. The duty was certainly not expected, nor was it the self-proclaimed motivation for Angelo's enlistment. He was more interested in the romanticized idea of adventurous military life and the promise of travel to the exotic locations of the Pacific. Protecting Yellowstone Park from poachers and tourists must have seemed a far cry from his reason for enlisting. Moreover, he was hardly alone. "Tramping" tourist Mode Wineman met and stayed a few days with a soldier stationed at the Fountain Flats outpost, to whom he only gave the name "Jack" from New York City. Wineman asked Jack why he enlisted, and Jack responded, "I thought we were going to the Philippines. I wanted to go far away."[20] Again, military adventure, not park protection, was the main reason for enlistment.

The soldiers who patrolled the park were probably more similar to Angelo and "Jack" than different. Every soldier's reasons for enlisting were unique, and there were probably countless reasons for enlisting in the army at the beginning of the twentieth century, adventure and travel being only two of them. However, protecting national parks was not likely among them. Nor were expectations apt to include patrolling the park, policing tourists, or fighting forest fires. Notwithstanding intent, the very minor mission of the army in the national parks of Yellowstone, Yosemite, and Sequoia

"Soldier Jack" photographed near the Fountain Soldier Station by Mode Wineman in 1908. Note the Marshall Hotel in the background. Wineman spent two days with the soldiers at the Fountain Station and built a rapport with them. "Jack," from New York, enlisted to fight in the Philippines but found himself in Yellowstone instead. (Yellowstone National Park Museum Collection)

undoubtedly was not a stimulus to enlist or among the expectations of new recruits after they did so.[21]

Even for those who may have enjoyed the duty, as Herbert Angelo admitted he did, the motivation and sense of mission of the soldiers were not entirely satisfied by patrols and incessant tourist questions and transgressions. Their self-identity and sense of mission perhaps contributed to the desertion problem that Major Miller was investigating. It is hard to imagine the later National Park Service ranger who enlisted to patrol Yellowstone having "a sense of dread in the mountains."[22] In fact, the self-identity of the latter would be much more tied to the concept of a defender of nature or a conservationist first. Soldiers were soldiers first and foremost, and their mission of protecting Yellowstone National Park may have been uninspiring, as noted separately by both Miller and Young.

The army did little to help persuade the more reluctant soldiers to shift their identity from imperialist agents of America to a constabulary force for nature. Military drill and preparedness were still required, and the army took that duty seriously. Use of sabers and machine guns would not be terribly useful against tourists, but these skills were instrumental in the employ of soldiers. In 1902, after a noted deficiency in military drill, the command practiced an attack upon Fort Yellowstone by an imaginary four-company enemy. The commanding officer concluded that

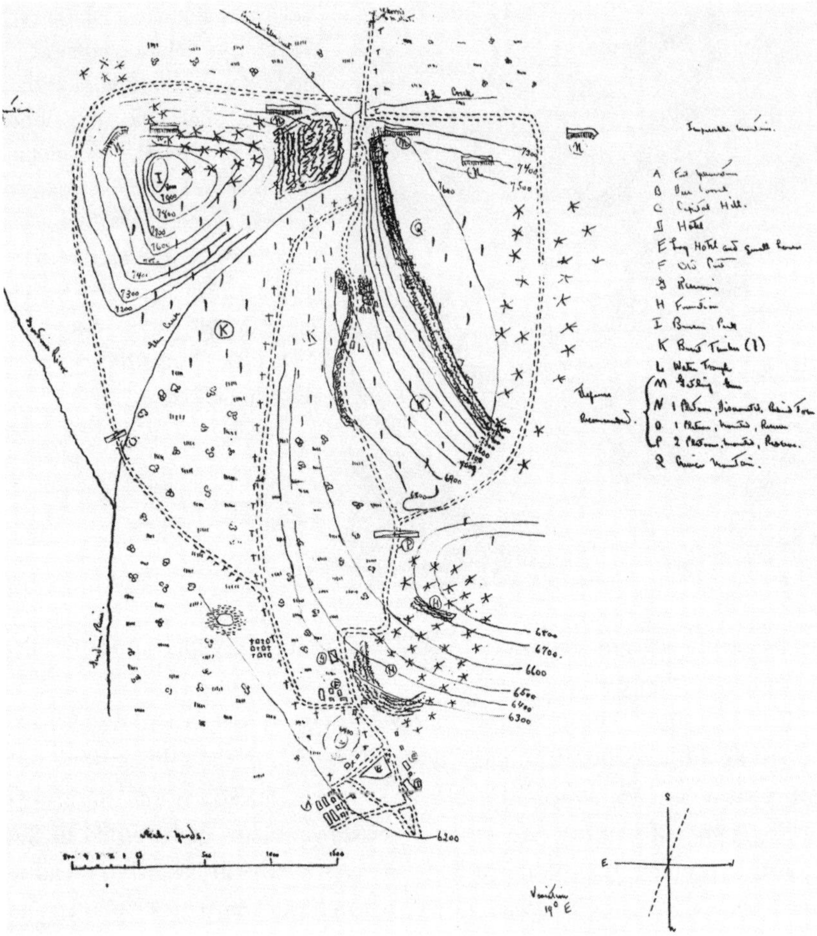

Map of the military exercise simulating a mock attack on Fort Yellowstone, included in the 1901 inspection report. (National Archives and Records Administration)

> This post would be difficult to defend against an attacking force of equal strength. . . . [There is a] need to prevent artillery from gaining the top of Mount Everts where [it] could demolish the fort without opposition. Station A commands the entrance to the canyon, overlooks the entire country to the westward making it impossible to flank this position on the right with anything except infantry, in which case the two troops of cavalry could easily fall back to position nearer post to block the attack. Artillery would be indispensable on account of the superb opportunities it would necessarily have. Two Co of infantry at station B, while acting as a reserve, [could] defend the post from flank attack from left front. [The] Gatling

gun at station C, commands large range extending from impassible bluffs on left around 180 degrees.[23]

Though such an assault upon Fort Yellowstone was unlikely by an enemy force or group of renegade tourists, the efforts required to stage such a war game were significant and distracted from the duty of patrolling the park. The need for and dedication of time and resources to such an effort demonstrate the difficulty of balancing the unique and diverging military and park duties. Still, based on Major Miller's investigation, a large contingent of soldiers resented the park duty to which they had been assigned.

Major Miller's conclusions also noted that there were social tensions that existed in the unique milieu of Yellowstone Park. Of particular note was that many men did not like the "disrespect shown the uniform by civilians," and that they were "not allowed to go into the hotels." This was partially because the public at large imposed its expectations and stereotypes about the social status of enlisted men, further limiting and affecting their sense of mission. These external identities were imposed on the soldiers and confirmed by Major Miller's findings that the social atmosphere of the park was unpleasant. As Rudyard Kipling noted, "America is a free country, but the citizens look down on the soldier." Moreover, Kipling's party of hotel tourists shunned them so much that he felt compelled to "entertain" one of the soldiers.[24]

The social class system of the late Victorian era was very much still in place, dictating rules of behavior within and between the classes. Where and how those rules applied to the soldiers stationed in the park affected not only the experience of the soldiers there but also their ability to perform their duties. In Yellowstone Park enlisted men found themselves in daily contact with people who naturally looked down upon them and wanted "nothing to do with them." Until the arrival of the automobile, Yellowstone had a distinct class orientation to the tourist, and the soldier operated in that world. Much like the transatlantic passenger ships of the time, which kept social classes segregated, there were three classes of visitors to the park. The largest was the first class, those who could afford the significant time and expense to travel to the park. The transportation and hotel companies favored these patrons and established the posh and well-appointed hotels for their comfort. The second were those of the growing middle class, such as schoolteachers, clerks, lawyers, and small businessmen, who could tour the park in the permanent camps for almost half the price of staying in the hotels. The lowest were the "sage brushers," or those who camped along the side of the road to limit their expense in the park.[25]

Machine-gun platoon at drill on the parade ground between Fort Yellowstone and the National Hotel, circa 1910. Notice the machine-gun pack on the front horse, center left. (Yellowstone National Park Museum Collection)

Though not official policy, the hotels and their guests indeed received favored treatment by the military superintendents. As late as 1909, hotel guests were shuttled into the park through the new Roosevelt Arch in Gardiner, while camping parties were forbidden to go through the arch and entered a few hundred yards away at a soldier station. This drew the ire of William F. Gossel, a union man from Butte, who wrote directly to President Taft. "I speak from personal observation and only as a citizen who desires that the 'poor camper' be given a 'square deal' and park affairs be administered with justice and fairness to all." The complaint made its way down the chain of command. Maj. H. C. Benson, the acting superintendent of Yellowstone National Park, replied to the secretary of the interior, confirming that the standard policy for campers required them to register at the soldier station rather than be able to go through the arch; he summarily dismissed the accusations, saying that "this complaint . . . means nothing." In other words, it was indeed an institutional policy to discriminate against those not staying in the hotels, or as Harry Child, the manager of the Yellowstone Park Association put it, the "right people" to whom the hotels catered.[26]

Ironically, while ordinary soldiers were of a perceived lower social class, they did have legal authority over their assumed social superiors. Even their mere presence at one of the park's features caused tourists to "instinctively put their hands behind their backs or guiltily move in the opposite direction."[27]

"Soldier at Play," photographed by Mode Wineman in 1908. Wineman's rapport with the soldiers gave him a glimpse into the more relaxed discipline at the remote stations. While soldiers may have enjoyed the more relaxed atmosphere in the park's interior, they were in a unique and uncomfortable position when interacting with park visitors. (Yellowstone National Park Museum Collection)

Yet the hotel tourists also had a refuge from these perceived lower-class soldiers who enforced the park rules and regulations. The soldiers' regulations stated, "Under no circumstances will any noncommissioned officer in charge of a station permit any of his men to go upon the premises or to enter any hotel in the park for the purpose of enforcing any rule or regulation." The soldiers were warned "not [to] loiter about the porches or entrances of the hotels." The hotel tourists were duly separated from the lower-class soldiers, at least within the confines of their intimate domestic space, even only temporarily in the hotel, where they slept, ate, and drank according to their own social rules. They may have been at the legal mercy of the soldiers outside that sphere, creating an awkward relationship at best; however, within the confines of the hotel and their sacred domestic sphere, the soldiers would have no authority over them.

The social entertainment within the park could be arbitrary and at the whim of hotel or camp managers. It was clear that off duty, "enlisted men are forbidden to enter the hotels" to enjoy their amenities. The only exceptions were upon "invitation of hotel guests to visit them, and to attend 'Formation Dances,' or other entertainments . . . on an invitation of the managers," but only if they wore "the dress uniform." While soldiers could receive such invitations to dances at one location, such as the Fountain Flats Hotel, at others they could be met with firm rebukes. During the inspection of 1914, the inspector general noted specifically that at the Wylie Camp near Canyon, "enlisted men are practically excluded from the dances and other entertainment." He noted that soldiers complained that "when enlisted men appeared upon the dance floor at these dances, the music was stopped." He added that this was directed specifically at the soldiers since "maids and other help pertaining to the camp and hotel were made welcome." It was not unique to the Canyon area since the inspector general "learned that such discrimination against the uniform existed at several places." He besieged the military superintendent to "give the matter his serious attention" and suggested "drastic action" to "enforce respect for the uniform of the United States Army."[28]

Naturally, soldiers viewed themselves differently from the way in which the upper-class tourists saw them. Soldiers thought of themselves as artisans or skilled workers of a particular craft—soldiering. They saw other duties as below them and often felt mistreated when asked to do something other than soldiering. This did not go unnoticed by civilians in Yellowstone, such as G. L. Henderson, who noted that "the soldiers do not like the new function of preserving a national park . . . because it is not a soldiers work." Their worldview was much more democratic, having grown up with the working-class idealism of the American cultural egalitarianism. Yet the reality of Yellowstone was unique in that the social-legal relationship added to the tension already present between the "American Dream," the unofficial class structure of America, and the general relationship of the US Army with society at large, all of which led to the "disrespect shown the uniform by civilians," as noted by Major Miller and others.[29]

While the enlisted men were looked down upon by the hotel tourist class, officers would be welcomed as members of the upper social strata. They may have lacked the financial affluence of the hotel class of visitors, but their education, genteel customs, beliefs, and habits gave them recognition as members of the upper class.[30] Enlisted men stationed at the main post, two hundred yards from the hotel at Mammoth Hot Springs, and even at some of the more isolated posts near other hotels, could see this lifestyle and these rituals from which they were fundamentally excluded despite their sense of egalitarianism. Yellowstone Park, with its semi-institutionalized class structure, made this divide more evident than at other posts where civilians were kept at a distance off the military reservation. This may have exacerbated a level of strain that led many to quietly rebel against the social structure or possibly even desert.

Deeper into the park, near the detached soldier stations, opportunities presented themselves away from the watchful eyes of commissioned officers, who only came through sporadically. In 1912 Pvt. Albert Beagle dressed in civilian clothes while stationed at the Upper Basin Soldier Station near Old Faithful.[31] Private John Gear donned civilian clothes at the Lake Soldier Station, walked the 300 yards to the opulent and well-appointed Lake Hotel, and registered for a room. While there he also drank and entertained women. All three actions were against the regulations for troops in the park.[32] Yet, for that brief night, Private Gear sampled the lifestyle of the upper-class hotel guests from which he was otherwise excluded but with which he was always in close contact while stationed in the park.

The detached soldier stations also provided the opportunity for amusements officially forbidden by the army. One of the most common court-martial offenses of troops stationed in the park was drunkenness. For the limited number of years for which records of summary courts-martial for minor offenses survive, the vast majority of prosecuted instances of drunkenness (sixty-eight cases, or 80 percent of all alcohol-related cases) were at the main post, Fort Yellowstone. Either the men at detached soldier stations drank less or the soldiers were merely not caught and prosecuted as frequently. Archaeology at the Fountain Flats Soldier Station suggests that alcohol was readily available at the outpost even if only two cases of court-martial exist. Officers tried to suppress excessive consumption but often to no avail, as soldiers would band together in solidarity. Lieutenant Frank Keller discovered that soldiers at the Thumb Soldier Station had two suitcases belonging to Sgt. Charles Leach full of whiskey, and he asked Pvts. Martin Lilienthal, William Wencil, and John Kane about their location. They all denied any knowledge of them but were eventually found out and court-martialed. On July 23, 1913,

Sgt. Richard Bohen allowed his entire detachment at the Riverside Soldier Station to become drunk despite "it being his duty to prevent liquor from being brought into the station occupied by the detachment."[33]

The drunkenness was not limited to the soldier outposts, often quietly out of sight from tourists' eyes. Sometimes, drunken and disruptive behavior was in plain view of the park visitors. One soldier, who was moonlighting or "spooning" as security for Mr. E. C. Waters on the boat that ran between the West Thumb and Lake Hotel, was so drunk he frightened the passengers. One passenger noted that he was "especially quarrelsome" and "conducted himself in a disgusting manner." The passenger told the boat captain that he had "no business to be on board a boat armed and as drunk as he is." The hotel tourist classes could readily see visibly drunk soldiers at Fort Yellowstone and outside the park at Gardiner. Incidents could become rather violent affairs, resulting in assault, destruction of private property, passing out in the streets or on the road to the post, and generally disorderly conduct. The cemetery records also show that at least two soldiers died because of alcohol-related causes on the road between Gardiner and the fort.[34]

The sight of intoxicated soldiers in Gardiner and along the road likely would not make a favorable impression on the hotel class of tourists. But it was not that the tourists, or even the army officers, were always strong temperance advocates, though some were, as the third wave of the temperance movement was building toward prohibition. The real problem would have been that soldiers were openly drinking alcohol and behaving in a way that was against the moral ethos of the higher classes who consumed alcohol. Army officers and their class peers were known to drink, sometimes heavily, but the social rules dictated that it be done more privately, with different types of alcohol, such as champagne, brandy, liqueurs, or wine, and only among peers who understood the rules of genteel consumption and behavior.[35] Despite official regulations that stated "no drinking saloon or barroom will be permitted within the limits of the park," the commanding officers and even the head legal authority, US Commissioner Judge John Meldrum, apparently did not enforce the rule.[36] In fact, there was a barroom directly across the hall from Meldrum's first office in the hotel at Mammoth frequented by the fort's officers. Meldrum also remembered meeting Acting Superintendent Capt. George Anderson for the first time at the "barroom" in the Fountain Hotel.[37] Besides, the Yellowstone Park Association provided post commanders directly with substantial amounts of alcohol, a curious procedure if they did not have barrooms.[38] The sight of the enlisted men's openly drunk and disruptive behavior would only reinforce the social differences between the soldiers and at least the hotel class of tourists, straining the paradox between their social and legal relationships.

This contradiction of social and legal authority seems to have played out in interesting ways, particularly in the interior of the park at the soldier stations. One of the primary missions of the army was to prevent poaching. To help enforce that edict, tourists were required to either bind and seal their guns or turn them in to the army and retrieve them upon leaving the park. While the soldiers may have enforced these rules against their social superiors, they themselves felt free to hunt at will and supplement their rations. An analysis of bones found at three of the remote soldier stations (Fountain, Tower, and Soda Butte) indicate that wild game was a pervasive food source and significantly more so than domestic meat sources.[39]

Sergeant Edward Offley openly mentioned hunting and evaluated the culinary talents of other soldiers stationed at the remote outposts in 1900. At the Riverside, Thumb, and Snake River Stations, he enjoyed "elk steaks," "elk chops," and "venison." Compounded with the archaeological evidence at other interior stations, it is clear that the soldiers were at least indifferent to following the hunting regulations they were called on to enforce against others. The question is whether the post commanders encouraged the soldiers to supplement their supplies with hunting. The evidence suggests otherwise. No such order appears in writing, the annual inspection reports only mention supplies of domestic meat provided to the outposts, and at least one soldier was court-martialed for hunting inside the park.[40]

Like hunting, there was evident apathy to the regulations against the use of firearms in the park. Gunplay at the stations seemed rather common, at least at the Fountain Flats Station, where a large number of bullets and cartridge cases were found around the front porch, the social center of the outpost. Drunkenness and gunplay at the soldier stations could lead to dangerous situations, such as when Pvt. Amil Moravek became drunk at the Fountain Soldier Station and "did fire his revolver . . . in the quarters of his detachment." But indifference to the regulations was only part of the experience in the remote soldier stations. Intentional corruption was also noted occasionally. Sergeant Knapp trafficked in the black market for elk teeth, and Maj. John Pitcher received correspondence that accused soldiers of letting known "trappers stay with them" and informing them when scouts would be in the region. In other cases the soldiers might identify the location of game or even drive it out of the park so poachers could hunt them.[41]

The worst accusations of corruption came from James Fullerton of Red Lodge, Montana. He wrote to the *Red Lodge Picket* that the soldiers were "venal and corrupt and that their acceptance of bribes is so open and notorious that westerners have long ceased to express surprise at it." He claimed, ironically, that one soldier retired from service and "bought a ranch in an adjoining state on the ridged [*sic*] economy of $13 a month," the monthly soldier's pay.[42] Though the *Picket* only printed the letter by Fullerton and an additional letter under the pen name Herman Strann, the letters were republished in the *Livingston Post* and the *Gardiner Wonderland* in a manner more like investigative news than unfounded accusations.[43]

Fullerton's accusations against the soldiers, while generally exaggerated or even false, played into the accepted stereotypes of the soldiers' lower-class status in order to bolster opinion for his real and more passionate concern about the sale of alcohol in the park. He accused Major Pitcher, perhaps correctly, of knowing about and turning a blind eye to barrooms being operated in the park. Even the canteen of the fort's post exchange was by all measures a barroom. Fullerton even traveled to Washington, DC, and attempted to meet personally with President Theodore Roosevelt to discuss the issue but was rebuffed. He continued his efforts against the military in the park almost exclusively along temperance lines in the future. Attending temperance meetings in Denver and Detroit, Fullerton offered resolutions "decrying the sale of intoxicants" in the park and even demanded a plank at the Democratic Party's 1904 national convention "looking for the impeachment of President Roosevelt on the alleged ground that the president condones unlawful sale of liquor in the Yellowstone Park and refuses to remove Superintendent Pitcher who is responsible for the alleged violation of the law."[44]

The presence of barrooms in the park aside, Fullerton's accusations of corruption against the common soldier were on the whole likely false, though readily believed because of a limited number of actual cases and the stereotypical bias against soldiers, as well as the local distaste for government regulation of the park. He had a more difficult time convincing people outside the region about his accusations. The editors of *Forest and Stream* pressed Fullerton for details when he unexpectedly visited their office with the same accusations of wholesale military corruption. However, the editors "found that he had no facts to give—that he was talking of matters of which he knew nothing." They concluded that "Fullerton knew nothing, that he was repeating a lot of traditionary gossip, much of it many years old, and reported to have happened between the years 1880 and 1890." Nevertheless, they sent an investigator "to inquire into the truth or falsity of the allegations," but he concluded that the allegations "against the soldiers stationed in the park are unjust and not correct." Sadly, two years later Fullerton was removed to an insane asylum. The editors of *Forest and Stream* noted that "this will hardly surprise those persons possessing any knowledge of the Park who talked with him when he came east to make his charges" and characterized him as a generally "malicious person."[45]

Though Fullerton's accusations were largely false, and many soldiers were serious about their responsibilities, it is clear that a few soldiers did wantonly succumb to occasional corruption and many more viewed their duties and obligations in the park with indifference. While soldiers enforced the park rules—such as the prohibitions on hunting, guns, and drinking—against the tourists, the same rules appear not to have applied to themselves, perhaps relieving some of the stress associated with the paradox of the social-legal relationship between soldiers and especially between soldiers and the hotel tourists. This social strain may have led to the soldiers' breaking the park's rules and regulations in a type of "reaction formation," where they developed their own subculture outside both the social norms of society and the legal expectations of the park. In the distant outposts they could assume a role of power where they could both enforce the rules on others and yet break them themselves nearly at will, relieving the tensions of the paradox in which they lived with a level of autonomy not present at the main post, Fort Yellowstone. This may partially explain why Major Miller found that being stationed at the soldier outposts was an attractive duty. They could even form a type of solidarity for those seeking to escape the whole system by assisting deserters even though they knew such assistance to be against military regulations, as Pvt. Frederick Moses did at the Riverside Soldier Station.[46] These violations of basic park rules and regulations, for whatever reason, certainly reinforced the idea that the soldiers likely had less buy-in to the mission of protecting the park than would be ultimately desired and evident in the later National Park Service ranger.

Concurrent with Major Miller's investigations into the high desertion rate, another experiment was taking shape that showed the beginning of the transition from military to civilian control of the park. For the first time since the military arrived, the post commander was not the acting superintendent of the park. That role was being filled by Ret. Gen. Samuel Baldwin Marks Young, who reported directly and only to the secretary of the interior. Despite his retirement, Young was a military man through and through. "Every inch a soldier," was how *Sunset Magazine* described him in their profile of him six years later in 1913. He had enlisted as a private in Company K of the Twelfth Pennsylvania Infantry on April 25, 1861, but received a commission as captain in the Fourth Pennsylvania Cavalry by August of that same year. He steadily rose through the ranks after the war and was no stranger to military administration in the national parks. He commanded the Fourth US Cavalry contingent and was the acting superintendent of Yosemite from 1893 until 1897, where he significantly improved the military administration of that park. He acted briefly as Yellowstone's acting superintendent from June 23, 1897, to May 18, 1898, before being assigned to lead volunteer troops in the Spanish-American War. After the war he continued to rise, becoming the army's first chief of staff in 1903.[47] Clearly, Young was in a unique position to understand the nature of a soldier's duties, even in places such as national parks, as well as the role of the US Army as it was becoming a global power.

Young's lament about the military's dual interest in keeping soldiers fit for duty and policing the park in 1907 and 1908 emphasized the problems of military administration and that the soldiers were ill-suited for the job. He noted that only a few of the soldiers "have taken interest in carrying out their instructions" to protect the park, but that "the majority are indifferent and appear to resent" their time there and its multiple responsibilities. "The enlisted men of the Army are not selected with special reference to the duties to be performed in police patrolling, guarding, and maintaining the natural curiosities and interesting 'formations' from injury by the curious, the thoughtless, and the careless people who compose a large percentage of annual visitors." He added that it was quite "obvious that any man assigned to duty in any capacity in the park should possess special qualification for the proper discharge of that duty." In other words, these caretakers of the park needed to have special characteristics that fit with their mission and personal sense of it. He even nodded to the social tensions between tourists and soldiers, implying that currently, the soldiers did not always act considerately. "A visiting tourist should always be favored by an intelligent and courteous answer on any subject pertaining to the park from any guard interrogated." Major Miller concurred with Young in his final report that the current enlisted men were ill-suited for the duties in the park. He claimed that the park at least needed "a better class of soldiers for this type of service," particularly in the more remote soldier stations where they had the most frequent contact with tourists but where military discipline was sometimes lacking.[48]

Young and Miller must have understood that they were creating a high list of expectations that the army could not easily fill. Young noted that "the pay of enlisted men in the Army is too meager to attract capable men who can fill these requirements, and the duties are too onerous for the remuneration." He added that the "proper and necessary military instruction and training cannot be carried on through discipline and cannot be maintained" under the current circumstances. The only answer was a civilian force selected for "their special fitness, their interest in the work, and their capacity to perform it." To make them agreeable to the hotel class of tourist, he noted that it would "be necessary to select men of good repute," and if they were found to have "incivility, dishonesty, habitual and inordinate use of intoxicants, neglect of duty, gross immorality or disorderly behavior . . . [they] should be dismissed." He was therefore clearly recommending individuals who would be more palatable to the class-conscious hotel guests than the enlisted men of the army, who were stereotyped as embodying almost all those negative characteristics. Major Miller concurred that enlisted men lacked the sense of mission to protect the park, though it was beyond his purview to suggest ceding control to civilians. All he could do was suggest that the command should "be composed only of officers and men particularly fitted for the unusual and peculiar service the troops are now and will be called upon to perform so long as it is garrisoned by U.S. Troops."[49]

By 1910 the irony of the situation was that it had changed completely since the congressional debate that brought the army into the park. In 1886 Lt. Gen. Philip Sheridan and the War Department were some of the biggest proponents of the military administration of Yellowstone, while the Department of the Interior only turned to soldiers as a last resort thrust upon them by Congress. At the turn of the second decade of the twentieth century, the army was searching for a way out, and the Department of the Interior was much more in favor of keeping the army in place.[50] The problem of park administration had taken on greater importance with the addition of Sequoia and Yosemite in 1890, Mount Rainer in 1899, Crater Lake in 1902, Wind Cave in 1903, Mesa Verde in 1906, and finally Glacier in 1910. After the addition of Glacier and the army's recent difficulties in Yellowstone, it seemed timely to explore the future of what the national parks were and how they fit into the American consciousness. The secretary of the interior called a "National Park Conference," which was held in Yellowstone in September of 1911.

The conference had "the purpose of discussing the difficulties met within the various parks, in order that the difficulties met within one park may be avoided in the others, and in order that the plans which have been found

Lake Hotel, circa 1900. The soldiers had little in common with the posh tourists who could afford to take time and travel across the country to the park and stay in its posh hotels. Regulations strictly forbade soldiers from entering the hotel, except upon invitation, thus segregating the tourists and soldiers. (National Park Service photo)

successful in one park may be adopted in the others," claimed Walter Fisher, the secretary of the interior, in his opening remarks. He focused on "three general heads—transportation, concessions within the parks, and the subject of park administration from the point of view of those charged with that duty."[51]

The various special interests were all represented. The superintendents from the different national parks, representatives from railroads, concessionaires in many parks, and members of several government agencies all attended. How to bring tourists to the park and accommodate them was a topic of considerable discussion. So was the topic of military administration. R. B. Marshall, the chief geographer for the United States Geological Survey, weighed in on the topic. "The question of whether or not troops should be stationed in the parks and monuments is a mooted one. The present policy of stationing Federal troops in the parks for brief periods is shortsighted, and the system is entirely inadequate for proper protection," Marshall said on the second day of the conference. However, he saw no foreseeable change. "The tendency appears to have been to continue and even to extend this policy. It is questionable whether troops should be stationed in the parks at all; but if they are they should be detailed for guard duty only and for periods of at least five years, and then not all changed at the same time. It requires at least one year of experience for a man to become at all familiar with the conditions in any one of the national parks." He proceeded to quote from the annual reports of previous military superintendents of Yellowstone, Yosemite, and Sequoia national parks.[52]

Colonel Lloyd M. Brett, the acting superintendent of Yellowstone, also spoke to the issue. He opened with an admission that he was "rounding out my first year in the park here and I do not feel competent as yet to discuss a great many questions." Clearly, though, he understood that the role of the army in the national parks was under extreme scrutiny. "I do not believe it is necessary for me to defend the Army and the work of the troops in these different parks, but as there has been an expression of the desirability of replacing the troops with civilian employees, I have concluded that it is best to give this assembly a little idea of the equipment and work of our men." Despite the problems that troops in Yellowstone had had in the past, he felt that "the military organization and its discipline is just as well suited for this kind of work as it is for any other military work, because this is military work." He then detailed the army's deployments in the park, and how it was administered. He concluded by saying, "When you take into consideration the cost of replacing all of this by civilian labor, it very soon runs into the hundreds of thousands of dollars. The only argument which can be adduced for replacing us by the other form is that the other form should have more permanency. I grant you that, but I do not grant its efficiency. I believe that the system is very efficient to-day and has been and that with the small change of detail—instead of ordering out all at once but half be so ordered and those who remain instruct the newcomers—I am convinced that our force would be as efficient as any that could be secured."[53]

By the time of the third National Park Conference four years later, held at the University of California at Berkeley, Colonel Brett had significantly more experience than at the first conference in 1911, where he praised the administrative structure of the army's management of Yellowstone. He understood his command beyond merely the administrative level. As he spoke at the conference, he focused his remarks less on the organizational structure and more on the qualities of what people needed to protect the park adequately. He could see that the days of soldiers patrolling Yellowstone were numbered, as Yellowstone was the only park that still had an army administration. He laid out what was needed for those who would succeed soldiers in patrolling and enforcing laws in the park. "It would be impossible to delve exhaustively into this subject without taking up too much of your time," he told the attendees, though he expounded on a lengthy list of requirements. First, he felt there should be a hierarchy of rangers, like military ranks, though in his mind the ranger would need to be paid significantly more than soldiers in order to attract a better quality of candidates. He proposed pay ranging from $1500 a year for the chief ranger to $900 a year for the lowest rank. The average soldier made considerably less. A brigadier general in the army only made $500 a year, so the lowest rank of ranger would make nearly twice that salary. However, with such high pay, the new rangers, he felt, should purchase their own mounts and equipment. He also felt they should be "of good character and correct habits" and be "tactful in handling people," something the soldiers occasionally lacked. They should also have "experience in outdoor life." He concluded that "men who will lend themselves conscientiously to this work are not common, and their training is of the greatest importance that their faculties of observation be cultivated to the extreme limit. These men must feel a pride in the work."[54] His description echoed that of Gen. S. M. B. Young eight years before, who called for similar qualities because the soldiers were often "indifferent" to their work. When the National Park Service was created and began to form the ranger program, Brett's recommendations were duly noted. All the best from the military could be kept and the shortcomings of the soldiers addressed. The qualities looked for in rangers, therefore, were a result of the common soldiers' experience, both in terms of the skills and attributes they had, but also those they did not.

# "Petty Grievances"

## Isolated Duty at the Soldier Outposts

The day was cold with a high only in the thirties, and the road from the Sylvan Pass Soldier Station had between one and three feet of snow on it. The arduous journey that the contingent made from that station was all the more difficult because they pulled a sled with a body of one of their own, Pvt. Frank J. Cunningham, who had died the previous night. Three of the four surviving soldiers all took solemn turns pulling and steering the sled with their comrade's body. The fourth, Pvt. Frank Carroll, could not, as his arm was severely injured and might need to be amputated. As the party neared Tex Holm's ranch, Sgt. Clarence A. Brittain turned to Pvt. William H. Mutch and asked him, "Do you have a pistol?"

"Sure, I've got a gun," Mutch told the sergeant.

"I thought you had sense enough to," Sergeant Brittain responded. "You're an old enough soldier to know."[1]

The awkwardness of the question was not lost on Mutch. There was a significant amount unspoken but understood in the exchange. As Mutch later recalled, nobody was really in charge of the soldiers at that moment, nor had anyone been for nearly a day and a half, even though Mutch had initiated almost all the critical decisions in the last thirty-six hours.[2] Ironically, for the first time in perhaps the last nine months, the group was working together to bring Cunningham's body down from the wintery isolation of the park. These men, together since July 3, 1911, had grown to show only disdain for each other. Tensions steadily developed over the winter until Sergeant Brittain, the commander of the Sylvan Pass Soldier Station, shot and killed Private Cunningham and severely wounded Pvt. Frank Carroll. How these men came to the point where they needed to make this grave journey reveals significant details about isolated duty deep within the park and its perils. From the moment they arrived at the station, they faced a unique confluence of forces that affected their ability to become a socially cohesive group that could withstand the psychological trials of extreme isolation required by their duty in the park. They were the wrong mix of men to be placed at one of the most isolated posts in the park, with a relatively unchallenging mission, and virtually no support from their headquarters. All of these would be needed for this small group of men to effectively cope in such severe isolation.

June 1912 was a big month for Clarence Allen Brittain of Company E, First US Cavalry. The thirty-one-year-old Pennsylvanian was promoted to sergeant and assigned to command the Sylvan Pass Soldier Station. Brittain was of slight build and had served over a decade in the army, including four years in the Philippine War, where he was promoted to corporal. He left the service briefly but rejoined it in 1910. Before being assigned to the Sylvan Pass Station, he was in charge of the target range at Fort Yellowstone. His troop commander, Capt. Robert Foy, thought he was a competent noncommissioned officer and "well fitted to take that [Sylvian Pass] station," despite the fact that Foy had only recently joined the company and Brittain's assignment to Sylvan Pass preceded his arrival. Brittain had done well at the target range but had a reputation for being harsh if his orders were not strictly followed. Private Alex Nelson of F Company had left his duties as the cook to shoot at the range. Brittain reprimanded Nelson and ordered him to return to barracks and cook, all while pointing his finger in Nelson's chest "in a way I didn't like," Nelson recalled. When Nelson refused to leave, Brittain hit Nelson in the face and the back of the head. At the same time, nobody else was known to have a problem with Brittain. Civilian Tex Holm, who lived near the Sylvan Pass Soldier Station just outside the park, thought that Brittain was one of the best commanders at the station he had met. However, Brittain did not like the posting. By the end of the summer, he would tell Private Mutch that "if I stay here six months longer, it will drive me crazy."[3]

Every spring the soldiers at the remote stations were rotated back to post and new soldiers assigned. Captain Foy stated that "as far as possible, the rule was to give the noncommissioned officers the men that they preferred." However, he added, "I don't remember in this particular case whether he asked for the men he got." Some soldiers volunteered for duty at certain stations, and if they reenlisted at the end of their term of service, they often would be given a choice of where they'd like to serve. Private William H. Mutch had reenlisted in November of 1910 and asked to be posted at the Sylvan Pass Station. "I just thought I would like to be on the boundary stations, I heard it was a good station," Mutch testified. He was a veteran soldier with more years of experience than Brittain. However, he also had a reputation of being a heavy drinker and a soldier who would do his duty but never anything more. According to Private Carroll, he was also "naturally nervous. [He] can't take up a cup of coffee without [his] hand shaking." Still, at first, Mutch seemed to revel in his duties at Sylvan Pass as others described him as "jolly." At one point, he even told Sergeant Brittain he "would stay another year if they'll let me."[4]

Private Frank L. Carroll was also assigned to the Sylvan Pass detachment. The twenty-nine-year-old from Pearl, Georgia, was five feet, eight inches tall with a dark complexion and somewhat "round and chunky." At first he was on friendly terms with everyone. He may have even been considered Sergeant Brittain's favorite until sometime in the winter. Not that he was never critical of Brittain or had harsh words with the sergeant, but he claimed that he "always forgot about them in a day or two." However, for reasons not entirely clear, he was replaced as the sergeant's pet by the unassuming Pvt. James G. May. May "was quiet. You never heard much from him," said Captain Foy, who went on to describe him as "unobvious" during his time in the troop. May admitted that he "always wanted to keep out of all trouble."[5] That would become increasingly difficult at the Sylvan Pass Station. As the contingent's time at the station progressed, May kept to himself more and more, and even during the court-martial of Sergeant Brittain, his answers were reluctant and evasive, forcing the court to remind him to answer more directly.

The fifth member of the Sylvan Pass detachment, and the one who would not survive the posting, was Pvt. Frank J. Cunningham of New York. Cunningham was imposingly large, "a husky lad" at six feet, four inches and over 190 pounds. His face was covered in scars from smallpox, acne, or something else unknown to anyone but him. He was very sensitive about his appearance. "If he thought you were laughing at him, he would ball you out," or if you dared to ask about them he would snap back at you, "None of your goddamned business." Once a tourist asked about them, and he snarled, "A fish bit me." He was not well liked by anyone at the station and was described by his fellow enlisted men as "sullen" and "sulky." He had a quarrelsome disposition and was prone to bouts of being very "grouchy." Jack Winters, the auto mechanic at the Irma Hotel in Cody, thought he was "a queer sort of fellow. . . . He acted queer at times." He "had problems with everyone on the station except [Private] May," though May considered him "a damned fool." He was such a lousy cook that the soldiers "could hardly eat his cooking," and he was removed from that duty after only two weeks into their posting. Partially because of this, Private Carroll became disgruntled, feeling

Cunningham did not do his fair share of the work. He testified that some of Cunningham's culinary limitations were out of "laziness, I think." When asked if he could think of anything positive to say about Cunningham, Carroll replied: "I couldn't say much for him."[6]

Problems for the Sylvan Pass contingent began before it even left Fort Yellowstone. About ten days before, Private Mutch heard rumors that Sergeant Brittain did not like him and preferred that Mutch not go along. This surprised Mutch, as he had never had any problem with the sergeant. The rumor persisted, and Private Thomas of E Troop even told him he heard Brittain say that "if [Mutch] went on station, he [Brittain] wouldn't." Mutch never approached Brittain about the rumors, and Brittain later denied any such feelings about him before their departure.[7] Regardless, the group set out from Fort Yellowstone on July 1, 1912. They traveled with Captain Foy and the supplies they needed for the summer from Fort Yellowstone to Norris, to Canyon, then Lake, and on to the east entrance at Sylvan Pass.

On July 3 Sergeant Brittain and his group took command of the station. After a winter of isolation, the place needed some work. Captain Foy left after a day but returned in a week for an inspection. Even after a week of hard work, the station was still in poor condition, but Foy still attributed that to the previous command. The captain directed Brittain how to clean it up. The soldiers at the Sylvan Pass Soldier Station were not only in charge of the east entrance to the park, but also had to make regular patrols to prevent violations by tourists and to search for poachers. During the summer regular patrols were to be made from the station to the soldier station near the Lake Hotel to watch over tourists. During both summer and winter, patrols were to be made to Crow and Jones Creeks to search for poachers. To do this, soldiers traveled to the Shoshone River, two miles outside the park near the civilian hotel named Pahaska Teepee. They then moved up the river to the creeks and then west up the creeks, returning by the same route. In the summer it could be done by horse, in the winter only on skis. The typical distance covered on these patrols was over fourteen miles.[8]

During the first inspection a week into the crew's posting, it should have become clear to Captain Foy that command was going to have problems. Sergeant Brittain asked to have Private Cunningham removed. Cunningham had been sent on patrol up Jones Creek but had returned after only a short time, too short a time to make the trip, in Brittain's opinion. In addition, Brittain felt he had poor morale and that it affected the others. Rather than relieve him, Foy dressed down Cunningham and told him "in the future to

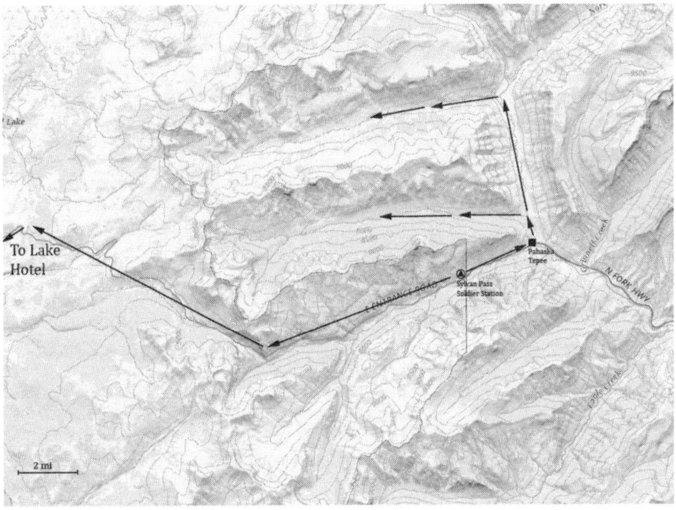


Sylvan Pass Soldier Station and vicinity with regular patrol areas marked on a topographic map. (United States Geological Survey)

carry out the orders of the noncommissioned officer strictly." Other than this incident, the soldiers all reported that they were generally on "good terms" with their comrades those first weeks. Even by the end of July, when Captain Foy performed another inspection, he asked Brittain whether he still wanted Cunningham removed. The sergeant replied that he "would just as soon have him remain on station rather than another man."[9]

Sergeant Brittain's second report to Captain Foy belies the already growing tensions that were brewing at the station during the short time the command had been there. In fact, Brittain testified that he had nearly constant "friction with Cunningham since I went out there."[10] Cunningham had been assigned to cook for the men, a duty that all took in turn. Everyone "found him to be a very poor cook" and complained that his food was virtually inedible. Also, one afternoon he "left dishes unwashed" late into the day. When Brittain found him lying on his bunk, he ordered him to wash them immediately. Cunningham only reluctantly did so after "growling." Another day, Cunningham left the post without permission and visited a civilian camping party about two miles away. Sergeant Brittain found him and ordered him to return to the station and cook dinner. "Let someone else get supper, I am busy," Cunningham snapped back, sitting among the women of the party. Brittain repeated the order, and Cunningham grudgingly got up slowly and accompanied him back to the station. Even so, Cunningham's cooking was so bad that he had to be relieved from kitchen duty before the end of his week, and he never again cooked at the post. Instead, he was put in charge of the stables, "where he did very well but had to be watched, or he would leave them without cleaning up."[11]

The growing tension at the station did not always center on Cunningham. Brittain and Mutch became disenchanted with each other over a girl. Wooing women was a favorite pastime with the soldiers and the civilian employees at the hotels in and around the park. The soldiers went to great lengths, often disobeying orders to seek out liaisons. Regulations forbade women from entering the soldier stations, but sometimes the reward could be worth the risk. Privates Daniel Becker, James Gearin, James Daley, and George Collins invited women into their quarters at the Lake Soldier Station and were court-martialed. Soldiers would also go into the hotels to pursue women, also forbidden by regulations. Impressing women and finding opportunities to woo them led Pvt. Van Sheffield, in charge of the post library at Fort Yellowstone, to kick other soldiers out and close it down early so he could invite two women employed at the hotel into a now-private space. The female hotel employees appreciated the attention. Lake Hotel employee Emilie Kryger and her friend Hanna would often stay out "with the soldiers until dark."[12]

For the soldiers at Sylvan Pass Soldier Station, the large Lake Hotel with its equally large female staff provided an ample opportunity. One of the regular summer patrols for the men from Sylvan Pass was to Lake Soldier Station, and every Saturday during the tourist season there was a dance. Sergeant Brittain made the sacrifice of regularly assuming the patrol to Lake on Saturdays and was thus available for the dances. This led to some resentment among his men.[13] But the woman who drove the wedge between the sergeant and Private Mutch was Sadie Meeks, an employee at the more conveniently located Pahaska Teepee just outside the park and only two miles away from the station. Like most of the accounts about Sylvan Pass that fateful season, the Pahaska stories are congruent and agree on the basic facts with only occasional details differing. The reasons, internal reactions, and professed motivations are the sources of disagreement.

In late July Sergeant Brittain and Private Carroll went from the station to Pahaska Teepee after dinner. Several times Brittain and Carroll had gone to Pahaska and met the girls who worked there. The girls at Pahaska would get off work between 7:30 and 8:00 p.m., and Brittain went down almost every evening around that time. One time, the sergeant and Carroll went to the

Pahaska Tepee, a hotel located only two miles from the Sylvan Pass Soldier Station. The hotel was built by William "Buffalo Bill" Cody around 1905. (Author's collection)

hotel, but Brittain stayed so long talking to Sadie Meeks that Carroll finally returned to the station alone in the dark. Another night things took a turn. The sergeant and Carroll went to the hotel to get some supplies that Brittain had ordered from Cody. On a hill above the road from the station were two women; one was Sadie Meeks. They called to the soldiers to come up and sit with them. Brittain jumped the fence and yelled, "Come on, Carroll!" They sat and talked with the girls for a while and then continued on to the hotel to pick up their supplies. On the way back, the girls were still there, and the men talked with them for a while longer. Soon Privates Mutch and May came along, walking toward Pahaska, and joined the group. They all talked for a while together before the girls left with May and Mutch. Carroll joked with the sergeant about the girls ditching them, but Brittain was in no mood. "Son of a bitch!" he said, "Others will be sorry." Later he added that he "simply would queer others," meaning he would make them look foolish.[14]

Brittain did not recall saying anything about the incident or even feeling jilted by Ms. Meeks, though he admitted that she and Mutch later became "pretty thick."[15] When the court asked if this affected his relationship with the sergeant, Mutch replied that it did "according to how a man would take a thing like that." It was becoming clear to people around the station that the feelings everyone had for each other were turning sour. Private Oliver Jordway, who was stationed at Lake but made the patrol from Lake to Sylvan Pass, was keenly aware that by midsummer there was some tension at the outpost.

Sylvan Pass Soldier Station, date unknown. (Yellowstone National Park Museum Collection)

When he was riding with Brittain to find Private May, who had gotten lost, the sergeant turned to him and said: "Only two men will come out [of Sylvan Pass] alive." Jordway did not think too much of it at the time. However, he noted that the privates were also unhappy, particularly about the food.[16]

Beyond the possible conflict over Sadie Meeks, Mutch grew increasingly discontent with how Brittain ran the station. A professional soldier despite his shortcomings, he felt that the patrols were not frequent enough to effectively patrol the area. Besides, when there were patrols, he felt that he did far more than his fair share. At another point during the summer, Mutch was sealing guns that tourists brought into the park. Regulations stipulated that tourists either had to turn in their weapons and retrieve them upon exiting the park or have them sealed and then inspected upon their departure to make sure the seal was intact. The hope was to prevent visitors from hunting the park's game. While Mutch was sealing the guns, Brittain came over and showed him another way of doing it, but Mutch said he would do it his way. "Don't talk back to me!" shouted Brittain. "I'm running this station."[17]

Millie Winter, the manager of Pahaska Teepee, sensed the growing unfriendliness among the garrison as well. The privates came down individually several evenings a week, but Brittain rarely did.[18] Private Cunningham went to Pahaska Teepee at some point during the summer and had dinner. He told Millie how much he hated it there. She asked the sulky Cunningham why, but he refused to elaborate, stating only that he "would get [Brittain]."[19] Cunningham must have been serious about the threat. In late summer, Winter said, Cunningham came to the hotel, excited, and asked for Mutch, who was upstairs. Cunningham told him that Brittain was coming down the road. "If we don't get him today we will when we are shut in." However, Mutch hesitated in "getting" the sergeant, and Cunningham left upset.[20]

Jack Winter of the Irma Hotel in Cody also noticed the rising friction. One day, when he brought the mail to Pahaska from Cody, Private Cunningham approached him and called out "Hello, Jack!"

"Hello, big fellow," Winters responded to the large and imposing private.

"Did you get the mail?" Cunningham asked.

"I have some right here," Winter said as he handed the station's mail to him. Cunningham looked through the envelopes, took a few and threw the rest in the toolbox of Winter's car.

"Here," snarled Cunningham. "I don't want these damn things!" The shocked Winters was surprised that he would not take the rest of the mail to the post.[21]

As summer turned to fall, the station's morale only continued to sink. In early September Private Mutch, who at one point claimed he would have stayed another year at the post, asked for permission to talk on the telephone and to request a transfer back to Fort Yellowstone. Brittain permitted him to talk to Captain Foy. The officer dutifully listened but did not think Mutch's complaints were "well-founded." An early snow made travel difficult, prompting Brittain and Foy to agree that Mutch should stay at the post.[22] The crestfallen Mutch later went to Pahaska. He talked with both Millie and Jack Winters. He had let it be known that he was going to seek a transfer so Jack asked him if he received it. "No," replied the disappointed private. "I was sent back and told to stay." He confided to Jack Winters, "Well, I would sooner go on out of there because I'm afraid there will be trouble."

"You're big enough to take care of yourself," reassured Jack Winters.

"That ain't the thing of it. The sergeant there was carrying a gun," replied Mutch.

Winters laughed and said, "All you fellows carry a gun with you when you come down here."

"I know it," replied Mutch before he fell silent for a minute or two. Then, with no warning, he became very agitated.

"What are you so excited about?" asked Winters. Mutch just shook his head.

"I want to get away from there because, believe me, fellow, there will be a shooting scrape before snow comes."

"You're wrong to think that way," exclaimed Winters, trying to calm the private down.

"Believe me, Jack, there's going to be trouble," said the dejected private. He gathered his parcels and walked out into the night on the road back to the station alone.[23]

The mood against Brittain was growing. At his court-martial, the surviving privates depicted Brittain as a man who did not hold the mission of protecting the park in high regard, especially if there was an opportunity for profit. Carroll and Brittain had been fishing on Jones Creek when the sergeant thought he saw something shiny, possibly gold, in the stream. He said they should come back once the pass was closed and check it out. Carroll said he never mentioned it again, for fear of getting in trouble with his superiors. He also testified that the sergeant said he would kill a beaver for its skin if he could find one, in blatant violation of park rules and regulations. It was not long after the time when Carroll was no longer considered the sergeant's favorite that Brittain also started "acting cool" to everyone else.[24]

As the tourist season was winding down, the garrison's food was becoming increasingly problematic. Everyone was complaining about the food, or lack of it. The last supply from Fort Yellowstone had occurred when the contingent assumed control on July 3. The fresh meat had run out long before because nearly 300 pounds had spoiled. There was also a problem with the number of rations provided by the fort. Taking it upon himself to help procure supplies, Brittain traded some government hay to a group of tourists for lard from Pahaska Teepee. This was not an uncommon occurrence. The soldier stations throughout the park could offer meals or supplies to tourists and park employees as long as they paid for it. The soldiers were to keep "all receipts for meals furnished" and the "books will be balanced at the end of each month . . . or whenever a non-commissioned officer is relieved from duty at any station." The money could be used to get future rations to replace those consumed or "divided pro rata among the members of the detachment." The deal with the hay was in line with those policies, but the disgruntled privates, ready to criticize Brittain for any excuse, saw it as an abuse of government property, even if it helped alleviate their own shortage of rations about which they always complained. Their superiors saw it differently. Colonel Brett, the commanding officer and acting superintendent of the park, stated that "I put these noncommissioned officers at these stations and they must solve the problems as they arise. If I am convinced that they are honest and solved those problems to the very best of their ability, I exonerate them from any mistakes."[25]

He added that the rationing at the stations was challenging to begin with, and this created problems that the noncommissioned officers needed to solve. "You see, the ration system has so changed that I thought that probably in making up their consignment some essential thing had been omitted because, as you know, . . . it is not confined to the rationed articles as it used to be, but there is a wide selection and [I] took it for granted that some important article had been omitted. But they should not be anywhere near out of rations." He added that trading hay for lard was an acceptable solution to the missing "important article."[26]

However, the lack of fresh meat was more perplexing. There were several reasons why the meat might spoil, and this had occurred at several other stations. If it was not properly stored or if wild animals got into it, the expected ration would become unavailable. However, neither Sergeant Brittain nor the privates explained why there was a lack of fresh meat. Sometime in the early fall Brittain and Cunningham brought in a deer so the men could have the long desired fresh meat. Though Brittain claimed he had killed it outside the park in the national forest, Cunningham claimed it was from inside the boundary. He told Carroll the meat was from inside the park and that if he got in trouble, he was taking the sergeant with him. In fact, Cunningham struck first. He wrote a letter to Captain Foy about the deer and included a litany of other complaints. Captain Foy dismissed them. After all, he had already had to dress down Cunningham at the beginning of the summer, and the letter seemed "written out of malice." He added that the private "struck me as a man who was not particularly keen on obedience to orders."[27]

Cunningham also struck Aaron "Tex" Holm as particularly vengeful. Holm lived on a ranch west of Cody and was in the transportation business. He employed forty men and twenty-five vehicles to bring tourists through the park. He also had his newfangled "machine," a personal automobile. Regularly Holm brought tourists through the park's east entrance, and he got to know the soldiers of the station well. He recalled chatting during the late summer with Cunningham, who said that "before spring it would be necessary to work the sergeant over and make a good soldier of him." The stunned Holm reminded him that Brittain had more authority over him, but Cunningham retorted that "after the phone was down, it wouldn't make any difference."[28]

Aron "Tex" Holm driving his automobile, circa 1923. Holm began leading fourteen- and eighteen-day camping parties into the park from Cody in 1903. He built several campsites within the park, but they were significantly less developed than the permanent camping establishments run by the Wylie and the Shaw & Powell companies. (Yellowstone National Park Museum Collection)

A remark of that kind often got fellows into trouble, Holm reminded the private.

"That don't make any difference up there," claimed Cunningham.

In mid-September, Holm's teamster, C. A. Richardson, brought what would be the last party of the 1911 tourist season through the entrance by the soldier station. On that cold day, when the rain was mixing with snow, Richardson brought his wagon to the post. "How many you got?" Sergeant Brittain asked.

"Eight of us all together," Richardson answered.

"The boys are just lunching and you better have your party come in and have dinner here," invited Brittain warmly. As the party entered the station and huddled around the stove, Richardson stayed outside to tend to the horses.

Cunningham came over to him. "It's a wonder that son-of-a-bitch would give you any accommodations here." Richardson continued his work, not replying. "He might just as well asked you to put the horses in the barn," continued Cunningham.

"I don't care to put them in the barn," answered the teamster. "I have oats here in the oat bags." Then he tried to make friendly small talk. "Are you going to stay in the station this winter?"

Cunningham replied, "If I do, I'll mix it with that son-of-a-bitch before the winter is over." Richardson decided it was best just to walk away from the cantankerous soldier.[29]

It was clear that there were problems between the sergeant and the soldiers. Brittain had asked Cunningham to be reassigned in the first week at the post but changed his mind a few weeks later. Both Cunningham and Mutch had asked to be reassigned, only to be rebuffed by Captain Foy. The higher command ignored the signs of trouble, and any support from Fort Yellowstone was minimal at best. Similar instances had occurred at different soldier stations before, and other officers took the initiative to solve them. In September of 1904, the four soldiers stationed at the Thumb Soldier Station asked to be relieved. They wrote: "We the undersigned request to be relieved from the Thumb Soldier Station as Corporal Clark is dissatisfied with us and we are dissatisfied with Corporal Clark and there are men in Fort Yellowstone that Corporal Clark would be more satisfied with. [signed] Pvt. Ludsen A. Conely, Pvt. John R. Passar, Pvt. A. R. Giles, Pvt. Foreland." Just like the privates at Sylvan Pass, these soldiers had reached their limit with their station commander by the end of summer. However, records find that they were all removed from Thumb by October.[30] Perhaps their collective action carried more weight than the individual appeals of the men at Sylvan Pass. Perhaps Foy did not take the signs of tension at Sylvan Pass seriously. Whatever the reason, the men remained in place as the winter approached. It would have fatal results.

The soldiers at the Sylvan Pass Soldier Station clearly disliked Sergeant Brittain, perhaps with good cause, perhaps not. However, the testimony is also somewhat skewed because the sergeant was the person on trial for the murder of Cunningham. Yet, in their testimony everyone admitted that, at one time or another, they were not on speaking terms with anyone else at the station. Even the quiet May could not get along with everybody all the time.[31] They all seemed on friendly terms at the beginning of the summer. Private May went so far as to say they all "were friends." However, by the late fall things had turned. At different times certain soldiers would not talk to each other. On the whole Mutch, Carroll, and Cunningham did not speak to each other much. Even when they did talk to each other, they did not do so "in the way they ought to, that is, to be friendly." Everyone admitted they had problems with Cunningham or were "out of sorts" with him most of the time.[32] The problems, therefore, seemed more widespread and not confined to Brittain alone.

With the tourist season over, the five soldiers set about preparing the station for winter. Wood needed to be collected and cut. The horses were sent back to Fort Yellowstone and the winter rations from the main fort brought in. Finally, fresh meat arrived in a large "Alaska ration" since the isolated post would have only minimal contact with headquarters for the next six months. Once winter set in, to get people or supplies to or from the fort, soldiers would need to travel fifty-three miles overland through the snow to Cody, then by train to Billings, Montana, where they would change trains and go to Livingston, change trains again and go to Gardiner. Finally, they would travel overland to the headquarters at Mammoth Hot Springs. Traditionally, snow slides on Sylvan Pass regularly cut the phone line to the post, adding to the post's isolation in the winter. As expected, on November 10, 1911, the telephone line was indeed cut by an avalanche during a heavy snowstorm on the west side of Sylvan Pass.[33] The five men of the station, who had grown to dislike each over the summer, now were very isolated and only had each other for company in a small four-room cabin surrounded by a hostile and deadly winter environment.

Life at the soldier stations in winter was an exceptional experience, perhaps not much different from the winters at a modern Antarctic research station. Some unique psychological and medical situations arise in those environments. "Winter-over syndrome" is common, where individuals exhibit increased anxiety, irritability, depression, insomnia, and even irritable bowel syndrome. The cause is not entirely known but may include stress, social isolation, extreme seasonal affective disorder, or perhaps a combination of all of these. People in Antarctica have also been known to have lower levels of the thyroid hormone T3. Low levels of T3 increase mood disturbances and forgetfulness, and result in cognitive impairment. Like "winter-over syndrome," the exact cause is not known.[34] For men who were already in a raw emotional state and generally disliked at least some of the other men at the detachment, these conditions might have added to an already toxic situation.

Even for men who liked each other, under the best circumstances the winters at soldier stations were severe, not only because of expected duties but also because of the social atmosphere. Corporal Thomas M. Connery, a contemporary of the men at Sylvan Pass, was in charge of the Upper Basin Soldier Station in 1911–1912 and described it this way for *Wide World Magazine*:

Soldiers prepare for a winter ski patrol, circa 1910. Given the elevation and extreme cold and unpredictable weather, soldiers needed to take precautions that included never going out alone. As seen at the Sylvan Pass Station, those regulations might routinely be ignored. (Yellowstone National Park Museum Collection)

> The reader may imagine, therefore, a sergeant from Tennessee in charge of four men—one from Brooklyn, another from New York, one from Chicago, the fourth from no place in particular—trying to live together "peacefully" for eight months, with no change or other society, and not another cabin or shack for twenty miles on either side. When the winter starts to drag and the playing cards are worn to rags, when the reading matter that has done years of service gets still older, and, as the lights in the cabin are extinguished for the night, the coyotes assemble and yelp. That is when the "old grouch" affects each man. Every morning a fellow gets up, looks at the same faces, puts on his skis, goes out for his patrol, comes back, eats, and lies down: to do the same thing next day.[35]

The patrol duties had to continue, but with the added dangers of extreme cold and snow at nearly eight thousand feet above sea level. After numerous deadly mishaps several precautions had been put in place to mitigate the dangers. Private David Mathews had been delivering mail alone in the winter of 1894 and disappeared. His body was not found until June the next year. The acting superintendent, Capt. George Anderson, concluded that "it was evident that he became lost, while in that condition became crazed and perished from cold."[36] In the winter of 1897–1898, Pvt. John Davis left his station at Mud Geyser to meet soldiers from the Snake River detachment to exchange mail, which they did twice monthly. After leaving the Lake Hotel, where he and another soldier spent the night, the weather turned decidedly sour. While the other soldier turned back, Davis pressed on but never met up with the men from Snake River. A dramatic search ensued in subzero temperatures until his frozen body was found several days later. The cold was not the only enemy to the soldiers in winter. An avalanche took the life of Cpl. Christ Martin in 1904.[37]

So, the men of Sylvan Pass continued their patrols up Jones and Crow Creeks, but without any regularity and much less often than the privates suspected they ought to. Sometimes weeks went by with no patrols, and nobody seemed to know the orders about how often they should be made.[38] The station log, which lists patrols during the later fall and winter of 1911–1912, shows a marked decrease in the number of patrols per week over the winter. From October through December, the soldiers averaged 2.4 patrols a week. After the new year, they averaged only 1.4 patrols a week.[39] As there were only two duties at the station over winter, cooking (done by one person each week) and patrolling (done by two or sometimes even just one person), there was significant downtime for the men at the station.

However, the entries are also suspect as there may have been even fewer patrols than those listed. Private Carroll was "positive" that "a dozen, twelve or fifteen" patrols entered in the log did not actually occur.[40] Cunningham was suspicious too and even approached Private May in the kitchen one day with the log. "Come here, I want to show you," he said to May. May was busy and tried to ignore him. Undeterred, Cunningham opened the log and showed May an entry to Crow Creek that listed them both as having made it. "Did you and I make that?"

"No," replied May. Cunningham claimed he did not either.[41]

The lack of patrolling added to the problematic situation. The soldiers at the post considered themselves on duty on only two occasions: when they were on kitchen duty or when they were on patrol. Since only one soldier a day was actually in the kitchen, on the majority of the days, when there were no patrols, the other men were not "on duty." During those times, they

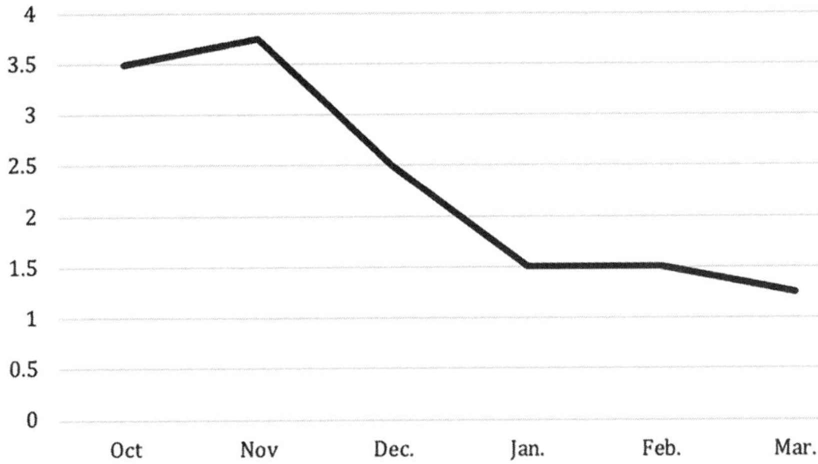


The average number of patrols a week at the Sylvan Pass Soldier Station over the winter of 1911–1912.

had to fill their days as best they could, reading, playing cards, or simply "spend[ing] all day on their bunk if they wanted."[42] The incredible amount of downtime led to a lessening of military discipline. The isolation and lack of direction, with men already on bad terms with each other, would naturally lead to significant tension, and the strain started to show very quickly.

As the winter set in, May moved into the sergeant's room because he claimed he needed an open window. Cunningham remained insolent, and Sergeant Brittain gave him "a calling down," which made him "sore" for several days.[43] Then, as the new year approached, the whole contingent save Private Mutch went to Wapiti, Wyoming, for a dance. The social atmosphere must have been a relief. Cunningham, Carroll, and May also asked and received permission to go to Cody afterward. Surprisingly, there things began to spiral, especially for Cunningham. At the Irma Hotel in Cody, his behavior became increasingly erratic. He sat in a corner by himself, mumbling things only he could hear, and then suddenly bolted out of the room. Jack Winters thought it very peculiar.[44] In the street his conduct was equally unpredictable. A young boy came up and offered him tickets to a show. Cunningham swore and kicked him.[45] His actions were so rude and aggressive that Jack Winter told May, "You better go along with that fella."

"Let him go," replied May. "He'll be all right."

Curious about May's dismissive reply, Winter asked: "Thought you were all in the same room?"

Incredulously, May replied, "No, I wouldn't go to bed with that damned fool!"[46]

Cunningham retired to his room at the Irma in a drunken state. For reasons unknown, he drew his revolver and shot at the brass ball atop the foot of his bedpost three times but missed. Nobody dared enter the room, so the bartender called the sheriff. As people gathered in the hallway, May suggested that he should go in first as Cunningham knew him and was less likely to be shot. He was almost dead wrong. As May entered the room, Cunningham put the revolver to May's head and pulled the trigger. Fortunately, the chamber was empty. May grabbed the gun and took out the rest of the shells. "What the hell do you want?" Cunningham snapped. At that point the sheriff entered and arrested the belligerent private, taking him to the jail. As he entered his jail cell, Cunningham told the current occupant, "Get out of the way, you son-of-a-bitch, I'm coming in." As the jailer locked the door, Cunningham told him it would be useless as he could break the door if he wanted. Ultimately, he proved himself right by breaking the lock, though he made no actual attempt to escape. For his escapades, he received a $50 fine plus restitution or confinement in jail while he worked it off.[47]

Even with the quarrelsome Cunningham isolated from the group at the station, things did not necessarily improve at Sylvan Pass. The problems ran deeper than one "bad apple." During that time, a nearly fatal fight broke out between Private Mutch and Sergeant Brittain. One evening, Mutch came back from patrol and went to the kitchen to get some bread and milk. According to Mutch and corroborated by the other privates, upon returning from patrol they could go after hours to get some food. Normally, they limited their rations in order to save money for the expensive daily bacon that everyone desired. Brittain chastised Mutch for getting the milk and bread. "You get permission when you want to get bread and milk." Dismissing the sergeant's animosity, Mutch sat down at the table and began to eat. Brittain grabbed a chair and struck Mutch across the back. A fight ensued. Mutch grabbed a glass oil lantern and thought about throwing it at Brittain, but after a moment of pause, he decided to put it back down. "I thought it would set the quarters on fire," he later testified. Then he added, "I thought nobody is allowed to hit a man with a lamp."[48]

Cunningham was released from jail early, and on February 1 the sergeant retrieved him from Cody and returned to the station. Adding Cunningham back into the social mix made things worse. For reasons that were unclear, Cunningham tried to provoke Mutch into a fight when he called him "a bad name in front of Private Carroll." Carroll broke up the altercation, though Cunningham "called Carroll down about it." On February 14 Cunningham let a mule out of the stables, and it wandered off. The fact that he also did not work in the kitchen, one of the only actual duties at the post that winter, irritated Private Carroll. On March 1 Carroll told Brittain, "I'm not going to dog-rob for no one no more!" and demanded that Cunningham do his share of the cooking. But the sergeant replied that he should "just do what you're told." Carroll retorted that no one in the station liked the sergeant as a commander and that he demanded to be taken back to the headquarters at Fort Yellowstone, a demand that Brittain denied. "Since that time all the men have been unfriendly," Brittain later claimed, and they were "speaking only when spoken to."[49]

The whole situation came to a head on Friday, March 29, 1912. Sergeant Brittain arose early and prepared to leave the post for the patrol up Jones Creek, a trip of over seventeen miles on skis. Private Carroll was helping Mutch in the kitchen, making pies. The sergeant entered as he was about to leave and asked Carroll, "Are you going up to Pahaska?"[50]

Carroll thought he might go there and exchange some reading material with the winter keeper. "I think I am," he told the sergeant.

"Bring back that saw," said Brittain. The post was running low on firewood, and the station's six-foot saw had been lent to winter keep at Pahaska in the fall. The question that was never fully answered was whether or not Brittain's words constituted an official order. Carroll and Mutch, who heard it, never considered it so. Brittain, on the other hand, considered his words a direct order. The rest of the day hinged on each man's interpretation as Brittain left the post around 8:30 in the morning, by himself. Going on winter patrol alone was against regulations for safety reasons, but according to the station log, Brittain had made several patrols alone, perhaps because of the general dislike the soldiers had for him and he for them.[51] Carroll apparently had a change of heart about going to Pahaska and decided to stay at the post. The saw would remain where it was.

In the afternoon, the sergeant passed Pahaska Teepee on the return leg of his patrol. Brittain noticed that the saw was still there and became angry. He refused to take it himself, and for the remaining two miles to the station, he stewed about the fact that Carroll had disobeyed what he considered a direct order. He intended to make sure Carroll would get it. When he arrived at the station, he took off his skis near the stables and started toward the main building. He claimed that his legs were tired and he needed a little support, so he grabbed a small stick off the woodpile to use as an improvised cane to

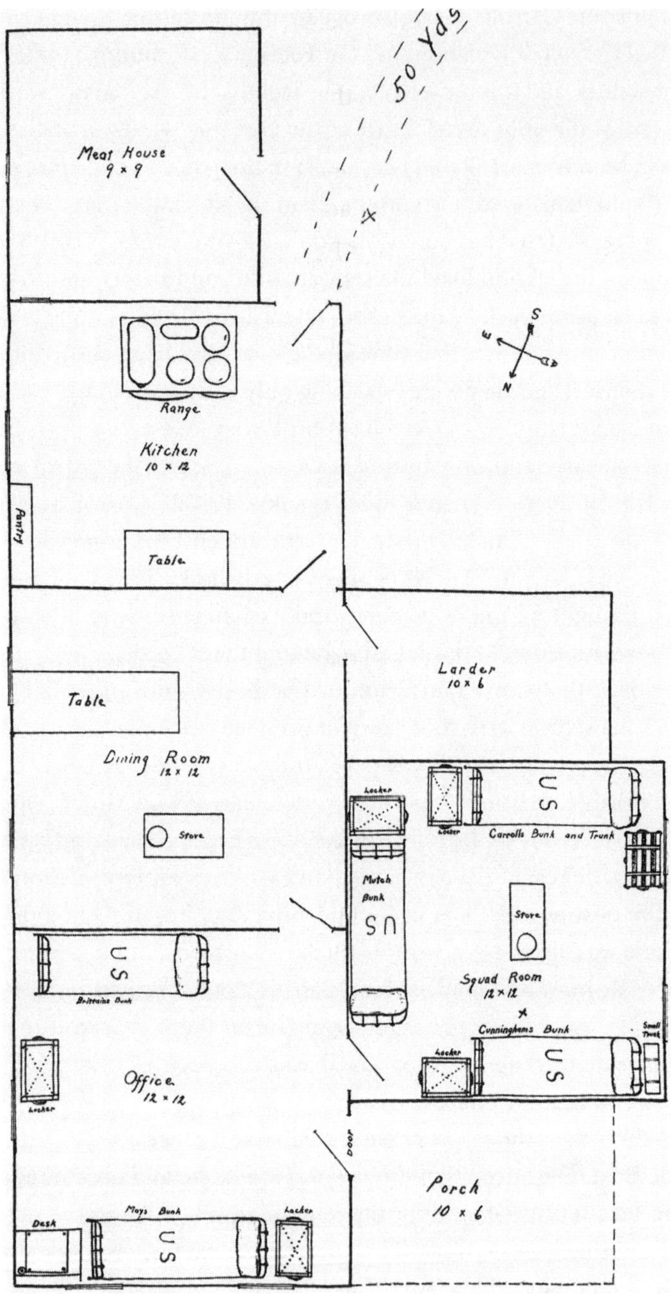


The plan of the Sylvan Pass Soldier Station in the winter of 1912, introduced as Exhibit A in the court-martial of Sgt. Clarence Brittain. (National Archives and Records Administration)

steady himself. Given his state of mind, and the fact that even by his own admission the piece of wood was only a little over two feet long, remarkably short for a cane, it seems more likely that it was going to be used at least for intimidation if not something worse.

Shortly after 2:00 p.m., Brittain entered the station through the main door and marched through the room that acted as his quarters and office. May's bunk was in that room as well, and the private was lying on it, asleep. Brittain then turned into the room where the other privates slept. They were all on their bunks, as usual. He barked at Carroll, "Did you get that saw?"

"I never went down to Pahaska," replied Carroll.

"No, damn you! You never went down because I told you to fetch that saw up," accused the sergeant. "Tomorrow you go walk every step of the way down there and get that saw and walk every step of the way back."

Carroll replied, "I will see if I can make it."

Britain took that as a snarky reply. "Don't talk back to me," he said. Then he walked right up to Carroll, with the stick still in his hand, and said, "You are under arrest."

Seemingly unmoved, Carroll retorted dismissively, "I've been under arrest before."

Brittain then left the room and went back into his room and woke up May, telling him to come with him. The private stirred and oriented himself as the sergeant went back to confront Carroll. After quickly assessing the situation, May quietly left out the front door to avoid the whole confrontation. As May was leaving the building, Brittain reentered the other room and looked at Mutch, reclining on his bunk, and told him to "jump him [Carroll]!"

The reluctant Mutch countered, "Why do you want me to do that?" Mutch later testified that he felt that if he had gotten involved "it would have made it worse." However, it was also becoming clear that the troop no longer recognized the authority of Sergeant Brittain.

Taking offense at the insubordination, Brittain snapped, "I told you to jump him!" He immediately swung the hand with the stick in it at Mutch, who fell back on his bunk and avoided the punch as Brittain's fist went harmlessly over the private's shoulder. At the same moment, Cunningham stood up and with the help of Carroll grabbed the sergeant, roughly shoving him out the door of their room and back into his own. The next few seconds were "cloudy" to the sergeant, but not to Mutch or Carroll. Brittain reached for his sidearm, a .38-caliber pistol he was wearing when he went out on patrol. He aimed it at Cunningham and Carroll, shooting three times. One bullet hit Cunningham in the chest; another passed through Carroll's upper arm and grazed his torso. The third bullet missed its mark entirely. Bleeding profusely, the wounded Carroll bolted out of the bedroom screaming. He ran through the sergeant's room, the dining room, and out the back door to hide in the stables behind the outpost, leaving a trail of blood. Cunningham fell to the floor, bleeding. Even Private May, who had left the building but only made it to the porch, heard the shots and the screams. He froze for a moment near the corner of the building and saw the wounded Carroll run to the stables bleeding. The skittish May decided that instead of aiding Carroll, he would go to Pahaska Teepee. When asked why, he claimed he thought it best he go to Pahaska to call a doctor in Cody. He admitted, however, that he was pretty "rattled."[52]

After the shots were fired, Mutch rose off his bunk and entered the other room. Confronting the sergeant, he said, "What in the hell are you trying to do? Throw down that gun!" The sergeant immediately threw his revolver on his bunk. From that moment on, it was clear that Mutch was unofficially in charge. Despite his nervous disposition, he remained clearheaded and asserted himself with authority in the chaotic situation. Though never directly spoken, even Sergeant Brittain acknowledged Mutch's unofficial authority, following the private's directives.

Mutch testified that even though he did not confiscate the pistol, he did not think Brittain would use it again. Mutch returned to the privates' room and helped Cunningham onto his bunk. "Well, I guess I got mine," the mortally wounded private said.[53] Mutch stood up and looked for Carroll. He followed the blood trail. As he passed Brittain, still standing dazed in his own room, the private commanded his sergeant to "look after that man," pointing to Cunningham. Snapping himself out of the daze, Brittain dressed Cunningham's wounds. Mutch found Carroll in the corner of the stables. He told Carroll to come back inside, that the situation was under control. In shock and having lost a significant amount of blood, Carroll was weak and lying in the snow. Mutch lifted him up and brought him back into the post, but the enfeebled Carroll could only make it to the kitchen where Mutch laid him out on the floor in the doorway between the dining room and the kitchen.

He got a butcher knife and cut open Carroll's sleeve to the shoulder. "I am shot in the stomach," protested Carroll, wanting Mutch to see what he thought might be a more serious wound. Mutch cut open the shirt but while there was bruising and light lesion, there was no gunshot wound. The serious wound was the bleeding arm with a possible severed artery. Mutch dashed to the medicine cabinet for a bandage to make a tourniquet. As he did, Sergeant Brittain passed him, took the silk handkerchief off his neck, and told him to use that. While Mutch went for some water, Brittain made a tourniquet for the man he had shot only a few moments before. Turning his attention to Cunningham, Mutch noticed there was very little blood coming from his wound. However, given that the shot was located in the right breast, there was likely internal bleeding. Both soldiers desperately needed a doctor, and the only way to get one would be to call Cody from Pahaska Teepee's telephone. With May's whereabouts unknown, one of the two remaining men would have to do it. Mutch decided it should be himself. He told Brittain to take care of the wounded men, a remarkable show of faith in his sergeant who had just tried to kill the men he was now caring for.

Mutch frantically arrived at Pahaska Teepee. He asked the winter keeper, Pat English, to call a doctor in Cody. A physician named Dr. Bennett answered the call. He wanted to speak directly with Mutch but English replied that it was against the rules for the soldiers to use the phone. Not in the mood, Mutch pushed English aside and told him, "Let me have it." He relayed the information as best he could to Dr. Bennett, who acknowledged that the wounds were very severe. However, he could not come because he had some serious cases in Cody that he needed to tend to. He would get another doctor to come. The other physician, a Dr. Wapples, was put on the phone. He would come but asked, "Will the government pay for it?"

"Yes, your money is sure!" snapped Mutch.

"Wait a minute," said the doctor. "I will telephone to see if I can get an automobile to start." After confirming that he could get at least partway by automobile, the call ended. Mutch then called to have a telegram sent to Fort Yellowstone, reporting the situation.

While he was at Pahaska, Mutch finally found Private May. They returned to the post together and awaited the doctor's arrival. When they arrived, they found that Cunningham was still alive but barely coherent and would remain so as the night progressed. At one point "he was talking foolish, [saying] something about a gold mine," May said. Brittain came in the room, and May said the sergeant "told me not to talk to him and stepped outside." An awkward calm settled on the station. Sergeant Brittain even continued to record the weather conditions in the post log, perhaps taking comfort in the routine duty.[54]

Dr. Wapples had made his way to the station using Tex Holm's automobile but could only get within ten to fifteen miles of the post. He brought with him Tex Holm and Harry Miller, a forest ranger stationed at the Wapiti Forest ranger station. The rest of the journey had to be made on horseback.[55] When the doctor arrived, he thought Cunningham's wound was severe and he needed to get him to Cody. Mutch and Brittain discussed the situation as they had not yet received instructions from their commanding officers. Mutch decided they would leave the next morning. In Mutch's mind, "really, there was nobody in command" of the garrison at that point.[56] Brittain never contradicted him but apparently was allowing Mutch to make the decisions for the group.

Cunningham passed away at 8:30 a.m., before they could leave. Mutch decided they would go to Cody anyway. The dead private's body was wrapped in an army blanket and put on a makeshift sled using skis for runners. Two men would be needed to move him down the mountain. One soldier would be in the front and the other in the back, steering. Mutch, Brittain, and May all took their turns. Carroll, also severely wounded, could not exert himself and was also put on a sled. They made their way to Pahaska Teepee, where they stopped for "a brief meal." Then they continued toward Holm's lodge, arriving at 6:30 p.m. They made approximately eleven miles in about six hours.[57] Partway down, Brittain suggested that perhaps he should consider himself under arrest, though it was never officially spoken. "Do you have a pistol?"

"Sure, I've got a gun," Mutch told the sergeant.

"I thought you had sense enough to," Sergeant Brittain responded. "You're an old enough soldier to know." They stayed the night at Holm Lodge; at 5:00 a.m. the next morning, the solemn procession continued to Cody in wagons. At the Wapiti Forest ranger station, they transferred into Holm's automobile, which took them the rest of the way to Cody.[58]

When they arrived, they found Captain Foy waiting. The captain had traveled by train to Livingston, then to Billings, and finally down to Cody. Foy could not leave Fort Yellowstone for Cody until March 31 as there was no train going to Cody from Billings any earlier. He originally wanted to go to the Sylvan Pass Station itself but, "when I got to Cody, I found that Private Cunningham had already died and that all the men of the station were on their way."[59]

Foy inspected Cunningham's body and Carroll's wounded arm. He confined Brittain to a hotel room and ordered him to go back to Fort Yellowstone on the next day's train under the charge of Private Mutch. Foy had great trust in his sergeant and added

> I believe he [Brittain] would have come back to the Post alone, without anyone to take charge of him. At the time I told him to confine himself

to the hotel I thought that I would come the next day myself, I thought I would be able to finish my duty at Cody and intended to have the accused come back with me without the aid of any guard or anyone. . . . When I found I couldn't go myself, I thought it best to have him under charge of someone as much for his own protection as for any reason.

When asked about the sergeant's demeanor, he described it as "decidedly that of a man who had done his duty," adding, "It occurred to me that perhaps that sometime during the trip he might be advised by some friend of his that he best get away as he was under serious charges, and I thought for that reason as much as any other that I had better have someone with him."[60]

An investigation and court-martial against Sergeant Brittain for murder were undertaken concurrently with court-martial proceedings for Mutch, Carroll, and May for mutiny. The investigation took most of April. The sensational nature of the incident garnered the attention of local newspapers, and the trial of the soldiers began in the public press long before the actual proceedings. Like Captain Foy, the benefit of the doubt had gone to the sergeant before all the facts could be gathered. The *Northern Wyoming Herald* in Cody reported that "while it is impossible to say what will be the outcome of the court-martial, still it is pretty generally believed here that the Sergeant acted in self-defense. The two men who were shot refused to obey orders and are said to have been the aggressors."[61] The *Park County Enterprise* claimed that "the men refused to obey his command and when he told them they were under military arrest, they turned on him." The paper quoted Dr. Wapples as saying "If [Brittain] had put on gloves and given one or two of the men a good thrashing early in the season, there would have been less blood."[62] While the newspapers were quick to judge, the proceedings were more thorough and definitely more nuanced.

Brittain's court-martial commenced May 13, 1912, and lasted for five days. He was charged with the manslaughter of Private Cunningham and assault and battery with intent to kill Private Carroll. Eighteen witnesses were called and 409 pages of testimony gathered. For the prosecution, the case was simple: Brittain had shot and killed a man under his command. The defense, on the other hand, had to show that the men at the station mutinied and that Brittain felt his life was threatened, forcing him to act in self-defense. What is remarkable about the extensive testimony was how much of it agreed. The witness testimony, whether on behalf of the prosecution or defense, correlated nicely, often down to the very words spoken. Of course, there were differences. Sergeant Brittain denied that he was put out by Mutch courting the same girl, saying that he was never interested in her anyway. Brittain also felt that the men had formed a clique against him. May, Carroll, and Mutch agreed that they were not terribly fond of their sergeant, but they did not like each other (especially Cunningham) very much either. The sergeant seemed oblivious to that. The real key to the case came down to whether or not Brittain's directive to Carroll about retrieving the saw from Pahaska on the morning of March 29 constituted an order. Added to that was whether or not May and Mutch, ignoring his orders to help subdue Carroll, constituted a pattern of mutiny by men at the post, particularly when Carroll and Cunningham scuffled with him. The scuffle had to be shown in a way that a reasonable man would assume his life was threatened. When looking at it, both the prosecution and the defense needed to take the same road to different destinations. The prosecution needed to demonstrate that the atmosphere at the post was such that Brittain had shirked his duties and that what happened was his fault. The defense needed to show that the atmosphere at the post was such that the men were against him and his life was in danger at that moment. Perhaps that accounts for the significant agreement in the testimony.

After all the evidence was presented, the court took less than an hour to deliberate the fate of Sgt. Clarence A. Brittain.[63] He was found "not guilty" on all charges. The officers of the court apparently believed the action that day constituted a pattern of mutiny and that Brittain acted in self-defense. However, for the historian, the case reveals much more than the simple answer to whether they mutinied or Brittain acted justly on that cold March morning. Instead, the testimony of the witnesses shows the trials and tribulations of duty in the park, particularly at isolated posts, and especially in the uniquely remote conditions of winter. The social and psychological tensions created by such duty are more meaningful than the simple decision of guilt or innocence.

The dramatic nature of the episode immediately garnered the attention of contemporaries. The first history of the men at Sylvan Pass Station was written by their comrade, Cpl. Thomas M. Connery of Company F, First US Cavalry. Corporal Connery was himself in charge of the Upper Geyser Basin soldier station and knew of the problems related to the isolation of posts. However, he was at his station when the court-martial of Brittain occurred and had no direct knowledge of the incident. Perhaps that accounts for the wild inaccuracies of his version. Maybe it was because he wrote for *Wide*

*World Magazine,* which emphasized dramatic masculine adventure. The cover of the issue that contained Connery's account, after all, depicted a man in a swimsuit wrestling an alligator. Even though Connery was a contemporary of the men, and therefore should have had valuable firsthand knowledge of the event, he got almost every important detail wrong when compared to the testimony of the men involved. He claimed the telephone line was still up when in fact it had been down since early November. His account has Cunningham "bent on running the station himself, the other privates backing him," turning them against Brittain. In fact, everyone at the station seemed to dislike Cunningham as much as their sergeant.

Connery has Brittain leaving the post on March 29 but breaking his ski pole after "he had gone but a hundred yards," compelling him to return after only a few minutes. However, all the men testified that Brittain left shortly after 8:00 a.m. and came back a little after 2:00 p.m. The actual confrontation by Connery differs so significantly from that point that it hardly seems like the same incident described by the soldiers actually there.

> When he [Brittain] opened the door of the cabin and stood there with the club [broken ski pole] in hand, Cunningham asked him gruffly what he was going to do with it, whereupon the sergeant told him it was none of his business. Cunningham then told him if he did not drop the club he would drop him, at the same time advancing towards the sergeant. The latter immediately pulled out his pistol, fired, the bullet striking Cunningham between the eyes, killing him instantly. Another private, named Carroll, advanced behind him, and the sergeant fired at him, the bullet penetrating the left arm, nearly severing the large vein. As no other man advanced, the sergeant ordered one of the remaining privates, who had previously been in the hospital corps, to put a tourniquet on Carroll's arm, which no doubt saved his life.[64]

Connery's version, as simple and dramatic as it is, obviously bears little resemblance to the agreed-upon facts. Unfortunately, this account has become the standard retelling of the incident used by future historians. The eminent Aubrey Haines and Lee Whittlesey use it in their accounts of the problems and ordeals in isolated park outposts. They can hardly be blamed for using Connery's nearly fictional account as it was published and more easily accessible than the court-martial records buried deep in the National Archives. It was told in a clear and succinct style, and presumably should have been accurate given Connery likely knew the men personally. While

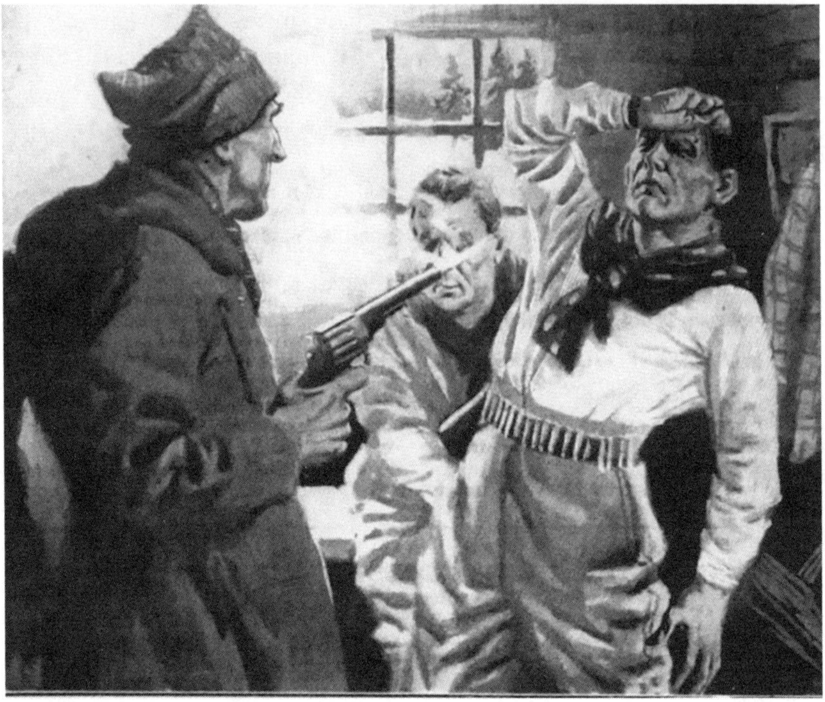

The illustration depicting the shooting of Pvt. Cunningham in the men's adventure magazine *Wide World*, June 1919. The illustration and account in the magazine are remarkably inaccurate in almost every detail.

Haines's and Whittlesey's general point that life at the outposts could be psychologically taxing and lead to such unfortunate events is accurate, the details revealed in the testimony of the men during the trial reveal a more complex and nuanced understanding of the forces that shaped the environment at the post that led to Cunningham's death.

The nature of the extreme isolation of duty at the park's outposts in winter is also much better understood today through the lens of later psychiatric and medical knowledge. With increased activity in isolated environments such as Antarctic bases, extended nuclear submarine missions, and prolonged space flight, the United States and other governments have invested heavily in understanding small-group isolation over prolonged periods in order to prevent incidents such as what happened at the Sylvan Pass Soldier Station. From these studies it becomes clear that the soldiers at Sylvan Pass faced difficulty not only from personal conflicts but also due to the physiological and psychological impacts of their isolation. Even cohesive small groups with strong external support suffer adverse effects. The men stationed at Sylvan Pass in the winter of 1911–1912 were neither cohesive nor well supported.

The psychological and social impacts of extreme isolation were only starting to be noticed, much less understood, by 1912. The negative emotional reactions were first documented in 1898 by polar explorer Frederick A. Cook. "Around the tables, in the laboratory, and in the forecastle, men are sitting about sad and dejected, lost in dreams of melancholy from which, now and then, one arouses with an empty attempt at enthusiasm."[65] Through the twentieth century, studies of small-group isolation have found a nearly ubiquitous increase in levels of depression, anxiety, and group hostility over the period of isolation. This has garnered the name "winter-over syndrome" because it was first identified in the crews of Antarctic research stations who remained at their station over the long dark winters. The longer the isolation, the more significant the symptomology. Yet, regardless of length, the symptomology peaked at about the three-quarter mark of the mission. This has resulted in terming the phenomenon "third-quarter syndrome."[66] If the beginning of October to the end of May is the period of the greatest isolation at Sylvan Pass, the shooting on March 29 happened at the beginning of the third quarter.

Even when members self-select for such missions and are thoroughly screened, they are not immune to the psycho-social impacts of isolation. At McMurdo Station in Antarctica in 1989, over 60 percent of the winter-over crew reported feeling depressed, and almost half of them described themselves as more irritable than usual, reporting memory problems and difficulties in completing tasks.[67] The symptoms may have a physiological basis as well. It has been discovered that people in Antarctic research stations have a lower level of the thyroid hormone T3, which is essential for standard brain functions.[68] Beyond simple psychology, the men at Sylvan Pass may have had genuine physiological responses to their isolation that made a problematic group dynamic even worse.

To a degree, the men at Sylvan Pass Station, and at the other stations in the park, were their own worst enemies. Unlike people engaged in prolonged space missions or wintering at Antarctic research stations, these men were neither screened nor trained in how to cope with anticipated problems. Several of the men already had dispositions that might exacerbate the psycho-social environment, and when things deteriorated, the climate became openly hostile. The irritability they showed to each other is perhaps on one level normal and to be expected in such isolated environments. The fight that ensued when Brittain chastised Mutch for getting bread and milk without permission is undoubtedly representative of that. Carroll's complaints about "dog robbing" for Cunningham are indicative of that as well. The sniping and complaining were clearly evident and admitted by all. It is not unusual for such behaviors to continue even after a respite from the isolation.[69] This was clear when Cunningham went to Cody. He continued that symptomology as displayed by his behavior toward the boy in the street, the employees at the Irma Hotel, May, the jailor, and even his fellow inmates.

Lessons learned in the later twentieth century suggested that people need to have the "right stuff" to cope effectively in an isolated small group. While there is no complete immunity from the problems that arise, those with a positive disposition who can express it interpersonally usually cope better. Those who have mastery of the tasks they are expected to perform and who are motivated to do the work will fare better as well. Conversely, those who are arrogant, hostile, and verbally aggressive tend to do exceedingly poorly as individuals in isolated small groups and can affect the group dynamic as a whole.[70] Indeed, we see more of the "wrong stuff" in Private Cunningham, with his negative demeanor and aggressive attitude toward others in the group. Sergeant Brittain too had a known aggressive side in his leadership at the Fort Yellowstone target range before being assigned to Sylvan Pass. Perhaps the skittish Private May did not have the "wrong stuff," but his lack of motivation, his seemingly limited ability to express positivity, and his lack of strong interpersonal skills was certainly not the "right stuff."

The stated mission, regulating tourist traffic in the summer and patrolling for poachers in both summer and winter, was problematic. If mastery of tasks is important, Brittain's criticism of Mutch's handling of the guns undermined the private's feeling of mastery of his duty. The lack of poachers, particularly that winter, and the infrequent level of patrolling, did not give the men the opportunity to feel the satisfaction of accomplishment or let them feel as though they were "masters" of those duties.

The individual character of each man also affected the cohesiveness of the group—another critical element in coping with the problems of isolation. If a small group can coalesce around an interconnected social core, it can develop essential coping skills.[71] Leadership, either formal or informal, is needed to build a social cohesion where individuals feel appreciated within the group. A cohesive group brought together by informal leaders can also positively affect the image of the formal or appointed leader. At

Sylvan Pass nobody exhibited even informal leadership, and the men never coalesced into a cohesive social group. The slight between Private Mutch and the formal leader, Sergeant Brittain, in July, impeded Brittain's ability to formally promote social cohesion. The almost immediate problems between Cunningham and Brittain exacerbated that. Since all the surviving members noted that they had problems with everyone else at one point or another to the extent that they would not even talk to each other, it is clear that group cohesiveness was lacking. Unfortunately, the lack of cohesiveness affects the perception of formal leaders. If a group forms a cohesive core, a leader's initial negative perception can change to a positive one.[72] This group's lack of cohesiveness may partially account for their negative view of Sergeant Brittain.

Modern missions in isolated situations also emphasize training leaders for the unique demands of such environments. Unfortunately, Sergeant Brittain was placed in command before there was a recognized need to train him for the role. Clearly, the army officers hoped that since he had risen to the rank of sergeant, his military skills were sufficient for him to be in command of a group in that unique environment. Formal leaders in isolated environments can promote social cohesion by promoting positive task leadership and rewarding accomplishments with praise. As an isolated group progresses, the leader needs to focus more on emotional support. In moments of crisis, large or small, the leader needs to be direct and decisive.[73] Sergeant Brittain did none of these. He was critical from the outset, and being emotionally supportive was apparently not his style, particularly when he thought one or more of his subordinates had wronged him.

Still, we cannot fault Brittain for being in command of a remote station before it was understood what qualities and training were needed to effectively lead a group in physical and social isolation. In fact, at times Brittain even sought assistance from his superior, Captain Foy, in addressing early issues with Cunningham. Even though Foy dressed down the troublesome Cunningham in the first week of their posting, he failed to recognize that a serious problem was brewing at Sylvan Pass. Mutch, Carroll, and Cunningham all reached out to Foy about the situation, and two directly asked to be relieved of duty. NASA and the Russian space agency have recognized that isolated groups in prolonged spaceflight need direct and specific support from the ground. It is not that there is a strong connection between ground personnel and astronauts; in fact, the astronauts often have a certain passive hostility toward certain ground-crew personnel. However, if the structure of the mission includes regulating tasks by making sure there are neither too few nor too many, being aware for subtle signs of psychological or social problems with the crew, and actively intervening in appropriate ways, the group will have increased productivity and better coping skills when the inevitable problems arise.[74]

Again, it may be hard to fault Captain Foy too much. Clearly, modern spaceflight preparation and mission structure are influenced by decades of research on isolated groups, something that the US Army did not have in 1912. Nor was it Foy's fault that a snowslide cut the telephone line in early November. Still, some signs of trouble must have called for an intuitive solution. Men who disliked each other at an outpost, such as when all the privates at West Thumb Station asked to be removed, was nothing new. In that case, all the men found themselves replaced at the station before the winter set in. Other officers had seen and recognized problems in a way that Foy missed; he responded instinctively without the benefit of modern research. Still, the mission in and of itself was part of the problem during the winter months. As the men noted, they were only on duty when they were cooking or on patrol. Only one man cooked each week and the patrols did not happen very often. When they did happen, nothing of note ever occurred to foster positive feelings of competence. Boredom in small isolated groups exacerbates the symptoms of depression, anxiety, and irritability.[75] Here, boredom may have turned deadly.

The men stationed at Sylvan Pass in 1911–1912 had the cards stacked against them from the start. They were the wrong mix of personalities, placed at one of the most isolated posts in the park, with a limited mission, a scant support structure, and inadequate leadership needed for a small group to effectively cope in such severe isolation. They faced a confluence of forces that transcended the pure guilt or innocence of any of them at their courts-martial. It is true that all of the privates, in one way or another, disobeyed their superior on March 29, 1912, and could arguably be guilty of mutiny. The guilty verdicts at their trials may, therefore, be justified. Each made choices that affected the fatal outcome, and there were alternatives they did not pursue. The same was true for Sergeant Brittain and Captain Foy. Still, there were mitigating circumstances beyond the control of anyone. The editor of the *Northern Wyoming Herald* rather insightfully acknowledged those circumstances during the initial reporting of the incident. "The fact is, that it seems inhuman to leave a small number of men in an almost inaccessible location, without other companionship and surrounded by snow which effectively shut them away from civilization for months at a time, and with nothing to occupy their time and attention except petty grievances."[76] Perhaps we should not look as much to what caused this fatal outcome at Sylvan Pass Soldier Station as we should seek to understand why such incidents did not happen more often at other stations throughout the park during the army's thirty-year tenure.

# "Patriotism . . . and the Love of Nature"

## The Close of the Military Era

In 1886, when soldiers arrived in Yellowstone, the head general of the army, Lt. Gen. Philip Sheridan, was one of the staunchest proponents of having the military administer the park while the secretary of the interior was more reluctant. As the second decade of the twentieth century dawned, the reverse was true. Sheridan died almost exactly two years after Capt. Moses Harris brought Troop M into the park. George Vest, the senator who originally supported the notion of soldiers protecting the park only to reject the idea as it came to fruition, had passed away in 1903. By 1911, when the first conference on the national parks convened in Yellowstone, the army had been in the park for a quarter century. The soldiers who had arrived in 1886 were stalwarts of the "old army" who had frontier and even Civil War experience. At the turn of the twentieth century, the new generation had cut their teeth on the imperial wars in Spain and Cuba in 1898, the Philippines from 1899 to 1902 (though hostilities would continue until 1913), the Boxer Rebellion in China in 1900, the Panama separation from Colombia in 1901 and 1904, Cuba again from 1906 to 1909, and other foreign incidents. The officers and soldiers of the army were decidedly oriented toward service outside the United States rather than focused on patrolling domestic soil.

Superintendent S. M. B. Young's proposal that a civilian guard replace the troops in 1907 was the opening salvo that would force Congress and the government to examine the increasingly popular parks carefully. For the Department of the Interior, using the troops was very economical as they did not have to recruit, train, or pay the personnel; this was all handled by the War Department though part of the administrative costs were covered through the Interior Department's appropriations. Presidents Roosevelt and

Cavalryman at Midway Geyser Basin, circa 1903. (Library of Congress)

Taft and the secretaries of war all supported transferring the parks back to civilian control by creating a specific bureau or service for that singular purpose. "Every consideration of patriotism and the love of nature and of beauty and of art requires us to expend money enough to bring all these natural wonders within easy reach of our people," implored Taft in a message to Congress in February of 1912. Still, Congress was unwilling to commit any funds to create such a service. The issue was pressed forward at the national park conferences held in 1911, 1912, 1915, and 1917, which all dealt in some way with how to transition the parks back to civilian control. Even though the new acting superintendent, Col. L. M. Brett, felt in 1911 that patrolling the park "is military work," others had openly criticized the use of the army, calling it "shortsighted," and arguing that "the system is entirely inadequate for proper protection." The debate over returning the park to civilian administration raged for another seven years.[1]

The army began to force the issue in California where it had been administering Yosemite, Sequoia, and General Grant national parks. From 1891 to 1914, the army had administered the California parks on a seasonal basis, marching from the Presidio in San Francisco to the parks and returning in the winter. However, in 1896 the War Department, wary of park duty as the nation's international obligations increased, questioned even the legality of park duty. By 1913 the army was facing increasing demand for troops along

Colonel Lloyd Military Brett, circa 1920. Brett was the military superintendent from 1910 to 1916. He had earned the Congressional Medal of Honor during the Indian wars at the Battle of O'Fallon's Creek in 1881 and would earn the army's Distinguished Service Medal during World War I. He retired in 1920 at the rank of brigadier general. (Library of Congress)

the Mexican border and Secretary of War Lindley M. Garrison wrote Secretary of the Interior Franklin Lane about ending military administration. Lane struggled to maintain military administration, but by 1914 Secretary Garrison ultimately simply refused to send troops to the parks, bringing an end to military administration in those parks.[2]

In Yellowstone the army took a more measured approach. In 1915 a special contingent was created: 250 soldiers drawn from multiple units who were "selected cavalrymen, preferably those having experience in the . . . park and having a natural taste and aptitude for the character of duties which they are to perform there." These men should have had the requisite skills and sense of duty for protecting the park and could be efficiently discharged and hired by the Department of the Interior should civilian control be returned to Yellowstone. These contingents were dubbed Troops 1 and 2 of the Yellowstone Park Detachment. Hopes prevailed that many of the noted issues could be solved. The intent was that this would help transition to ultimate civilian control when the political climate was favorable. However, the summary court-martial records of Troops 1 and 2 indicate that most of the same problems remained, with multiple offenses regarding drunkenness, lack of military discipline and insubordination, theft, animal abuse, and even poaching. The vetting of soldiers for the detachment must have been less than thorough since at least one soldier, Pvt. George Miller, deserted on July 23, 1916, before he was arrested in Butte. Ironically, notes on the court-martial paperwork indicate that he was one of the soldiers who had also deserted in 1908 and was noted by name in Major Miller's investigation.[3]

A group of four permanent and two seasonal civilian "rangers" replaced the old scouts and supplemented Troops 1 and 2 of the Yellowstone National Park detachment. Just like the scouts, these rangers were more skilled in mountain work and were paid significantly better than the soldiers. George Dustman was selected as a "first-class ranger" and earned an annual salary of $1,200, while the enlisted men in Troops 1 and 2 made $156 a year. Using Troops 1 and 2 combined with the new "rangers" was meant to facilitate the transition to civilian control, but it still took another three years to accomplish the task. After significant bureaucratic wrangling with a skeptical Congress, the National Park Service Act of 1916 was passed, and the new civilian ranger force started to take shape.

To the relief of the War Department, with the creation of the National Park Service and the concurrent entry of the United States into World War I, the troops in the park could finally be redeployed and made ready for combat. Political pressure mounted from Montana's congressional delegation to keep the troops in the park. Local citizens, who once despised the military's role in enforcing park regulations, grew alarmed about what the withdrawal of two hundred soldiers and their paychecks would mean to the local economy. Gardiner catered to tourists three months of the year, but in the lean winter months, the soldiers could keep cash flowing through the local barrooms, restaurants, hotels, and brothels. Losing two hundred men to be replaced by a couple of dozen rangers was a genuine concern. As a result, Montana's delegation prevented financial support for the new Park Service for hiring rangers to enforce the park's rules and regulations.

Reluctantly, the army had to repost troops in the park. The Yellowstone Park detachment had already been disbanded and the Seventh and Eleventh US Cavalry, units with no park experience, arrived. Commanders no longer held any responsibility for park administration beyond directing the troops since a new civilian superintendent appointed by the Park Service had assumed those duties. However, with World War I taking precedence, troops and officers were rotated through the park with only weeks on location. The

Department of the Interior expressed concern that the fort was merely being used as a temporary post for troops waiting to be assigned to other units en route to the trenches of Europe and that the soldiers were provided little if any training and even less incentive to perform their duties in the park. One trooper even questioned why over four hundred trained combat men were needed to replace a few dozen rangers for peaceful patrol work when they could be better used fighting on the western front. He alleged that if it would not bring shame to his family, he would desert and join the Canadian army. The war even assuaged local opposition to troop removal. Watching their friends and family members be drafted and sent to combat while so many soldiers were stationed in the relative safety and comfort of the park did not sit well with many Montanans. With mounting pressure to fully fund the National Park Service and use troops in the role for which they were both trained and desperately needed, Congress removed their funding limitations in the 1918 sundry bill, and the military withdrew from the park and turned over buildings of Fort Yellowstone to the Department of the Interior. On October 1, 1918, Capt. Myer S. Silven of the Eleventh US Cavalry wrote the final document of the military era in Yellowstone with the simple words: "The undersigned hereby relinquishes command of Fort Yellowstone, Wyoming."[4] With that, protecting the park fell squarely on the new National Park Service and its rangers.

The policing of the park could start afresh without the inertia and expectations of the past. By transferring park management back to civilian control, the problems that confronted soldiers could be addressed. In fact, the qualities described by Young in 1907 provided the basis for what would become the National Park Service ranger. They would, just as Young suggested, have the skills and a sense of duty lacking in the army's enlisted men. The Department of the Interior attempted to sweeten the idea by giving a ranger the "fullest incentive to give his best service" to the job through the promise of quick advancement based on character and merit. Some soldiers who had shown real interest in Yellowstone Park were given opportunities to enlist in the new ranger program. Horace Albright, the new superintendent of the park, wanted "a number of sergeants and corporals who had such experience in leadership and had shown real interest . . . to be appointed park rangers" to supplement those others who had experience in the park. Lastly, Albright fought the head concessionaire, Harry Child, to remove the social distinction between law enforcement and the hotel tourist by securing the right of the rangers to enter the hotels, unlike the enlisted men before them. This would

Civilian Superintendent Albright (*center front*) and the new National Park Service rangers in Mammoth, 1919. The new rangers carried on the duties of the army with new force and vigor. The reimagined protectors of the park learned from the military's experience, both its successes and struggles. The new force was able to do the work of the soldiers with more efficiency, using only a couple of dozen rangers rather than a couple of hundred soldiers. (Yellowstone National Park Museum Collection)

be easier for Child and hotel guests, given that rangers would not have the same preconceived biases against them as the enlisted soldiers had. Besides, the increased use of the automobile in the park, and in America in general, had signaled a shift away from the old Victorian values that stressed work and delayed gratification toward the values of consumption and self-realization among all classes. As automobiles became more affordable, more people of lesser means could visit the parks, resulting in a "democratization" of tourism.[5] The fact that Albright had to fight for the right of rangers to enter hotels suggests that it was far from a smooth transition.

The military experience in Yellowstone, like so many things in history, was complex. Historians have rightly noted that the army's administration was a success, providing stability and preserving the park when its future was far from certain. Yet, the army was an imperfect solution, and when looking below the administrative decisions to the experience of the men who served

The new National Park Service rangers carried on many of the same traditions established by the army, such as monitoring bear feedings at hotels dumps as seen here at Old Faithful, circa 1929. (National Park Service photo)

in Yellowstone for a generation, a more complete and complicated picture evolves. Certainly, many soldiers enjoyed their time in Yellowstone, but to assume they all did is not borne out by the facts. Numerous soldiers disliked their time in the park and considered it "an undesirable" station because of the isolation, the climate, and the disrespect shown them by tourists and civilians. While the noncommissioned officers may have gained some command experience being in charge of the remote soldier stations throughout the park, their duties were unlike anything for which they had trained. Monitoring tourists on the formations, sealing guns, and reprimanding civilians for minor violations were all things they had neither trained for nor were likely to use at other stations. Patrolling for poachers provided some field experience, but it too was unlike their training as they operated in one- or two-man teams rather than the squad or platoon as was their drilling norm. Besides, they were often overseen and directed by a civilian scout, reducing them to little more than armed support. In the winter their patrolling on skis was, again, unlike their training or typical deployment elsewhere as cavalrymen.

The army, unlike the future rangers, was a polyglot of different personalities and backgrounds with varied motivations and investment in their duties. People like the sullen and cantankerous Private Cunningham at Sylvan Pass or the "dirty" and "foul" Private Simpson would only reinforce tourists' stereotypes of the lowly soldiers. Most if not all men had joined the army for

As it had been for the soldiers, recreation was a part of the life of the new NPS rangers, seen here playing baseball in their off-hours sometime in the 1930s. (Yellowstone National Park Museum Collection)

reasons other than patrolling the park and consequently did not always fully embrace the mission. Many, such as Herbert Angelo or "soldier Jack" had enlisted to seek adventure in the Philippines or elsewhere, and the nonmilitary duties of Yellowstone were not always seen as soldiering. The evidence suggests that while the soldiers enforced the rules, such as the ban against hunting in the park, they also broke them with great regularity. At the Sylvan Pass Station in 1912, there is reason to believe that even the sergeant in charge did not perform the required number of patrols and may have been interested in poaching. Officers at the time, and even modern historians, noted that the remote soldier stations were often appealing because of their lax military discipline. Yet, as seen in the tragic events at Sylvan Pass, the relaxed discipline and duties, when combined with the wrong personalities, weak leadership, and limited support, could be fatal.

Perhaps most uncomfortable for the soldiers was the daily reminder of how upper-crust civilians perceived them in the unique milieu of the park. In its early years Yellowstone attracted mostly wealthier tourists who could afford the travel and accommodations. These people embraced a social outlook that respected class and status and imposed that view on the soldiers, whom they felt were considerably below them. However, the enlisted men, with a more democratic outlook, balked at this and took advantage of their power by, at times, ruthlessly enforcing the regulations of the park. This caused

Future president Gerald R. Ford, seen here in 1936, carried on the ranger tradition in Yellowstone, whose foundation was laid by the army. He was stationed at the Canyon and always recollected his experience fondly. (National Park Service photo)

significant tension but also set a precedent for strict adherence and protection of the park, at least enforced on the tourists since, as noted, the soldiers often broke the regulations themselves. The soldiers' reactive enforcement robbed the wealthy tourists of their traditional influence and privileges and emphasized that they too had to adhere to the ideals of the national park. By the time the thirty-year tenure of the military ended in Yellowstone, the democratizing influence of the Progressive Era had further weakened the old Victorian social class paradigm, and when the National Park Service rangers took over, it was a new era both within and outside the park.

While the soldiers may have enjoyed the relaxed discipline at the park's soldier stations, working in the park actually increased their workload, particularly at the main post in Mammoth. The daily duties in the park had to be done in addition to the regular military drills. The officers did their best to maintain the military readiness of their command, performing drills that were unlikely to be useful in the park but would be if the men were deployed into combat. However, some of those maneuvers had to be neglected in order to perform the park duties. This was a concern, even for the first commander, Captain Harris. By 1907–1908 it was clear, from the War Department all the way down to the privates, that the soldiers saw Yellowstone as an "undesirable posting" and the army wanted out of the park. By that time the country had changed, and locals, once resentful of the park and particularly of the military's enforcement of its rules, had become more accommodating, understanding the true value the park provided.[6]

Yet, it would be wrong to paint too negative a picture of the military experience in Yellowstone. Clearly for many the posting in Yellowstone was "undesirable." For perhaps an equal number, it was pleasant and enjoyable. The rest (and perhaps the majority), as Young noted in 1907, were likely "indifferent" to Yellowstone. It was merely another in a long list of stations. Its duties, though unique, were simply to be executed, even if there were opportunities in private to embrace one's personal moral decision regarding them. The men performed their duty despite any personal misgivings about being in the park. Soldiers through American history often had postings that were "undesirable," whether on the isolated frontier in the American West, in the South during Reconstruction, in the trenches of Europe during World War I, at small isolated posts in the Arctic during the Cold War, or even in the jungles of Vietnam or the deserts of Iraq. When their country called upon them, the American soldier responded and performed his duty. At times there were inevitable tensions and often a type of coping resistance to such places, and Yellowstone was no different. The country called upon the soldiers to serve there, as in other unplesant stations, and for the most part, the majority responded professionally. Since Congress was reluctant to support the parks in any substantive way from the creation of Yellowstone in 1872 to the creation of the National Park Service forty-five years later, the army and its soldiers answered the call and performed one of its most significant and long-lasting services to the country.

As the military's tenure in the park came to a close, much had been accomplished. The military administrators had brought order to the park, and legal transgressions had been significantly reduced. This created a model the civilian administrators could follow. However, the imperfect role the enlisted men had played in enforcing the park regulations contributed to the future as well. The experience of the ordinary soldier in the unique physical and social environment of the park added not only to the impetus for civilian control but also shaped the conceptual development of the future National Park

The mounted NPS rangers ready for duty in the early 1920s. (Yellowstone National Park Museum Collection)

Service ranger program. Through their strengths and their deficiencies, the soldiers had demonstrated the type of person needed for the program to be successful, the talents required by the rangers, and the individual focus and investment required by the mission. As the army recognized the shortcomings of the soldier's experience, it created the base job description for future rangers by emphasizing the need to recruit men with a sense of mission and a particular skill set focused solely on park management, men who would be accepted by the tourists of the park without negative social class expectations. Not every future ranger would perfectly fit these criteria, but the social experience of the soldiers in the park went a long way toward establishing the much more successful ranger program. In short, the rangers were shaped not only by what the soldiers were but also by what they were not.

# Notes

## PREFACE

1. Kenneth Karsmizki, *Soda Butte Soldier Station (48YE88): Report of Research and Testing Prepared for the National Park Service Intermountain Region* (Bozeman, MT: Museum of the Rockies, 1998), 81.

## INTRODUCTION: "TO CORRECT AND REMEDY THE EXISTING STATE OF THINGS"

1. US Statutes at Large, vol. 17, chap. 24, pp. 32–33. "An Act to set apart a certain Tract of Land lying near the Head-waters of the Yellowstone River as a public Park." [S. 392]: United States Congress, *The Congressional Globe: Containing the Debates and Proceedings of the Second Session of the Forty-First Congress* (Washington, DC: John C. Rivers Publishers, 1871), 697; Cornelius Cole to Secretary of the Interior Carl Schurz, Feb. 21, 1878, in 45th Cong., 2d Sess., House, Ex. Doc. No. 75, April 11, 1878.

2. Karl Jacoby, *Crimes against Nature: Squatters, Poachers, Thieves, and the Hidden History of American Conservation* (Berkeley: University of California Press, 2001), 129–130; Aubrey L. Haines, *The Yellowstone Story* (Boulder: Yellowstone Library and Colorado Associate University Press, 1977), 1: 323–325; H. Duane Hampton, *How the U.S. Cavalry Saved Our National Parks* (Bloomington: Indiana University Press, 1971), 31, 34–36, 55–56; Kikki Rydell and Mary Culpin, *Managing the "Matchless Wonders": A History of Administrative Development in Yellowstone National Park, 1872–1965* (Yellowstone National Park, WY: National Park Service, Center for Resources, 2006), 11–15; Richard Bartlett, *Yellowstone: A Wilderness Besieged* (Tucson: University of Arizona Press, 1985), 234–238, 248–250, 257.

3. Hampton, *How the Cavalry*, 65; Aubrey Haines, "A Review of Certain Attempts to Make Adverse Use of Yellowstone National Park" (Vertical File, Yellowstone National Park Library, Gardiner, MT, undated).

4. Hampton, *How the Cavalry*, 54; P. H. Conger to the Secretary of the Interior, Sept. 20, 1882, in Department of the Interior, Patents and Miscellaneous Division, Letters Received, 1872–1882, Record Group (hereafter RG) 48 (Washington, DC: National Archives and Record Administration (hereafter NARA)); S. Rep. No. 47-911, at 1–11 (1881).

5. P. H. Sheridan to Brig. Gen. R. C. Drum, Adjutant General, Nov. 1, 1882, in Records of the Adjutant General's Office, Letters Received (hereafter LR), RG 94, Washington, DC: NARA.

6. George B. Grinnell, "Mr. Vest's Victory." *Forest and Stream: A Journal of Outdoor Life, Travel, Nature Study, Shooting, Fishing, Yachting* 20, no. 5 (March 8, 1883): 101; Hampton, *How the Cavalry*, 52–69; Haines, *Yellowstone Story*, 1: 261–265; Bartlett, *Yellowstone*, 122–127.

7. *Congressional Record* (hereafter CR): 47th Cong., 2nd Sess., XIV, Part 4 (Washington, DC: GPO, 1881): 3193–3194; Carole E. Scott, "Racism and Southern Anti-Imperialists: The Blounts of Georgia," *Atlanta History* 31, no. 3 (June 1987): 24–29.

8. Eric Foner, *Reconstruction: America's Unfinished Revolution, 1863–1877* (New York: Harper Collins, 1988), 35–76, 176–198, 228–251, 274–278, 316–333; Mark L. Bradley, *The Army and Reconstruction, 1865–1877* (Washington, DC: United States Army Center of Military History, 2015), 9–24, 49–54, 71–72; James Sefton, *The United States Army and Reconstruction, 1865–1877* (Baton Rouge: Louisiana State University Press, 1967), 5–15, 25–26, 50–73, 120–128; Edwin C. Brouse, *The U.S. Army and Constabulary Operations* (Leavenworth, KS: School of Advanced Military Studies, 2006), 22–21; Gabrial Chin, "The Voting Rights Act of 1867: The Constitutionality of Federal Regulations of Suffrage during Reconstruction," *North Carolina Law Review* 82 (2004): 1581.

9. "An Act making appropriations for sundry civil expenses of the government for the fiscal year ending June thirtieth, eighteen hundred and eighty-four, and other purposes." CR, 47th Cong., 2nd Sess. XIV, Part 4 (Washington, DC: GPO, 1883): 3193–3195, 3482–3483, 3488; Act of Mar. 3, 1883 (22 SL, 626); Haines, *Yellowstone Story*, 1: 324; Hampton, *How the Cavalry*, 78–79.

10. W. Scott Smith, Special Agent, Department of the Interior, to H. M. Teller, Secretary of the Interior, Oct. 15, 1883, LR 1883–1884, RG48, Washington, DC: NARA.

11. P. H. Conger to H. M. Teller, Secretary of the Interior, Nov. 27, 1883. Records of the Office of the Secretary of the Interior, General Correspondence, LR 1883–1884, RG48, NARA; J. S. Crosby, "Report of the Governor of Montana Territory," in *Department of Interior Report, 1884*, vol. 2 (Washington, DC: GPO, 1885): 562; Governor of Wyoming to P. H. Conger, Mar. 13, 1884, Letters Received, Vol. 5, Yellowstone National Park Archives (hereafter YNPA).

12. W. H. Phillips to H. L. Muldrow, Acting Secretary of the Interior, Sept. 21, 1885, LR 1885–1886, RG 48, NARA.

13. D. W. Wear to L. Q. C. Lamar, Secretary of the Interior, Sept. 21, 1885, Office of the Secretary of Interior, LR 1883–1884, RG 48, NARA; Hampton, *How the Cavalry*, 78–80; Bartlett, *Yellowstone*, 1: 248–250.

14. Bartlett, *Yellowstone*, 1: 139–140; Hampton, *How the Cavalry*, 113–125; M. Paul Holsinger. "Senator George Graham Vest and the 'Menace' of Mormonism, 1882–1887," *Missouri Historical Review* 65 (October 1970): 23–36; Manuel I. Kuhr, "How George Vest Came to Missouri," *Missouri Historical Review* 59 (April 1965): 424–427.

15. CR, 49th Cong., 1st Sess., XCII, Part 7, (Washington, DC: GPO, 1886): 7220, 7473; CR, 49th Cong., 1st Sess., XCII, Part 8 (Washington, DC: GPO, 1887): 7844–7846.

16. P. H. Sheridan to Secretary of War, Aug. 9, 1886, LR, RG 94, NARA; Special Orders No. 79, Headquarters, Dept. of Dakota, Ft. Snelling, MN, Aug. 13, 1886, Special Orders Department Dakota 1866–1891, RG 393, NARA.

17. Hampton's *How the U.S. Cavalry Saved Our National Parks* focuses almost entirely on the administrative and legal development of Yellowstone and devotes only two paragraphs to the experience of soldiers, noting that it was generally a pleasant assignment though "many deserted," 175; Richard A. Bartlett, in *Yellowstone: A Wilderness Besieged*, provides a chapter on the military superintendents though he does give some anecdotal descriptions of duty in the park with the strain between military duties and policing, and he notes that there were some discipline problems with "alcohol, sex, desertion, and insubordination" but that overall "army discipline prevailed," 272. He adds that "from the commanding officer down to the lowest buck private it was considered a good assignment," 268; Aubrey L. Haines, *The Yellowstone Story*, in volume 2, devotes a chapter to anecdotal stories of soldier who occasionally "smirched the reputation for general good management that the army had earned" but that for the soldiers, the "Yellowstone experience was their idyll" (207–208); similar comments are noted by Elizabeth Watry and Lee Whittlesey, *Images of America: Fort Yellowstone* (Charleston, SC: Arcadia, 2012), 43; Karl Jacoby, *Crimes against Nature: Squatters, Poachers, Thieves, and the Hidden History of American Conservation*, focuses on the military's administrative success but gives greater attention to the local criticisms of soldiers, especially as a reflection of local resistance to federal conservation efforts by locals in Montana and Wyoming. Kikki L. Rydell and Mary S. Culpin, *Managing the Matchless Wonders: A History of Administrative Development in Yellowstone National Park, 1872–1965* (Yellowstone National Park, WY: National Park Service, Center for Resources, 2006) take greater account of the discipline problems, noting the high desertion rate in 1907 and 1908 and again some anecdotal stories of life at Fort Yellowstone with little analysis, but they conclude that "the army brought a proven management structure that encouraged accountability and responsibility" and "built the park's administrative infrastructure," (25) ignoring the impact of the social experience of the soldiers and their impact on the development of the later national park ranger.

18. Richard Kohn, "The Social History of the American Soldier: A Review and Prospectus for Research," *American Historical Review* 86, no. 3 (June 1981): 553–567. For more discussion on the military social history, see also Edward M. Coffman, "The New American Military History," *Military Affairs* 48, no. 1 (January 1984): 1–5; David F. Trask, "The 'New' Military History and Army Historians," *Army Historian* 5 (Fall 1984): 7–10; William H. Woodward, "The Citizen-Soldier Historian and the 'New Military History,'" *Army Historian* 9 (Fall 1995): 13–15; John W. Chambers, II, "The New Military History: Myth and Reality," *Journal of Military History* 55, no. 3 (1991): 395–406; James R. Harris, "'What Really Interests Me Are the People': Edward M. Coffman on Soldiers, Scholars, and the New Military History," *Register of the Kentucky Historical Society* 99, no. 2 (Spring 2001): 123–152; Robert M. Citino, "Military Histories Old and New: A Reintroduction," *American Historical Review* 112, no. 4 (October 2007): 1070–1090. For examples of social history of the soldier and the

history of the relationship between the military and society, see Kevin Adams, *Class and Race in the Frontier Army: Military Life in the West, 1870–1890* (Norman: University of Oklahoma Press, 2009); Douglas C. McChristain, *Regular Army O!: Soldiering on the Western Frontier, 1865–1891* (Norman: University of Oklahoma Press, 2017); James McPherson, *For Cause and Comrades: Why Men Fought in the Civil War* (New York: Oxford, 1998); Thomas Childers, *Soldier from the War Returning: The Greatest Generation's Troubled Homecoming from World War II* (New York: Mariner Books, 2010); Reid Mitchell, *Civil War Soldiers* (New York: Penguin Books, 1997); John Keegan, *The Face of Battle: A Study of Agincourt, Waterloo, and the Somme* (New York: Penguin Books, 1983); Fred Anderson, *Crucible of War: The Seven Years' War and the Fate of Empire in British North America, 1754–1766* (New York: Vintage, 2001).

19. See Georgy G. Iggers, *Historiography in the Twentieth Century: From Scientific Objectivity to the Postmodern Challenge* (Hanover, NH: Wesleyan University Press, 1997), 108; Sigurdur G. Magnusson, "The Singularization of History: Social History and Microhistory within the Postmodern State of Knowledge," *Journal of Social History* 36 (Spring 2003): 701–735; Edward Muir and Guido Ruggiero, eds., *Microhistory and the Lost People of Europe*, trans. Eren Branch (Baltimore, MD: Johns Hopkins University Press, 1991); For examples of microhistory, see Natalie Zemon Davis, *The Return of Martin Guerre* (Cambridge, MA: Harvard University Press, 1983); Carlo Ginzburg, *"Just One Witness," Probing the Limits of Representation: Nazism and the "Final Solution"* (Cambridge, MA: Harvard, 1992); Gene Brucker, *Giovanni and Lusanna: Love and Marriage in Renaissance Florence* (Berkeley: University of California, 2004); Carlo Ginzburg, *The Cheese and the Worms: The Cosmos of a Sixteenth-Century Miller*, trans. John and Anne Tedeschi (Baltimore: Johns Hopkins Press, 1980); Thomas V. Cohen, *Love and Death in Renaissance Italy* (Chicago: University of Chicago Press, 2004); Carlo Ginzburg, "The Philosopher and the Witches: An Experiment in Cultural History," *Acta-Ethnographica-Academiae-Scientiarum-Hungaricae* 37 (1991–1992): 283–292.

20. Kenneth Karsmizki, *Soda Butte Soldier Station (48YE88): Report of Research and Testing Prepared for the National Park Service Intermountain Region* (Bozeman, MT: Museum of the Rockies, 1998): 81.

## CHAPTER ONE: "THE WORK IS NOT A MILITARY DUTY"

1. Capt. Moses Harris, *Report of the Acting Superintendent of the Yellowstone National Park to the Secretary of the Interior, 1886* (Washington, DC: GPO, 1886), 6–11.

2. United States Department of the Army, *Cavalry Drill Regulations, United States Army*, adopted Oct. 3, 1891 (Washington, DC: GPO, 1891), 44–46, 124, 197, 229, 314, 361.

3. National Research Council. *The Context of Military Environments: An Agenda for Basic Research on Social and Organizational Factors Relevant to Small Units* (Washington, DC: National Academies Press, 2014), 42; Gerd Gigerenzer and Dan Goldstein, "Reasoning the Fast and Frugal Way: Models of Bounded Rationality,"

*Psychological Review* 103, no. 4 (1996): 650–651, 669; Daniel Kahneman and Dale Miller, "Norm Theory: Comparing Reality to Its Alternatives," *Psychological Review* 93, no. 2 (1986): 142–144.

4. Bvt. Brig. Gen. Theophilus F. Rodenbough and Maj. William L. Haskin (eds.), *The Army of the United States: Historical Sketches of Staff and Line with Portraits of Generals-in-Chief* (New York: Maynard, Merrill, 1886), 171; National Research Council, *Context of Military Environments*, 42–46; Kahneman and Miller, "Norm Theory," 136; Robert M. Grant, "Prospering in Dynamically-Competitive Environments: Organizational Capability as Knowledge Integration," *Organization Science* 7 (1996): 375.

5. Maintenance Record Book of the Post Quartermaster, 1886–1912. Item No. 167, Yellowstone National Park Archives (hereafter YNPA).

6. Richard Upton, *Fort Custer on the Big Horn, 1877–1898: Its History and Personalities as Told and Pictured by Its Contemporaries* (Glendale, CA: Arthur H. Clark), 285; Pvt. James O. Purvis, "Fort Custer News," in Upton, *Fort Custer*, 78.

7. Quoted in Lee Whittlesey, "In Yellowstone Park, 1886–1889: George Tutherly's Reminiscences," *Montana: Magazine of Western History* 33, no. 1 (Winter 1983): 4–5.

8. Kevin Adams, *Class and Race in the Frontier Army: Military Life in the West, 1870–1890* (Norman: University of Oklahoma Press, 2009), 154–162.

9. Adams, *Class and Race*, 87; Purvis, "Fort Custer News," in Upton, *Fort Custer*, 79–80.

10. Capt. Frazier A. Boutelle, *Report of the Acting Superintendent of the Yellowstone National Park to the Secretary of the Interior, 1890* (Washington, DC: Government Printing Office, 1890), 5; quoted in Elizabeth A. Watry and Lee H. Whittlesey, *Images of America: Fort Yellowstone* (Charleston, SC: Arcadia Publishing, 2012), 43.

11. Capt. Frazier A. Boutelle to the Secretary of the Interior, August 29, 1890, Letters Sent, Bound Volume 2, YNPA; Lt. Col. Theo J. Wint, to the Adjutant General, Department of Dakota, 18 November 1899. Annual Inspection of Fort Yellowstone, 1899 (hereafter Inspection Report 1899), 4. Records of the Office of the Inspector General (Army), Inspection Reports, 1891–1913, in United States Department of War, National Archives and Records Administration (hereafter NARA), Washington, DC, Record Group (hereafter RG) 159; Lt. Col. Theo J. Wint to the Adjutant General, Department of Dakota, 15 September 1900. Annual Inspection of Fort Yellowstone (hereafter Inspection Report 1900), NARA, RG 159, p. 2; Lt. Col. Philip Reade, Inspector General Department of Dakota, to Adjutant General, Department of Dakota, June 10, 1901. Annual Inspection of Fort Yellowstone, WY (hereafter Inspection 1901), 30–31. NARA RG 93; Maj. Alfred Reynolds to the Adjutant General, Department of Dakota, 13 June 1902. Annual Inspection of Fort Yellowstone (hereafter Inspection Report 1902), NARA, RG 159, p. 5; Capt. Moses Harris, *Report of the Acting Superintendent of the Yellowstone National Park to the Secretary of the Interior, 1889* (Washington, DC: GPO, 1889), 11; Samuel M. B. Young, *Report of the Superintendent of the Yellowstone National Park to the Secretary of the Interior 1907* (Washington, DC: GPO, 1907), 25–26.

12. Capt. George S. Anderson, *Report of the Acting Superintendent of the*

*Yellowstone National Park to the Secretary of the Interior 1893* (Washington, DC: GPO, 1893), 7.

13. Capt. Frazier A. Boutelle, *Report of the Acting Superintendent of the Yellowstone National Park to the Secretary of the Interior 1891* (Washington, DC: GPO 1891), 5.

14. Boutelle, *Report 1890*, 4.

15. Boutelle, *Report 1890*, 4–5.

16. Boutelle, *Report 1890*, 3.

17. Boutelle, *Report 1890*, 3; "Fires in the Park," in *Helena Independent*, August 31, 1889.

18. Harris, *Report 1889*, 21–22; Boutelle, *Report 1890*, 4; Boutelle, *Report 1890*, 4–5.

19. Capt. George S. Anderson, *Report of the Acting Superintendent of the Yellowstone National Park to the Secretary of the Interior, 1895* (Washington, DC: GPO, 1895), 6–7.

20. Capt. George S. Anderson, *Report of the Acting Superintendent of the Yellowstone National Park to the Secretary of the Interior, 1896* (Washington, DC: GPO, 1896), 7; Anderson, *Report 1893*, 7; Harris, *Report 1886*, 7.

21. Harris, *Report 1889*, 3–4.

22. Harris, *Report 1889*, 22; Samuel B. M. Young, *Report of the Superintendent of the Yellowstone National Park to the Secretary of the Interior, 1897* (Washington, DC: GPO, 1897), 9–10; Karl Jacoby, *Crimes against Nature: Squatters, Poachers, Thieves, and the Hidden History of American Conservation* (Berkeley: University of California Press, 2001), 3, 107–108, 137, 193–198; Samuel Hays, *Conservation and the Gospel of Efficiency: The Progressive Conservation Movement, 1890–1920* (Pittsburgh: University of Pittsburgh Press, 1959), 147–173, 261–268; Douglas Brinkley, *The Wilderness Warrior: Theodore Roosevelt and the Crusade for America* (New York: Harper Collins, 2009), 13–21, 357, 689–692; Char Miller, *Seeking the Greatest Good: The Conservation Legacy of Gifford Pinchot* (Pittsburgh, PA: University of Pittsburgh Press, 2013), 35–38, 56–59, 68–70, 137–139; Young, *Report 1897*, 9–10.

23. "Scouts for Park Poachers," *Forest and Stream* 42 (June 30, 1884): 551; Aubrey L. Haines, *The Yellowstone Story* (Boulder: Yellowstone Library and Colorado Associate University Press, 1977), 2: 22–25; Kikki L. Rydell and Mary S. Culpin, *Matchless Wonders: A History of Administrative Development in Yellowstone National Park, 1872–1965* (Yellowstone National Park, WY: National Park Service, Center for Resources, 2006), 37; Jacoby, *Crimes against Nature*, 111; Anderson, *Report 1893*, 7.

24. Capt. George S. Anderson, *Report of the Acting Superintendent of the Yellowstone National Park to the Secretary of the Interior, 1894* (Washington, DC: GPO, 1894), 9–10; Haines, *Yellowstone Story*, 2: 64.

25. Haines, *Yellowstone Story*, 2: 22–25, 107; Jacoby, *Crimes against Nature*, 108; H. R. Rep. 49-1076, at 248 (1885); Report of Scout Peter Holte, Doc. 7095, in United States Department of the Interior, YNPA, Army Era Records, "Employees," Jan. 1 1904–Dec. 13, 1907; Young, *Report 1907*, 23–24; Young, *Report 1897*, 24; quoted in Rydell and Culpin, *Matchless Wonders*, 26–50.

26. George Whittaker, Nov. 13, 1898, Diary 32, "Scout Diaries," Manuscript 92–94, YNPA; Anderson, *Report 1895*, 12.

27. George Whittaker, Diary, "Scout Diaries," Manuscript, YNPA, Gardiner, MT, Nov. 13, 1898, 92–94; Capt. James B. Erwin, *Report of the Acting Superintendent of the Yellowstone National Park to the Secretary of the Interior, 1898* (Washington, DC: GPO, 1898), 36, 39, 41; Haines, *Yellowstone Story*, 2: 22–25, 107; Jacoby, *Crimes against Nature*, 108; H. R. Rep. 49-1076, at 248 (1885); Young, *Report 1907*, 23–24.

28. Young, *Report 1907*, 23–24, 26; Testimony of Pvt. William Mutch, General Court Martial of Clarence A. Brittain, in United States Department of War, Records of the Judge Advocate General, NARA, Record Group 153 (hereafter RG 153), p. 56; Testimony of Pvt. Frank Carroll, General Court Martial of Clarence A. Brittain, NARA, RG 153, pp. 90, 157; Testimony of Pvt. James May, General Court Martial of Clarence A. Brittain, NARA, RG 153, p. 180; Report for Week of March 9, 1912. United States Department of the Interior, Yellowstone National Park Army Era Records, Sylvan Pass Weekly Station Log, July 1910 to January 1916 (Gardiner MT: YNPA), Box 126; Carroll, in NARA, RG 153, pp. 88, 104.

29. Edward M. Offley, Diary, Vertical File (hereafter VF), (Yellowstone National Park Library (hereafter YNPL), Gardiner, MT), Letter of October 4, 1900, 25–26, 30; Carroll, General Court Martial of Clarence A. Brittain, NARA, RG 153, p. 117; Testimony of Capt. Robert Foy, General Court Martial of Clarence A. Brittain, NARA, RG 153, p. 256; Danny Walker, "Faunal Remains from Three Military Soldier Stations, Yellowstone National Park, Wyoming," in Kenneth Karsmizki, *Fountain Soldier Station (48YE727): Report of Research and Mitigation Prepared for the National Park Service, Rocky Mountain Region* (Bozeman, MT: Museum of the Rockies, 2001), 5–7, 9–10; Jacoby, *Crimes against Nature*, 3, 133–137; Robert Kane, "The Social Ecology of Police Misconduct," *Criminology* 40, no. 4 (2002): 867–868, 891; David J. Dodd, "Police Mentality and Behavior," *Issues in Criminology* 3, no. 1 (1967): 54–55; Bethan Loftus, "Police Occupational Culture: Classic Themes, Alter Times," *Policing and Society: An International Journal of Research and Policy* 20, no. 1 (2010): 13.

30. Elmer Lindsley, "A Winter Trip through the Yellowstone," *Harper's Weekly* 42 (January 19, 1898): 107.

31. Lindsley, "Winter Trip," 107.

32. Anderson, *Report 1896*, 11; Anderson, *Report 1895*, 12.

33. Roy Talbert Jr. *Negative Intelligence: The Army and the American Left, 1917–1941* (Jackson: University Press of Mississippi, 1991), 3–4.

34. Theodore M. Becker, "The Place of Private Police in Society: An Area for Research in Social Sciences," *Social Problems* 21, no. 3 (1974): 438–453; Office of the General Counsel, United States General Accounting Office to Senator John C. Stennis. "Comments Concerning the Anti-Pinkerton Act, March 6, 1980" (Washington, DC: US GAO, 1980), http://www.gao.gov/assets/180/171215.pdf.

35. Frank Morn, *The Eye That Never Sleeps: A History of the Pinkerton National Detective Agency* (Bloomington: Indiana University Press, 1982), 188–189, 192; Joan M. Jensen, *Army Surveillance in America, 1775–1980* (New Haven, CT: Yale University Press, 1991), 36–38.

36. White to Anderson, July 27, 1895. Letters "S-Z, Jan 1. 1894–Dec. 31, 1909." Item 7, YNPA.

37. Lindsley, "Winter Trip," 106; Jacoby, *Crimes against Nature,* 129–130; "Veritas" to Anderson, September 18, 1895. Letters "S-Z, Jan 1. 1894–Dec. 31, 1909." Item 7, YNPA.

38. Marshall to Anderson, Aug. 27, 1895. Letters "L-R, January 1, 1892–December 31, 1895," Item 6, YNPA; Report of Lt. Elmer Lindsley, January 16, 1898, in United States Department of the Interior, Yellowstone National Park Army Era Records, Employees, January 1, 1898–December 31, 1903, Item 20, YNPA; Leigh to Lindsley, February 20, 1898, in United States Department of the Interior, Yellowstone National Park Army Era Records, Employees, January 1, 1898–December 31, 1903, Item 20, YNPA; Charles "Buckskin Charley" Marble, "Fifty Years in and around Yellowstone Park," typewritten manuscript, Theodore Roosevelt Digital Library. Dickinson State University, http://www.theodorerooseveltcenter.org/Research/Digital-Library/Record?libID=020158, p. 6. In reality, the evidence suggests that Mathews became lost in a snowstorm and died from exposures. See Anderson, *Report 1895*, 7.

39. Jacoby, *Crimes against Nature,* 133.

40. *Livingston (MT) Enterprise,* January 1, 1898, 3.

41. Romey to Pitcher, January 18, 1903, in United States Department of the Interior, Yellowstone National Park Army Era Records, Employees, January 1, 1898–December 31, 1903, Item 29, YNPA.

42. David Ammerman, *In the Common Cause: American Response to the Coercive Acts of 1774* (New York: Norton, 1974), 9–10, 15; Robert Middlekauff, *The Glorious Cause: The American Revolution, 1763–1789* (New York: Oxford University Press, 2005), 238–241; Ian Christie and Benjamin Labaree, *Empire or Independence, 1760–1776* (New York: Norton, 1976), 188; Ira Gruber, "The American Revolution as a Conspiracy: The British View." *William and Mary Quarterly* 26, no. 3 (1969): 360–372; Jack Sosin, "The Massachusetts Acts of 1774: Coercive or Preventative?" *Huntington Library Quarterly* (1963): 235–252; on the use of martial law in the British colonies before the American Revolution, see Ian Steele, "Governors or Generals?: A Note on Marital Law and the Revolution of 1689 in English America," *William and Mary Quarterly* 46, no. 2 (April 1989): 304–314; Mathew Warhauser, *Andrew Jackson and the Politics of Martial Law: Nationalism, Civil Liberties, and Partisanship* (Knoxville: University of Tennessee Press, 2007); Roy Morris Jr. *Sheridan: The Life and Wars of General Phil Sheridan* (New York: Crown Publishing, 1992), 335–338; Paul A. Hutton, *Phil Sheridan and His Army* (Lincoln: University of Nebraska Press, 1989), 208–212.

43. Eric Foner, *Reconstruction: America's Unfinished Revolution, 1863–1877* (New York, NY: Harper Collins, 1988), 35–76, 176–198, 228–251, 274–278, 316–333; Mark L. Bradley, *The Army and Reconstruction 1865–1877* (Washington, DC: United States Army Center of Military History, 2015), 9–24, 49–54, 71–72; James Sefton, *The United States Army and Reconstruction, 1865–1877* (Baton Rouge: Louisiana State University Press, 1967), 5–15, 25–26, 50–73, 120–128; Edwin C. Brouse, *The U.S. Army and Constabulary Operations* (Leavenworth, KS: School of Advanced Military Studies, 2006), 22–21; Gabrial Chin, "The Voting Rights Act of 1867: The Constitutionality of Federal Regulations of Suffrage During Reconstruction," *North Carolina Law Review* 82 (2004): 82; Hutton, *Sheridan,* 22–71.

44. Robert K. Wright Jr. *Military Police* (Washington, DC: United States Army Center of Military History, 1992), 6–9.

45. For more on how soldiers adapt to unfamiliar situations and missions, see National Research Council, *Context of Military Environments*, 23; Gary A. Fine, "Enacting Norms: Mushrooming and the Culture of Expectations and Explanations," in *Social Norms*, ed. Michael Hechter and Karl-Dieter Opp (New York: Russell Sage Foundation, 2001): 139–164; B. W. Tuckman, "Developmental Sequence in Small Groups," *Psychological Bulletin* 63, no. 6 (1965): 384–399; National Research Council, *Context of Military Environments*, 32.

46. Dodd, "Police Mentality," 47–53; Kane, "Social Ecology," 867, 891.

47. Kane, "Social Ecology," 891; Lawrence Felson and Marcus Cohen, "Human Ecology and Crime: A Routine Activity Approach," *Human Ecology* 8, no. 4 (1980): 384; Dodd, "Police Mentality," 55; Richard Sykes and John Clark, "A Theory of Deference Exchange in Police-Civilian Encounters," *American Journal of Sociology* 81, no. 3 (November 1975): 584–586; Adams, *Class and Race*, 144–145; C. Robert Haywood, *Victorian West: Class and Culture in Kansas Cattle Towns* (Lawrence: University Press of Kansas, 1991), 12, 15, 13; Daniel Howe, *Victorian America* (Philadelphia: University of Pennsylvania Press, 1976), 9; Lawrence Levine, *Highbrow/Lowbrow: The Emergence of Cultural Hierarchy in America* (Boston: Harvard University Press, 1990), 3, 200, 255; John F. Kasson, *Rudeness and Civility: Manners in Nineteenth-Century America* (New York: Hill & Wang, 1990), 43, 54, 115, 147–148, 173, 212; Thomas C. Rust, *Lost Fort Ellis: A Frontier History of Bozeman* (Charleston, SC: History Press, 2015), 98–101, 150–156, 117–119, 132–135.

48. Thomas J. Schlereth, *Victorian America: Transformations in Everyday Life, 1876–1915* (New York: Harper Perennial, 1991), xiii; Collin D. Wells, "Social Darwinism," *American Journal of Sociology* 12, no. 5 (1907): 695–696; Carl Degler, *In Search of Human Nature: The Decline and Revival of Darwinism in American Social Thought* (New York: Oxford University Press, 1991), 285; Haywood, *Victorian West*, 11–12; Joseph Kahl, *The America Class Structure: A New Synthesis* (Chicago: Dorsey Press, 1987), 21.

49. Ibid. *Oxford English Dictionary*, definition of "swaddie"; definition of "swad." Aubrey Haines, with no explanation, suggests the term originated from the British-Indian army's term, "swattie." Haines, *Yellowstone Story*, 2: 102. *The Oxford English Dictionary*, however, makes no such connection and has no entry for the term "swattie."

50. Howe, *Victorian America*, 8; Don Rickey, *Forty Miles a Day on Beans and Hay*, (Norman: University of Oklahoma Press, 1963), 26–28; Edward M. Coffman, *The Old Army: A Portrait of the American Army in Peacetime, 1784-1898* (Oxford: Oxford University Press, 1988), 400–404; Robert Utley, *Frontier Regulars: The United States Army and the Indian, 1866–1991* (Lincoln, NE: Bison Books, 1973), 22; Adams, *Class and Race*, 212; Haines, *Yellowstone Story*, 2: 102. Maj. Samuel W. Miller, Inspector General United States Army to Maj. Gen. Frederick C. Ainsworth, Adjutant General United States Army, November 20, 1908. Letters Received, Fort Yellowstone, RG 393, NARA. Rudyard Kipling, *From Sea to Sea:*

*Letters of Travel* (New York: Doubleday & McClure, 1899), 2: 49, 91; Dodd, "Police Mentality," 49.

51. Circular, March 6, 1908. Orders and Circulars, Fort Yellowstone, RG 393, NARA.

52. Georgina Synge, *A Ride through Wonderland* (London: Sampson, Low, Marston, 1892), 60; Gardner S. Turrill, *A Tale of the Yellowstone or, In a Wagon through Western Wyoming and Wonderland* (Jefferson, IA: G. S. Turrill, 1901), 98–99; Order No. 5, August 21, 1886, Camp Sheridan, Wyoming, Fort Yellowstone, RG 393, NARA. Harris, *Report 1886*, 11; General Order No. 10, May 31, 1902. Special Orders, General Orders, and Circulars 1896–1902, Fort Yellowstone, RG 393, NARA; Park Order No. 6, Park Orders, Fort Yellowstone, RG 393, NARA.

53. Lt. Col. L. M. Brett, Acting Superintendent, Yellowstone National Park, to Managers of Hotels. Letter No. 43. June 6, 1914. Park Orders. RG 393, NARA; United States Secretary of the Interior, *Rules, Regulations, and Instructions for the Information and Guidance of Officers and Enlisted Men of the United States Army, and of the Scouts Doing Duty in the Yellowstone National Park* (Washington, DC: GPO, 1907); YNPL, VF, 21; Park Orders No. 12, June 1, 1914. Park Orders, Fort Yellowstone. RG 393, NARA.

54. Sykes and Clark, "Deference Exchange," 586–589.

55. Mr. F.W. Trible to Lt. Col. Lloyd Brett, Commanding Officer and Acting Superintendent, August 3, 1914, Letter Box 46, Complaints 1909–1914, YNPA.

56. "Despotism in the Park," *Livingston Enterprise*, October 15, 1887, 3.

57. Harris, *Report 1888*, 4.

58. "A Tourist's Grievance," *Livingston Enterprise*, September 27, 1887, 3.

59. Sykes and Clark, "Deference Exchange," 589; Jack Ellis Haynes, *Yellowstone Stage Holdups* (Denver, CO: Brand Book, 1952), 17.

60. Quoted in Haynes, *Yellowstone Stage Holdups*, 19.

61. Owen Wister, "Old Yellowstone Days" *Harper's Magazine*, 157 (March 1936): 45–46; Haines, *Yellowstone Story*, 2: 29.

## CHAPTER TWO: "PECULIAR, PERPLEXING AND SEVERE DUTIES"

1. United States Department of War, Records of the Adjutant General's Office, Post Returns, Fort Yellowstone, WY (hereafter Post Returns), National Archives and Record Administration (hereafter NARA), Washington, DC, 1900–1915, April 1901, Record Group 94 (hereafter RG 94); U.S. Army, U.S. Military Post Returns, 1800–1916, NARA.

2. "George W. Goode, 1880," No. 2873, in George W. Cullum, *Biographical Register of Officers and Graduates of the U.S. Military Academy at West Point, N.Y., from Its Establishment in 1802 to 1890; with Early History of the United States Military Academy by Brevet Major General George W. Cullum* (hereafter Cullum, *Register)* (Saginaw, MI: Seeman & Peters, 1910): 5: 44; ibid.; Edward M. Offley, Diary, Nov. 17, 1900, Vertical File (hereafter VF), Yellowstone National Park Library (hereafter YNPL),

13; "George W. Goode, 1880," No. 2873, in Cullum, *Register* (1941): 9: 44; "George W. Goode," No. 2873, in Cullum *Register* (1901): 4: 337; United States Military History Institute, "Army Officer—Records from the Adjutant General (Biographical Data), VF, YNPL; "George W. Goode," No. 2873, in Cullum, *Register* (1910): 5: 312.

3. Lt. Col. Theo J. Wint to the Adjutant General, Department of Dakota, September 15, 1900, Inspection of Fort Yellowstone (hereafter Inspection Report 1900), in United States Department of War, Records of the Inspector General (Army), Inspection Reports, 1891–1913, NARA, Washington, DC, Record Group 159 (hereafter RG 159), 60.

4. Offley, Diary, Nov. 17, 1900, 13; Inspection Report 1900, RG 159, 60.

5. Eben Swift, "Obituary, John Pitcher, No. 2634, Class of 1876," in United States Military Academy, *Sixteenth Annual Report of the Association of Graduates of the United States Military Academy at West Point, New York* (Newburgh, NY: Moore Printing Co., 1929), 269.

6. For example, see Memorandum, March 22, 1911, and Memorandum, March 27, 1911, Records of Continental Commands 1821–1920, Fort Yellowstone, WY, General Orders and Memoranda, 1910-1918, NARA, Record Group 393 (hereafter RG 393).

7. "Memorial, Charles B. Drake, 1896, Cullum No. 3696," *West Point Association of Graduates*, http://externalapps.westpointaog.org/Memorials/Article/2873/; Lt. Col. Philip H. Reade, Inspector General to Adjutant General, Department of Dakota, June 10, 1901, Inspection of Fort Yellowstone, in United States Department of the Interior, Records of the Office of the Inspection Reports, 1891–1913, NARA, RG 159 (hereafter Inspection Report 1901), 22.

8. Reade, Inspection Report 1901, 22; K.H.A., "Obituary, Frank Porter Amos, No. 3968, Class of 1900," in *Sixty-Second Annual Report of the Association of Graduates of the United States Military Academy at West Point, New York* (Chicago: R. R. Donnelley & Sons, 1931): 369.

9. Inspection Report 1900, 2; United States Department of the Interior, Yellowstone National Park Army Era Records, Journal of the Acting Superintendent, 1900–1903, Gardiner, MT: YNPA, May 26, 1901, 145: 67.

10. Philip H. Reade, "General Reade's War Record," in *Epochs in U.S. History: A Series of Military, Historical, Educational and Interesting Lectures, Replete with Narrative and Personal Reminiscences* (Lowell, MA: Courier Citizen, 1906), 47–49.

11. US Dep't of Interior, Journal of the Acting Superintendent, May 24, 1901, 145: 67; Lt. Col. Theo J. Wint, to the Adjutant General, Department of Dakota, November 18, 1899, in Inspection of Fort Yellowstone, 1899, NARA, RG 159, 6 (hereafter Inspection Report 1899); Inspection Report 1900, 23; Lt. Col. Philip H. Reade to the Adjutant General, Department of Dakota, May 1901, in Inspection Report 1901, 31.

12. Offley, Diary, Nov. 15, 1900, 11; Inspection Report 1901, 69–70.

13. Inspection Report 1901, 69–70.

14. Inspection Report 1901, 69–70.

15. Inspection Report 1901, 69–43.

16. Inspection Report 1903, 3; Yellowstone Park Association to Maj. John Pitcher, May 31, 1903, and July 31, 1904, in United States Department of the Interior,

Yellowstone National Park Army Era Records, Miscellaneous Receipts, etc. 1900–1905, Gardiner, MT: YNPA, Box 88. There are a number of similar receipts from the hotel over Major Pitcher's tenure in the park.

17. Bessie Haynes-Arnold, "An Interview—1975," VF, 3. YNPL, Gardiner, MT; Kevin Adams, *Class and Race in the Frontier Army: Military Life in the West, 1870–1890* (Norman: University of Oklahoma Press, 2009), 68, 78; Emily Post, *Etiquette in Society, in Business, in Politics and at Home* (New York: Funk & Wagnalls, 1922), 73, 83–84, 86–87, 89–91.

18. Quoted in Lee Whittlesey, "In Yellowstone Park, 1886–1889: George Tutherly's Reminiscences." *Montana: The Magazine of Western History* 33, no. 1 (Winter 1983): 11.

19. Haines, *The Yellowstone Story, Vol. 2* (Boulder: Yellowstone Library and Colorado Associate University Press, 1977), 2: 105; Adams, *Class and Race*, 68, 78.

20. Bessie Haynes-Arnold, Jan. 20, 1915. "Diary of Bessie Haynes Arnold, Fort Yellowstone, 1915." YNPL, VF; quoted in Whittlesey, "Yellowstone Park," 4–5.

21. Whittlesey, 5, 10.

22. Haynes-Arnold, "Interview," 3; Haynes-Arnold, "Diary," January 20, 1915, YNPL, VF.

23. Haines, *Yellowstone Story*, 175; quoted in Whittlesey, "Yellowstone Park," 11.

24. Inspection Report 1901, 2.

25. Memorandum, January 4, 1911, in United States Department of the Interior, Records of the United States Continental Commands 1821–1920, Fort Yellowstone, WY, General Orders and Memorandum, 1910–1918, NARA, Record Group 393; Fort Maj. Alfred Reynolds to the Adjutant General, Department of Dakota, June 13, 1902; Inspection of Fort Yellowstone in United States Department of the Interior, Records of the Office of the Inspector General (Army), Inspection Reports, 1891–1913, NARA, RG 159 (hereafter Inspection Report 1902), 3; Inspection Report 1900, 7; Inspection Report 1900, 7; Inspection Report 1899, 3; Inspection Report 1902, 3; Capt. Wallace DeWitte, Surgeon Medical Corps to Adjutant Fort Yellowstone, February 12, 1910. Letter Received, Fort Yellowstone, RG 393, NARA; Inspection Report 1900, 7, RG 159, NARA; Inspection Report 1901, 6, RG 159, NARA; Inspection Report 1901, 6, RG 159, NARA.

26. Offley, Diary, November 11, 1900, 10; November 16, 1900, 13.

27. Offley, Diary, November 19, 1900, 15; January 31, 1901, 20; Memorandum, March 23, 1911, in General Orders and Memorandums, RG 393; General Order No. 10, May 31, 1902, in United States Department of the Interior, Records of United States Continental Commands 1821–1920, Fort Yellowstone, WY, Special Orders, General Orders, and Circulars 1896–1902, NARA, RG 393; quoted in Whittlesey, "Yellowstone Park," 12.

28. Inspection Report 1900, 29; Inspection Report 1902, 4.

29. Memorandum, March 1, 1911, in General Orders and Memorandums 1910–1918, RG 393, NARA.

30. Summary Court-Martial Pvt. William Fitzgerald, Company G, Fifth US Cavalry, July 28, 1909, in United States Department of the Interior, Records of

United States Continental Commands 1821–1920, Fort Yellowstone, WY, Summary Court-Martial Records, Fort Yellowstone, NARA, Record Group 393; Summary Court-Martial Pvt. George Collins, Company E, First US Cavalry, June 6, 1911in ibid.; Summary Court-Martial Achilles Taitt, Company E, First US Cavalry, December 5, 1911 in ibid.; Pvt. James Todd, Company E, Fifth US Cavalry, May 21, 1910; Pvt. Henry Herton, Company G, Fifth US Cavalry, August 3, 1911; Pvt. John O'Mara, Company E, Eleventh US Cavalry, September 29, 1916, Records of United States Continental Commands 1821–1920, Fort Yellowstone, WY, Summary Court-Martial Records, Fort Yellowstone, Record Group 393, NARA, Washington, DC.

31. Inspection Report 1899, 12; Inspection Report 1901, 25; Inspection Report 1901, 17; Inspection Report 1900, 17; Joseph Joffe, "John W. Meldrum," *Annals of Wyoming* 13, no. 2 (April 1941): 109–110.

32. William Gossel to Secretary of the Interior, September 20, 1911 in United States Department of the Interior, Yellowstone National Park Army Era Records, Complaints 1909–1914, Gardiner, MT, YNPA, Letter Box 92.

33. Maj. Henry C. Benson to the Secretary of the Interior, May 27, 1909, in Complaints 1909–1914; Maj. Henry C. Benson to the Secretary of the Interior, September 21, 1910, in Complaints 1909–1914, Letter Box 92.

34. Offley, January 18, 1901, 18.

35. Inspection Report 1901, 26.

36. Inspection Report 1901, 17, 25–26; Inspection Report 1899, 12; Inspection Report 1900, 17; Inspection Report 1901, 17; Inspection Report 1901, 17; Inspection Report 1903, 2.

37. Inspection Report 1902, 5, 10; Inspection Report 1903, 2.

38. Testimony of Hughey Hollins, General Court-Martial of Pvt. Laurence E. Moon, in United States Department of War, Records of the Judge Advocate General, Court-Martial Case Files and Related Records, NARA, Record Group 153 (hereafter RG 153), 54.

39. Robert Nye, "Western Masculinities in War and Peace," *American Historical Review* 112, no. 2 (April 2007): 428; Axel Bungaard, *Muscle and Manliness: The Rise of Sport in American Boarding Schools* (Syracuse, NY: Syracuse University Press, 2005), 109; Michael Oriard, *Reading Football: How the Popular Press Created an American Spectacle* (Chapel Hill: University of North Carolina Press, 1993), 189–276; Testimony of First Sgt. Henry Bauder, Court-Martial of Pvt. Laurence E. Moon, in Court-Martial Case Files, Records of the Judge Advocate General, Court-Martial Case Files and Related Records. Record Group 153, NARA, Washington, DC, 135; Testimony of Capt. E. A. Hickman, Court-Martial of Pvt. Laurence E. Moon, in Court-Martial Case Files, Records of the Judge Advocate General, Court-Martial Case Files and Related Records. Record Group 153, NARA, Washington, DC, 138–139, 142.

40. "Livingston Beats Fort Yellowstone," *Great Falls (MT) Tribune*, May 2, 1904; "The Livingston Team Successful," *Billings (MT) Gazette*, July 23, 1907; Jack Ellis Haynes, *Yellowstone Stage Holdups* (Denver, CO: Brand Books, 1952), 6.

41. "Players Had a Royal Time," *Billings (MT) Gazette*, Dec. 1, 1903.

42. Inspection Report 1899, 9–10; Inspection Report 1900, 23, 35, 38; Inspection Report 1901, 44–45; Inspection Report 1902, 8; Offley, Diary, January 19, 1901, 18.

43. Inspection Report 1899, 9–10; Court-Martial of Pvt. Robert Norman Jr., Dec. 14, 1914, in United States Department of War, Records of United States Continental Commands 1821–1920, Fort Yellowstone, WY, Summary Court-Martial Records, Fort Yellowstone, NARA, RG 393; see Court-Martials of Pvt. Emil Simminger, Jan. 30, 1912; Pvt. Clyde Rhodes, September 13, 1912; Pvt. Blaine Werr, Jan. 4, 1911; Pvt. Archie Parris, Mar. 28, 1910, in ibid.

44. Inspection Report 1902, 8.

45. Inspection Report 1901, 44–45; Offley, Diary, January 18, 1901, 18.

46. Inspection Report 1900, 26.

47. Special Order No. 13, in Orders 1915–1917, RG 393; see, for example, Court-Martial of Pvt. Frances Smith, Nov. 12, 1906, in Summary Court-Martial Records, RG 393; for details on the soldiers visiting the brothels in Gardner, see the Court-Martial of Pvt. Lawrence Moon in Court-Martial Case Files, RG 153; Maj. Wallace DeWitt, Medical Corps to Post Adjutant, March 21, 1910 in United States Department of War, Records of United States Continental Commands 1821–1920, Fort Yellowstone, WY, Letters Received, NARA, RG 393; Summary Court-Martial of Pvt. James Severns, Nov. 26, 1908, in Summary Court-Martial Records, RG 393.

48. Memorandum, Nov. 17, 1910, in General Orders and Memoranda, RG 393; Court-Martial of Pvt. Ernest Freeman, Oct. 19, 1911, in Summary Court-Martial Records, RG 393.

49. Special Order 54, June 1, 1898, in Special Orders, RG 393; Special Order 37, June 4, 1902, in Special Orders, RG 393.

50. Testimony of Pvt. James Mutch, General Court-Martial of Clarence A. Brittain, in Court-Martial Case Files, RG 153, 191; Thomas M. Connery, "The Winter Tragedy of the Yellowstone," *The Wide World: A Magazine for Everybody* (June 1919): 146.

51. Ellwood Bergey, *Why Soldiers Desert from the United States Army* (Philadelphia: William F. Fell, 1903), 86, 108–111, 131–134.

52. Inspection Report 1900, 5, 13, 20–21; Inspection Report 1901, 7, 29.

53. Offley, Diary, December 1, 1900, 16.

54. Offley, Diary, February 8, 1901, 21.

55. Offley, Diary February 2 and 15, 1901, 23.

56. Inspection Report 1900, 59–60.

57. Inspection Report 1900, 59–60.

58. Inspection Report 1901, 43.

59. Special Order 95, Oct. 4 1899, in Special Orders, RG 393.

60. Haines, *Yellowstone Story*, 2: 176.

61. Capt. Moses Harris, *Report of the Acting Superintendent of the Yellowstone National Park to the Secretary of the Interior, 1889* (Washington, DC: GPO, 1889): 11; Inspection Report 1899; Inspection Report 1900, 2; Inspection Report 1901, 30–31.

62. Inspection Report 1902, 5; Inspection Report 1899, 5; see Court-Martials of William Steward, April 23, 1909; William Fitzgerald, April 23, 1909; Joseph Congel,

May 17, 1909; George Collins, April 1, 1912; Willis Mullin, April 26, 1911; Fred Hoffman, May 5, 1911; William Griffin, May 15, 1911; James Nelson, June 6, 1911; Skelt Smith, August 1, 1911, in Summary Court-Martial Records, RG 393.

63. John Pitcher to the Adjutant General, November 30, 1903, in United States Department of War, Records of United States Continental Commands 1821–1920, Fort Yellowstone, WY, Letters Sent, NARA, RG 393.

64. Inspection Report 1899, 4.

65. Inspection Report 1902, 5.

66. Inspection Report 1899, 4–5; Inspection Report 1900, 48; Inspection Report 1903, 3.

67. Inspection Report 1899, 11–12; see also Inspection Report 1900, 34–35; Offley, Diary, December 1, 1900, 17.

68. Inspection Report 1901, 41–42; Inspection Report 1902, 10.

69. Inspection Report 1901, 73; Daniel Howe, *Victorian America* (Philadelphia: University of Pennsylvania Press, 1976), 8; Hiram M. Chittenden, *The Yellowstone National Park: Historical and Descriptive, Illustrated with Maps, Views, and Portraits* (Cincinnati, OH: Robert Clarke, 1900), 138, 284.

## CHAPTER THREE: "CONDITIONS . . . RESEMBLE THOSE EXISTING 30-ODD YEARS AGO"

1. United States Department of the Interior, Records of the Office of the Inspector General (Army), Inspection Reports, 1891–1913, NARA, RG 159 (hereafter Inspection Report 1901), 24.

2. United States Department of the Interior, Yellowstone National Park Army Era Records, Journal of the Acting Superintendent, 1900–1903, Gardiner, MT: YNPA, June 2, 1901; Journal of the Acting Superintendent 1900–1903, YNPA, 145: 147; Lt. Col. Philip H. Reade, Inspector General to Adjutant General, Department of Dakota, June 10, 1901, Inspection of Fort Yellowstone (hereafter Inspection Report 1901), 6; Records of the Office of the Inspector General (Army), Inspection Reports, 1891–1913, NARA, Record Group 159 (hereafter RG 159).

3. Inspection Report 1901, 6.

4. Aubrey L. Haines, *The Yellowstone Story* (Boulder: Yellowstone Library and Colorado Associate University Press, 1977), 2: 181–183.

5. Park Order No. 5, June 1, 1914, in United States Department of War, Records of United States Continental Commands 1821–1920, Fort Yellowstone, WY, Park Orders, NARA, RG 393.

6. Circular Sept 30, 1901, in United States Department of War, Records of United States Continental Commands 1821–1920, Fort Yellowstone, WY, Special Orders, General Orders, and Circulars, 1896–1902, NARA, RG 393; Circular, August 8, 1902, in United States Department of the Interior, Yellowstone National Park Army Era Records, Circulars and Other Instructions to Stations, Gardiner, MT: YNPA Bound Volume 239; Circular Sept 30, 1901, in Special Orders, RG 393.

7. Lt. Col. Theo J. Wint to the Adjutant General, Department of Dakota, September 15, 1900, Inspection of Fort Yellowstone (hereafter Inspection Report 1900), in United States Department of War, Records of the Inspector General (Army), Inspection Reports, 1891–1913, NARA, RG 159, 49.

8. Inspection Report 1901, 62–63; soldiers testifying at the court-martial of Sgt. Clarence Brittain anticipated the phone going down months before it actually did on Nov. 10, 1911; United States Department of the Interior, Records of the Judge Advocate General, Court-Martial Case Files, RG 153: testimony of "Tex" Holm, 269; testimony of Pvt. William Mutch, 69; testimony of Pvt. William Carroll, 87; Park Order No. 3, June 1, 1913; Park Order No. 11, June 1, 1914; Park Order No. 2, June 28, 1917, in Park Orders, RG 393.

9. Jack Ellis Haynes, *Haynes Official Guide: Yellowstone National Park: Descriptive, Geological, Historical* (St. Paul, MN: F. Jay Haynes, 1912): 31; Inspection Report 1901, 53.

10. Capt. George Anderson, *Report of the Acting Superintendent of the Yellowstone National Park to the Secretary of the Interior, 1893* (Washington, DC: GPO, 1893): 614, 617–618; Capt. Moses Harris, *Report of the Acting Superintendent of the Yellowstone National Park to the Secretary of the Interior, 1887* (Washington, DC: GPO, 1887): 8; H. R. Rep. No. 52-1956, at 272, 275; Haines, *Yellowstone Story*, 2: 8; Jack Haynes, *Official Guide*, 31–32.

11. Haines, *Yellowstone Story*, Vol. 2, 8; Inspection Report 1900, 42–43.

12. Lt. Col. Theo J. Wint, to the Adjutant General, Department of Dakota, November 18, 1899. Inspection of Fort Yellowstone, 1899 (hereafter Inspection Report 1899), in United States Department of War, Records of the Inspector General (Army), Inspection Reports, 1891–1913, NARA, RG 159, 14–15; Inspection Report 1901, 53, 61; United States Secretary of the Interior, *Rules, Regulations, and Instructions for the Information and Guidance of Officers and Enlisted Men of the United States Army, and of the Scouts Doing Duty in the Yellowstone National Park* (Washington, DC: GPO, 1907): 17, 23–24, 33 (hereafter *Rules, Regulations, and Instructions*); Circular No. 11, June 15, 1913, Park Orders, RG 393.

13. Pitcher, *Annual Report*, 1904.

14. Herbert Angelo, Diary, Vertical File, Yellowstone National Park Library, August 26, 1902, 74.

15. C. S. Bannerman to Capt. Anderson, Aug. 2, 1893, in United States Department of the Interior, Yellowstone National Park Arm Era Records, Letters Received, Jan. 1, 1897 to May 31, 1899, YNPA, Letter Box 7, Doc. 681.

16. Mode Wineman, typed manuscript, 1908, VF, YNPL, 22–23.

17. Wineman, manuscript, 24.

18. Angelo, Diary, August 25, 1902, 73.

19. Summary Court-Martial of Pvt. Frank Bedell, Co. F, First US Cavalry, August 18, 1913, Summary Court-Martial of Pvt. Joe Sattler, August 18, 1913, and Summary Court-Martial of Pvt. Louis Bradshaw, Company F, First US Cavalry, August 18, 1913, in United States Department of War, Records of United States Continental Commands 1821–1920, Fort Yellowstone, WY, Summary Court-Martial Records, NARA, RG 393; for other alcohol-related cases, see the summary courts-martial of

Pvt. Joseph Peters, Company G, First US Cavalry, Sept. 5, 1912; Pvt. Harry Sturst, Company G, Fifth US Cavalry, June 9, 1909, in ibid.

20. Post Returns, August 1897, in United States Department of the Interior, Records of the Adjutant General's Office, Fort Yellowstone, WY, NARA, RG 94 (hereafter Post Returns).

21. Sgt. Maxwell R. Welch, "Special Report to the Commanding Officer, Fort Yellowstone, Wyoming, August 16, 1897," in United States Department of the Interior, Yellowstone National Park Army Era Records, Monthly Reports, Canyon Station, 1897, YNPA; for a more detailed account of the robbery and the hunt for the robbers, see Haines, *Yellowstone Story*, 2: 203–206.

22. Col. Lloyd M. Brett to Secretary of Yellowstone Park Hotel Company, December 5, 1912, Letter Box 78, Letters Employees, YNPA.

23. Inspection Report 1901, 53.

24. Inspection Report 1901, 61; *Rules, Regulations, and Instructions*, 26, 34.

25. Capt. George Anderson, *Report of the Acting Superintendent of the Yellowstone National Park to the Secretary of the Interior, 1896* (Washington, DC: GPO, 1896), 11–12; Charles "Buckskin Charley" Marble, "Fifty Years in and around Yellowstone Park," typewritten manuscript, Theodore Roosevelt National Park, Theodore Roosevelt Digital Library, Dickinson State University, http://www.theodorerooseveltcenter.org/Research/Digital-Library/Record?libID=020158, 6; Capt. George Anderson, *Report of the Acting Superintendent of the Yellowstone National Park to the Secretary of the Interior, 1895* (Washington, DC: GPO, 1895), 7.

26. Karl Jacoby, *Crimes against Nature: Squatters, Poachers, Thieves, and the Hidden History of American Conservation* (Berkeley: University of California Press, 2001), 3, 27, 32, 36–37, 136, 146, 198.

27. Edward M. Offley, Diary, VF, YNPL, Oct. 4, 1900, 25.

28. Summary Court-Martial of Pvt. George Miller, Company D, Fifth US Cavalry, Troop 1, Yellowstone National Park Detachment, July 29, 1916; Summary Court-Martial of Pvt. Frederick Moses, Company C, Eighth US Cavalry, Troop 1, Yellowstone National Park Detachment, July 29, 1916; in Summary Court-Martial Records, RG 393.

29. Summary Court-Martial of Corporal George Desrosiers, Company H, First US Cavalry, July 24, 1913; Summary Court-Martial of Sgt. Richard J. Bohen, Company H, First US Cavalry, July 24, 1913, in Summary Court-Martial Records, RG 393.

30. Inspection Report 1900, 47.

31. Inspection Report 1900, 36.

32. Inspection Report 1901, 61; *Rules, Regulations, and Instructions*, 33–34; Special Order No. 68, Oct. 18, 1901, in Special Orders, RG 393.

33. Lee Whittlesey, "'Music, Song, and Laughter': Yellowstone National Park's Fountain Hotel, 1891–1916," *Montana Magazine of Western History* 53, no. 4 (Winter 2003): 24–26; Haines, *Yellowstone Story*, 2: 116.

34. Inspection Report 1899, 15; *Rules, Regulations, and Instructions*, 24; Whittlesey, "Music, Song," 31; Inspection Report 1900, 36.

35. *Rules, Regulations, and Instructions*, 21; Park Order No. 8, June 1, 1914, in Park Orders, Fort RG 393.

36. Summary Court-Martial of Pvt. Archie Lane, Company G, First US Cavalry, Sept. 10, 1911, in Summary Court-Martial Records, RG 393; Haines, *Yellowstone Story*, 2: 116; Angelo, Diary, July 24, 1902, 70; Summary Court-Martial of Pvt. Clarence Williams, August 14, 1912, in Summary Court-Martial Records, RG 393; Kenneth Karsmizki, *Fountain Soldier Station (48YE727): Report of Research and Mitigation Prepared for the National Park Service, Rocky Mountain Region* (Bozeman, MT: Museum of the Rockies, 2001), 147, 148.

37. Summary Court-Martial of Pvt. Archie Lane, Company G, First US Cavalry, Sept. 10, 1911; Summary Court-Martial of Pvt. Amil Moravek, Company G, First US Cavalry, July 14, 1913, in Summary Court-Martial Records, RG 393; Summary Court-Martial of Pvt. Amil Moravek, Company G, First US Cavalry, July 14, 1913, in Summary Court-Martial Records, RG 393; Karsmizki, *Fountain Soldier Station*, 116–117.

38. Karsmizki, *Fountain Soldier Station*, 107–109, 114; Angelo, Diary, August n.d., 1902, 70.

39. Haines, *Yellowstone Story*, 2: 189; Karsmizki, *Fountain Soldier Station*, 115; Danny Walker, *Faunal Remains from Three Military Soldier Stations, Yellowstone National Park, Wyoming* (Bozeman, MT: Museum of the Rockies, 1999), 9, 21.

40. Corporal Frank Notruba to Commanding Officer, Fort Yellowstone, December 6, 1902, in United States Department of the Interior, Yellowstone National Park Army Era Records, Employees, Jan. 1, 1898–Dec. 31, 1903, Gardiner, MT: YNPA, Letter Box 10.

41. Post Returns, RG 94; Angelo, Diary, May 12–June 4, 1902, 47–59; Post Returns, June 1902, RG 94; Angelo, Diary, June 6–8 and July 4, 1902, 61–64.

42. Angelo, Diary, July 4, 1902, 64; August 14, 1902, 72; July 2, 1902, 63; July 2, 1902, 63.

43. Angelo, Diary, July 6–July 10, 1902, 64–65; August n.d., 1902, 70; August 29 and August 31, 1902, 75–76.

44. Inspection Report 1901, 61.

45. Lt. Traub to the Adjutant, July 14, 1900, in Employees Jan. 1, 1898–Dec. 31, 1903, Letter Box 10.

46. *Rules, Regulations, and Instructions*, 25; Summary Court-Martial of Pvt. Albert Beagle, Company E, Fifth US Cavalry, August 5, 1912, in Summary Court-Martial Records, RG 393.

47. Inspection Report 1900, 54–55; Offley, Diary, Oct. 4, 1900, 26; Second Lt. F. J. Arnold to Acting Superintendent Capt. James Erin, September 22, 1898, in Employees Jan. 1, 1898–Dec. 31, 1903, Letter Box 10.

48. Inspection Report 1899, 15; Inspection Report 1900, 54–55; Edwin Ingalls, *New York Sun*, in United States Department of the Interior, Yellowstone National Park Army Era Records, Complaints 1909–1914, Gardiner, MT: YNPA, Letter Box 46.

49. Offley, Diary, Oct. 4, 1900, 26; Angelo, Diary, July 6, 1902, 65.

50. Statement of Jerome Chapin, Esq., of Battle Creek, Michigan, July 23, 1907, in United States Department of the Interior, Yellowstone National Park Army Era Records, Letters Received 1906–1909, Gardiner, MT: YNPA, Box 15.

51. [Illegible] to Capt. John Pitcher, August 22, 1902, in Employees, Jan. 1, 1898–Dec. 31, 1903, Letter Box 10.

52. Summary Court-Martial of Pvt. William Wencil, July 29, 1912; Summary Court-Martial of Pvt. John Kane, July 29, 1912; Summary Court Martial of Pvt. Martin Lilienthal, July 29, 1912, in Summary Court-Martial Records, RG 393; Mr. Henry Child, Manager Yellowstone Park Association to Acting Superintendent, October 19, 1909, in Complaints, 1909–1914, Letter Box 46.

53. Inspection Report 1900, 51, 60.

54. *Rules, Regulations, and Instructions*, 30.

55. Inspection Report 1901, 60.

56. Offley, Diary, October 4, 1900, 30; Corporal Travis Bauer to Commanding Officer, Fort Yellowstone, August 16, 1899, in Letters Received, Jan. 1 1897 to May 31, 1899, Letter Box 7.

57. Exhibit A, Affidavit, James M. Webb, Sergeant Troop 2, Yellowstone National Park Detachment, in in United States Department of the Interior, Yellowstone National Park Army Era Records, Property, Gardiner, MT: YNPA, Box 62.

58. Col. Lloyd M. Brett, Acting Superintendent, Yellowstone National Park, to Claimants, November 23, 1914, in Property, Box 62.

59. Inspection Report 1901, 40–41.

60. *Rules, Regulations, and Instructions*, 28, 34.

61. Testimony of Pvt. Oliver Jordway, General Court-Martial of Clarence A. Brittain, in Court-Martial Case Files, RG 153, 234; Summary Court-Martial of Pvt. Daniel Becker, August 1, 1909; Summary Court-Martial of Pvt. James Gearin, Sept. 5, 1912; Summary Court-Martial of James Daley, Sept. 5, 1912; Court-Martial of Pvt. George Collins, September 5, 1912, in Summary Court-Martial Records, RG 393; Clara Green, Diary, July 19, 1892, VF, YNPL, Gardiner, MT, 13–14.

62. Affidavit, Frank Starboard of Rexburg, Fremont County, Idaho, August 1913, in Complaints, 1909–1914, Letter Box 46.

63. Capt. Sweezy to Col. L. M. Brett, Jan. 9, 1914, in Complaints 1909–1914, Letter Box 46.

64. Col. L. M. Brett to Mr. John Kauer Jr., Jan. 15, 1914, in Complaints 1909–1914, Letter Box 46.

65. Inspection Report 1901, 9; *Rules, Regulations, and Instructions*, 28–29, 34.

66. Mr. F. W. Trible to Lt. Col. Lloyd Brett, Commanding Officer, and Acting Superintendent, August 3, 1914, in Complaints 1909–1914, Letter Box 46.

67. Offley, Diary, October 4, 1900, 27.

68. Angelo, Diary, July 8, 1902, 66–67.

69. Ken Karsmizki, *Tower Falls Soldier Station (48YE163): Historical Archaeology, Report of Research Prepared for the National Park Service Intermountain Region* (Bozeman, MT: Museum of the Rockies, 2000), 52; Inspection Report 1901, 32, 62; Lee Whittlesey, *Yellowstone Place Names* (Helena, MT: Montana Historical Society, 1988), 82; Haines, *Yellowstone Story*, 2: 188; quoted in Karsmizki, *Tower Falls*, 49; Inspection Report 1901, 32.

70. Inspection Report 1901, 62; *Rules, Regulations, and Instructions*, 31, 35.

71. Special Order No. 104, Sept. 18, 1902, in Special Orders, RG 393; Kenneth Karsmizki, *Soda Butte Soldier Station (48YE88): Report of Research and Testing Prepared for the National Park Service Intermountain Region* (Bozeman, MT: Museum of the Rockies, 1998), 63, 81.

72. Karsmizki, *Soda Butte*, 30, 80; Lee Whittlesey, *Yellowstone Album: A Photographic Celebration of the First National Park* (Boulder, CO: Robert Rinehart, 1997), 96; Maj. Harry C. Benson, to Secretary of the Interior, September 17, 1910, in Complaints 1909–1914, Letter Box 46.

73. Carl E. Schmidt, *A Western Trip* (Detroit, MI: Herold Press, 1901), 59.

74. Maj. Henry C. Benson to Secretary of Interior, August 22, 1910, in United States Department of the Interior, Records of the National Park Service, 1939, Liquor Traffic, Parks, Reservations, and Antiquities, Yellowstone National Park, Central Files 1907–1939, College Park, MD: NARA, RG 79; Inspection Report 1901, 60.

75. Journal of the Acting Superintendent, 1900–1903, YNPA, June 10, 1901, 145; Inspection Report 1901, 8.

76. Inspection Report 1901, 24; Report of Elmer Lindsey, January 16, 1898, in Employees, Jan. 1, 1898–Dec. 31, 1903, Letter Box 10; Jacoby, *Crimes against Nature*, 2–4.

## CHAPTER FOUR: AN "UNDESIRABLE STATION"

1. Fredrick C. Ainsworth to Samuel W. Miller, Oct. 2, 1908, in Correspondence, Record Group (hereafter RG) 94, Records of the Adjutant General's Office 1780s-1917, National Archives and Record Administration, Washington, DC.

2. Kathy Mason, *Natural Museums: U.S. National Parks, 1872–1916* (East Lansing: Michigan State University Press, 2004), 71; Samuel B. M. Young, *Report of the Superintendent of the Yellowstone National Park to the Secretary of the Interior, 1907* (Washington, DC: GPO, 1907): 25–26.

3. Capt. Moses Harris, *Report of the Acting Superintendent of the Yellowstone National Park to the Secretary of the Interior, 1889* (Washington, DC: GPO, 1889): 11–12; Capt. George S. Anderson, *Report of the Acting Superintendent of the Yellowstone National Park to the Secretary of the Interior, 1895* (Washington, DC: GPO, 1895): 6; Lt. Col. Philip Reade, Inspector General Department of Dakota, to Adjutant General, Department of Dakota, June 10, 1901, Annual Inspection of Fort Yellowstone, WY, 1901, RG 159, NARA, 24.

4. Maj. Samuel W. Miller, Inspector General United States Army to Maj. Gen. Frederick C. Ainsworth, Adjutant General United States Army, November 20, 1908, in United States Department of War, Records of United States Continental Commands 1821–1920, Fort Yellowstone, WY, Letters Received, NARA, RG 393, 2, 5, 9–10, 16.

5. Post Returns, Fort Yellowstone 1900–1915, Adjutant Generals Office, RG 94, US Army, US Military Post Returns, 1800–1916, Fort Yellowstone, WY, NARA; Robert Fantina, *Desertion and the American Soldier, 1776–2006* (New York: Algora, 2007), 216–217; testimony of Judson Conoley, October 3, 1906, in United States Department

of the Interior, Records of the Judge Advocate General, Court-Martial Case Files and Related Records, NARA, RG 153, General Court-Martial of Judson Conoley, 3.

6. Edward M. Offley, Diary, VF, YNPL, Gardiner, MT, 18.

7. Testimony of Frank Anderson, November 28, 1913, in Court-Martial Case Files, RG 153, General Court-Martial of Frank Anderson, 5.

8. Testimony of Richard Condus, December 3, 1912, in Court-Martial Case Files, RG 153, General Court-Martial of Richard Condus, 8–9.

9. Letter of J. F. and Coral Paul Willis to Nathan Willis, May 11, 1911, YNPL, Accession Number 92-70.

10. Testimony of Sgt. Frank Maricle, March 30, 1904, in Court-Martial Case Files, RG 153, General Court-Martial of Charlie Altvater, 9.

11. Testimony of Second Lt. Robert L. Lounsbury, March 15, 1912; testimony of Sgt. John Cahill, December 8, 1911, in Court-Martial Case Files, RG 153, General Court-Martial of George Collins, 4–6.

12. Miller to Ainsworth, November 20, 1908, in United States Department of War, Records of United States Continental Commands 1821–1920, Fort Yellowstone, WY, Letters Received, NARA, RG 393, 15.

13. Miller to Ainsworth, in Letters Received, RG 393, 10–12.

14. Inquirer, "Wants to Know," *Wonderland* (Gardiner, MT), June 18, 1903, 2.

15. L.S.T., "Wants Some Law and Order," *Wonderland* (Gardiner, Mont.), October 11, 1902.

16. L.S.T., "Wants Some Law and Order."

17. Testimony of Adelaide Lester and Myrtle Gregg, July 10, 1912, in Court-Martial Case Files, RG 153, General Court-Martial of Pvt. Laurence E. Moon, 86–92.

18. Testimony of Lester and Gregg, RG 153, Court-Martial of Pvt. Laurence Moon, 10–12, 15.

19. Herbert Angelo, Diary, May 1901, VF, YNPL, Gardiner, MT, 7.

20. Angelo, Diary, June 2, 1902, 58; Mode Wineman, typed manuscript, VF, YNPL, Gardiner, MT4.

21. Both political elites and the public in general saw the mission of the US military as changing significantly between 1890 and 1910. It became less an instrument for Manifest Destiny than a more imperial force emphasizing the cultural and economic "White Man's Burden" with the motivation to spread American ideals globally. Allan Millet and Peter Maslowski, *For the Common Defense: A Military History of the United States from 1607–2012*, 3rd ed. (New York: Free Press, 2012), 264–265, 275, 317–318.

22. Miller to Ainsworth, November 20, 1908, in Letters Received, RG 393, 15.

23. Maj. John Pitcher, Addendum, in Inspection Report 1902.

24. Rudyard Kipling, *From Sea to Sea: Letters of Travel* (New York: Doubleday & McClure, 1899), 2: 91.

25. Richard Bartlett, *Yellowstone: A Wilderness Besieged* (Tucson: University of Arizona Press, 1985), 47; Kevin Adams, *Class and Race in the Frontier Army: Military Life in the West, 1870-1890* (Norman: University of Oklahoma Press, 2009), 144–145; Kipling, *From Sea to Sea*, 91; Everett Judson, "A Report of the Sanitary Survey of

the Water Supplies of Yellowstone National Park, June 1918," YELL-01528, Gardiner, MT: YNPA, 1; Bartlett, *Yellowstone*, 175, 186; Haines, *Yellowstone Story*, 2: 112, 136.

26. Bartlett, *Yellowstone*, 274; William F. Gossel to President William Howard Taft, May 10, 1909, in United States Department of the Interior, Yellowstone National Park Army Era Records, Complaints 1909–1914, Gardiner, MT: YNPA, Letter Box 92; according to the *Butte Daily Post*, May 24, 1917, Gossel was elected to the Sick Committee of the Local 126; Maj. H. C. Benson to the Secretary of the Interior, May 27, 1909, Complaints 1909–1914, Letter Box 92; Bartlett, *Yellowstone*, 186; Haines, *Yellowstone Story*, 2: 112. Child, however, ultimately realized that he needed to soften this outlook because over time more people were able to afford the camping system and there was significant profit to be made there; he began buying controlling stock in some companies as early as 1906.

27. Georgina Synge, *A Ride through Wonderland* (London: Sampson, Low, Marston, 1892), 60.

28. United States Secretary of the Interior, *Rules, Regulations, and Instructions for the Information and Guidance of Officers and Enlisted Men of the United States Army, and of the Scouts Doing Duty in the Yellowstone National Park* (Washington, DC: GPO, 1907), 21; Park Order No. 8, June 1, 1914, in United States Department of War, Records of United States Continental Commands 1821–1920, Fort Yellowstone, WY, Park Orders, NARA, RG 393; Col. J. L. Chamberlain, Inspector General, Western Department, to Commanding Officer, Fort Yellowstone, Wyoming, August 24, 1914, in Letters Received, RG 393.

29. Adams, *Class and Race*, 144–145, 134, 154–162; quoted in Elizabeth Watry and Lee Whittlesey, *Images of America: Fort Yellowstone* (Charleston, SC: Arcadia, 2012), 43; Miller to Ainsworth, Nov. 20, 1908, in Letters Received, RG 393, 10.

30. Adams, *Class and Race*, 78.

31. Summary Court-Martial of Pvt. Albert Beagle, n.d. in United States Department of War, Records of United States Continental Commands 1821–1920, Fort Yellowstone, WY, Summary Court-Martial Records, NARA, RG 393.

32. Summary Court-Martial of Pvt. John Gearin, August 10, 1912, in Summary Court-Martial Records, RG 393.

33. Kenneth Karsmizki, *Fountain Soldier Station (48YE727): Report of Research and Mitigation Prepared for the National Park Service, Rocky Mountain Region* (Bozeman, MT: Museum of the Rockies, 2001): 116–117; Summary Court-Martial of Pvt. William Wencil, July 29, 1912; Summary Court-Martial of Pvt. John Kane, July 29, 1912; Summary Court-Martial of Pvt. Martin Lilienthal, July 29, 1912, in Summary Court-Martial Records, RG 393; Summary Court-Martial of Sgt. Richard J. Bohen, July 29, 1913, in Summary Court-Martial Records, RG 393.

34. Statement of Jerome Chapin, Esq. of Battle Creek, Michigan, July 23, 1907, in United States Department of the Interior, Yellowstone National Park Army Era Records, Letters Received, 1906–1909, Gardiner, MT: YNPA, Letter Box 15; the court-martial cases for drunkenness in Gardiner are very numerous, but see, for example, the summary court-martials of Wagoneer James Lewis, October 8, 1912; Pvt. Emil Hebding, May 18, 1911; Pvt. James McBee, January 1, 1911; Pvt. James Healey,

September 3, 1911, in Summary Court-Martial Records, RG 393; Pvt. Presley H. Vance, October 16, 1908; Pvt. Frank F. Monaghan, November 22, 1910, in Fort Yellowstone Cemetery Records, VF, YNPL, Gardiner, MT.

35. Adams, *Class and Race*, 118–119; Oliver Knight, *Life and Manners in the Frontier Army* (Norman: University of Oklahoma Press, 1978), 93; Robert Utley, *Life in Custer's Cavalry* (New Haven, CT: Yale University Press, 1977), 20, 94, 174.

36. *Rules, Regulations, and Instructions*, 12.

37. Joseph Joffe, "John W. Meldrum," *Annals of Wyoming* 13, no. 2 (April 1941): 109–110.

38. Receipts indicate that between April 1903 and August 1905, Major Pitcher ordered seven bottles of vermouth, sixteen bottles of Old Tom Gin, twenty-four bottles of Haut Sauterne wine, three cases of bitters, seven bottles of whiskey, twelve bottles of Riesling, two bottles of port wine, eighteen bottles of Mumm's Extra Dry Wine, one bottle of rum, twenty-five bottles of claret, and two bottles of burgundy, all delivered by the Yellowstone Park Association hotel's commissaries; receipts in Yellowstone Park Association to Maj. John Pitcher, April 1, 1903; May 2, 1903; August 31, 1903; February 1, 1904; April 30, 1904; June 30, 1904; July 31, 1904; August 19, 1905, United States Department of the Interior, Yellowstone National Park Army Era Records, Miscellaneous Receipts, etc. 1900–1905, Gardiner, MT: YNPA, Letter Box 88.

39. Danny Walker, *Faunal Remains from Three Military Soldier Stations, Yellowstone National Park, Wyoming* (Bozeman, MT: Museum of the Rockies, 1999), 5–7, 9–10. Report also included in Karzmiski, *Fountain Soldier Station (48YE727): Report of Research and Mitigation Prepared for the National Park Service, Rocky Mountain Region* (Bozeman, MT: Museum of the Rockies, 2001).

40. Offley, Diary/Letter, October 4, 1900, 25, 26, 30; Summary Court-Martial of Pvt. Amil Moravek, July 14, 1913, in Summary Court-Martial Records, RG 393.

41. Karsmizki, *Fountain Flats*, 107–109, 114; Summary Court-Martial of Pvt. Amil Moravek, July 14, 1913, in Summary Court-Martial Records, RG 393; D.W. Spaulding to Major Pitcher, February 5, 1902, in Letters A to E, Letter Box 15, YNPA; Romey to Pitcher, April 12, 1902, Romey to Pitcher, March 10, 1902, in Letters Received, Bound Volume III, YNPA.

42. *Red Lodge (MT) Pickett*, December 12, 1902.

43. *Livingston (MT) Post*, December 11, 1902; *Wonderland*, (Gardiner, MT), February 5, 1903.

44. *Red Lodge (MT) Pickett*, December 12, 1902; *Billings (MT) Gazette*, July 24, 1903; *Fort Benton (MT) River Press*, July 13, 1904.

45. Karl Jacoby, *Crimes against Nature: Squatters, Poachers, Thieves, and the Hidden History of American Conservation* (Berkeley: University of California Press, 2001), 110; Anon., "The Yellowstone Park," *Forest and Stream: A Journal of Outdoor Life, Travel, Nature Study, Shooting, Fishing, Yachting* 60 (January 17, 1903), 1; *Billings (MT) Gazette*, December 19, 1902; *Red Lodge (MT) Pickett*, December 19, 1902; Anon., "The Fullerton Park Criticisms," *Forest and Stream* 64, no. 4 (March 1905): 1.

46. For more on the social strains theories of criminology, see Albert Cohen,

*Delinquent Boys* (Glencoe, IL: Free Press, 1955); Richard Cloward, "Illegitimate Means, Anomie, and Deviant Behavior," *American Sociological Review* 24 (1959): 164–177; especially Steven Messner and Richard Rosenfeld, *Crime and the American Dream* (Belmont, CA: Wadsworth, 1997); Miller to Ainsworth, November 20, 1908, in Letters Received, RG 393, 13; Summary Court-Martial of Pvt. Frederick Moses, July 29, 1916, in Summary Court-Martial Records, RG 393.

47. Anon., "Every Inch a Soldier," *Sunset Magazine* (August 1913): 350–355; United States Military History Institute, "Army Officer—Records from the Adjutant General (Biographical Data)," YNPL, Gardiner, MT, VF; Harvey Meyerson, *Nature's Army: When Soldiers Fought for Yosemite* (Lawrence: University Press of Kansas, 2001), 166–169, 172–180; Army Officer—Biographical Data, 24.

48. Army Officer—Biographical Data, 25–26; Miller to Ainsworth, Nov. 20, 1908, in Letters Received, RG 393, 7. Major Miller's investigation also discovered that when soldiers reenlisted and were given their choice of duty, they preferred units stationed deeper in the park at the soldier stations because they were not under the supervision of commissioned officers. See Miller to Ainsworth, Nov. 20, 1908, in Letters Received, RG 393, 13.

49. Adams, *Class and Race*, 114; Miller to Ainsworth, Nov. 20, 1908, in Letters Received, RG 393, 15, 25–26.

50. Haines, *Yellowstone Story*, 2: 285–286; H. Duane Hampton, *How the U.S. Cavalry Saved Our National Parks* (Bloomington: Indiana University Press, 1971), 176–182.

51. Walter L. Fisher, "Introductory Remarks," in United States Department of the Interior, *Proceedings of the National Park Conference Held at the Yellowstone National Park, September 11 and 12, 1911* (Washington, DC: GPO, 1912), 3.

52. R. B. Marshall, "Park Administration," in *Proceedings of the National Park Conference Held in the Yellowstone National Park, September 11 and 12, 1911* (US Department of the Interior: GPO, 1912), 116.

53. Col. L. M. Brett, "Yellowstone National Park," in *National Park Conference 1911*, 154–155.

54. Col. L. M. Brett, in United States Department of the Interior, *Proceedings of the National Park Conference Held at Berkeley, California, March 11, 12, and 13, 1915* (Washington DC: GPO, 1916): 42–43; https://www.navycs.com/charts/1908-military-pay-chart.html; Brett, *National Park Conference 1915*, 43–47.

## CHAPTER FIVE: "PETTY GRIEVANCES"

1. United States Department of the Interior, Yellowstone National Park Army Era Records. Monthly Reports, Sylvan Pass Weekly Station Log (hereafter Sylvan Pass Weekly Log), July 1910—January 1916, Gardiner, MT: YNPA, Box 126, March 31, 1912; "Insubordinate Soldiers Shot Down by Officer: Pvt. Frank Cunningham Seriously Hurt," *Park County (WY) Enterprise*, March 31, 1912; testimony of Pvt. William Mutch, General Court-Martial of Clarence A. Brittain, in United States Department

of War, Records of the Judge Advocate General, Court-Martial Case Files, NARA, Washington, DC, RG 153, 53.

2. Testimony of Mutch, General Court-Martial of Clarence A. Brittain, in Court-Martial Case Files, RG 153, 34.

3. "Cunningham Dies from Wound and Carroll Will Lose His Left Arm," *Park County Enterprise*, April 3, 1912; testimony of Capt. Robert Foy, General Court-Martial of Clarence A. Brittain, in Court-Martial Case Files, RG 153, 5–6; testimony of Pvt. Alexander Nelson, General Court-Martial of Clarence A. Brittain, in Court-Martial Case Files, RG 153, 246; testimony of Tex Holm, General Court-Martial of Clarence A. Brittain, in Court-Martial Case Files, RG 153, 271; testimony of Mutch, General Court-Martial of Clarence A. Brittain, in Court-Martial Case Files, RG 153, 82.

4. Maj. Gen. Fredrick C. Ainsworth, Adjutant General's Office United States Army, to Maj. Samuel W. Miller, Inspector General, October 2, 1908, in United States Department of War, Records of the Adjutant General's Office, Letters Sent, NARA, RG 94, 13; testimony of Mutch, General Court-Martial of Clarence A. Brittain, in Court-Martial Case Files, RG 153, 54; testimony of Foy, General Court-Martial of Clarence A. Brittain, in Court-Martial Case Files, RG 153, 293; testimony of Pvt. Frank Carroll, General Court-Martial of Clarence A. Brittain, in Court-Martial Case Files, RG 153, 87; testimony of Carroll, General Court-Martial of Clarence A. Brittain, in Court-Martial Case Files, RG 153, 82; testimony of Pvt. James May, General Court-Martial of Clarence A. Brittain, in Court-Martial Case Files, RG 153, 209.

5. Testimony of Holm, General Court-Martial of Clarence A. Brittain, in Court-Martial Case Files, RG 153, 271; testimony of Carroll, General Court-Martial of Clarence A. Brittain, in Court-Martial Case Files, RG 153, 87; testimony of Carroll, General Court-Martial of Clarence A. Brittain, in Court-Martial Case Files, RG 153, 88; testimony of Foy, General Court-Martial of Clarence A. Brittain, in Court-Martial Case Files, RG 153, 293; testimony of May, General Court-Martial of Clarence A. Brittain, in Court-Martial Case Files, RG 153, 171.

6. Testimony of Foy, General Court-Martial of Clarence A. Brittain, in Court-Martial Case Files, RG 153, 263; testimony of Holm, General Court-Martial of Clarence A. Brittain, in Court-Martial Case Files, RG 153, 271; testimony of Jack Winter, General Court-Martial of Clarence A. Brittain, in Court-Martial Case Files, RG 153, 320; "Insubordinate Soldiers Shot Down by Officer: Pvt. Frank Cunningham Seriously Hurt," *Park County Enterprise*, March 30, 1912; testimony of Mutch, General Court-Martial of Clarence A. Brittain, in Court-Martial Case Files, RG 153, 69; testimony of May, General Court-Martial of Clarence A. Brittain, in Court-Martial Case Files, RG 153, 231; testimony of Carroll, General Court-Martial of Clarence A. Brittain, in Court-Martial Case Files, RG 153, 155; testimony of Mutch, General Court-Martial of Clarence A. Brittain, in Court-Martial Case Files, RG 153, 105; testimony of Carroll, General Court-Martial of Clarence A. Brittain, in Court-Martial Case Files, RG 153, 87; testimony of May, General Court-Martial of Clarence A. Brittain, in Court-Martial Case Files, RG 153, 163; testimony of Jack Winter, General Court-Martial of Clarence A. Brittain, in Court-Martial Case Files, RG 153, 320; testimony of Mutch, General Court-Martial of Clarence A. Brittain, in Court-Martial Case Files, RG

153, 37; testimony of May, General Court-Martial of Clarence A. Brittain, in Court-Martial Case Files, RG 153, 163; testimony of Mutch, General Court-Martial of Clarence A. Brittain, in Court-Martial Case Files, RG 153, 37; testimony of Carroll, General Court-Martial of Clarence A. Brittain, in Court-Martial Case Files, RG 153, 160; testimony of Sgt. Clarence A. Brittain, General Court-Martial of Clarence A. Brittain, in Court-Martial Case Files, RG 153, 350; testimony of Carroll, General Court-Martial of Clarence A. Brittain, in Court-Martial Case Files, RG 153, 159.

7. Testimony of Mutch, General Court-Martial of Clarence A. Brittain, in Court-Martial Case Files, RG 153, 5; testimony of Brittain, General Court-Martial of Clarence A. Brittain, in Court-Martial Case Files, RG 153, 339.

8. United States Secretary of the Interior, *Rules, Regulations and Instructions for the Information and Guidance of Officers and Enlisted Men of the United States Army, and of the Scouts Doing Duty in the Yellowstone National Park* (Washington, DC: Government Printing Office, 1907), 29–30.

9. Testimony of Foy, General Court-Martial of Clarence A. Brittain, in Court-Martial Case Files, RG 153, 6.

10. Testimony of Brittain, General Court-Martial of Clarence A. Brittain, in Court-Martial Case Files, RG 153, 362.

11. Testimony of Mutch, General Court-Martial of Clarence A. Brittain, in Court-Martial Case Files, RG 153, 37; testimony of Carroll, General Court-Martial of Clarence A. Brittain, in Court-Martial Case Files, RG 153, 160; testimony of Brittain, General Court-Martial of Clarence A. Brittain, in Court-Martial Case Files, RG 153, 350.

12. Summary Court-Martial of Daniel Becker; Summary Court-Martial of James Gearin; Summary Court-Martial of James Daley; Summary Court-Martial of George Collins, in United States Department of War, Records of United States Continental Commands 1821–1920, Fort Yellowstone, WY, Summary Court-Martial Records, Fort Yellowstone, NARA, RG 393; Summary Court-Martial of James Gearin, in Summary Court-Martial Records, RG 393; Summary Court-Martial of Van Sheffield, in Summary Court-Martial Records, RG 393; Clara Green, Diary, VF, YNPL, Gardiner, MT, July 19, 1892, and July 25, 1892, 14.

13. Testimony of Pvt. Oliver Jordway, General Court-Martial of Clarence A. Brittain, in Court-Martial Case Files, RG 153, 234.

14. Testimony of Carroll, General Court-Martial of Clarence A. Brittain, in Court-Martial Case Files, RG 153, 121; testimony of Brittain, General Court-Martial of Clarence A. Brittain, in Court-Martial Case Files, RG 153, 367; testimony of May, General Court-Martial of Clarence A. Brittain, in Court-Martial Case Files, RG 153, 223; testimony of Brittain, General Court-Martial of Clarence A. Brittain, in Court-Martial Case Files, RG 153, 367; testimony of Carroll, General Court-Martial of Clarence A. Brittain, in Court-Martial Case Files, RG 153, 121; testimony of Carroll, General Court-Martial of Clarence A. Brittain, in Court-Martial Case Files, RG 153, 224.

15. Testimony of Brittain, General Court-Martial of Clarence A. Brittain, in Court-Martial Case Files, RG 153, 367.

16. Testimony of Mutch, General Court-Martial of Clarence A. Brittain, in Court-Martial Case Files, RG 153, 82; testimony of Jordway, General Court-Martial of Clarence A. Brittain, in Court-Martial Case Files, RG 153, 235.

17. Testimony of Carroll, General Court-Martial of Clarence A. Brittain, in Court-Martial Case Files, RG 153, 123; testimony of Mutch, General Court-Martial of Clarence A. Brittain, in Court-Martial Case Files, RG 153, 34.

18. Testimony of Jack Winter, General Court-Martial of Clarence A. Brittain, in Court-Martial Case Files, RG 153, 318.

19. Testimony of Millie Winter, General Court-Martial of Clarence A. Brittain, in Court-Martial Case Files, RG 153, 324.

20. Testimony of Millie Winter, General Court-Martial of Clarence A. Brittain, in Court-Martial Case Files, RG 153, 324.

21. Testimony of Jack Winter, General Court-Martial of Clarence A. Brittain, in Court-Martial Case Files, RG 153, 318–319.

22. Testimony of Foy, General Court-Martial of Clarence A. Brittain, in Court-Martial Case Files, RG 153, 9.

23. Testimony of Jack Winter, General Court-Martial of Clarence A. Brittain, in Court-Martial Case Files, RG 153, 311.

24. Testimony of Carroll, General Court-Martial of Clarence A. Brittain, in Court-Martial Case Files, RG 153, 88, 104–105.

25. Testimony of May, General Court-Martial of Clarence A. Brittain, in Court-Martial Case Files, RG 153, 188; testimony of Mutch, General Court-Martial of Clarence A. Brittain, in Court-Martial Case Files, RG 153, 29; Circular, August 8, 1902, in United States Department of the Interior, Yellowstone National Park Army Era Records, Circulars and Other Instructions to Stations, Gardiner, MT: YNPA, bound vol. 239; testimony of Lt. Col. L. M. Brett, General Court-Martial of Clarence A. Brittain, in Court-Martial Case Files, RG 153, 311.

26. Testimony of Brett, General Court-Martial of Clarence A. Brittain, in Court-Martial Case Files, RG 153, 311–312.

27. Testimony of Brett, General Court-Martial of Clarence A. Brittain, in Court-Martial Case Files, RG 153, 311–313; testimony of Carroll, General Court-Martial of Clarence A. Brittain, in Court-Martial Case Files, RG 153, 117; testimony of Foy, General Court-Martial of Clarence A. Brittain, in Court-Martial Case Files, RG 153, 256.

28. Testimony of Holm, General Court-Martial of Clarence A. Brittain, in Court-Martial Case Files, RG 153, 269.

29. Testimony of C. A. Richardson, General Court-Martial of Clarence A. Brittain, in Court-Martial Case Files, RG 153, 273–274.

30. Pvts. Conely, Passar, Giles, and Foreland to Commanding Officer, Fort Yellowstone, in United States Department of the Interior, Yellowstone National Park Army Era Records, Employees, Jan. 1, 1904–Dec. 31, 1907, Gardiner, MT, YNPA, Letter Box 14; Post Returns, September and October 1904, in United States Department of War, Records of the Adjutant General's Office, Post Returns, Fort Yellowstone, WY, 1886–1915, RG 94, NARA, Washington, DC .

31. Testimony of May, General Court-Martial of Clarence A. Brittain, in Court-Martial Case Files, RG 153, 163.

32. Testimony of Carroll, General Court-Martial of Clarence A. Brittain, in Court-Martial Case Files, RG 153, 87; testimony of May, General Court-Martial of Clarence A. Brittain, in Court-Martial Case Files, RG 153, 163; testimony of May, General Court-Martial of Clarence A. Brittain, in Court-Martial Case Files, RG 153, 163; testimony of Mutch, General Court-Martial of Clarence A. Brittain, in Court-Martial Case Files, RG 153, 69; testimony of Carroll, General Court-Martial of Clarence A. Brittain, in Court-Martial Case Files, RG 153, 87.

33. Report for Week of November 12, 1911, in Sylvan Pass Weekly Log, Box 126; testimony of Foy, General Court-Martial of Clarence A. Brittain, in Court-Martial Case Files, RG 153, 258, 276.

34. Lawrence A. Palinkas, "On the Ice: Individual and Group Adaptation in Antarctica." Unpublished manuscript (2000), www.bec.ucla.edu/papers/Palinkas_On_The_Ice.pdf; H. Lester Reed et al., "Changes in Serum Triodothyronine (T3) Kinetics after Prolonged Antartic Residence: The Polar T3 Syndrome," *Journal of Clinical Endocrinology & Metabolism* 70, no. 4 (1990): 965.

35. Thomas M. Connery, "The Winter Tragedy of the Yellowstone," *Wide World: A Magazine for Everybody* (June 1919): 143.

36. Capt. George Anderson, *Report of the Acting Superintendent of the Yellowstone National Park to the Secretary of the Interior, 1895* (Washington, DC: GPO, 1895), 7.

37. Capt. George Anderson, *Report of the Acting Superintendent of the Yellowstone National Park to the Secretary of the Interior, 1898* (Washington, DC: GPO, 1898), 26; Edward H. Moorman, "Yellowstone Park Camps History," VF, YNPL, Gardiner, MT, 11.

38. Testimony of Mutch, General Court-Martial of Clarence A. Brittain, in Court-Martial Case Files, RG 153, 56; testimony of Carroll, General Court-Martial of Clarence A. Brittain, in Court-Martial Case Files, RG 153, 90.

39. Weekly Reports, October 1911 to March 1912, in Sylvan Pass Weekly Log, Box 126.

40. Testimony of Carroll, General Court-Martial of Clarence A. Brittain, in Court-Martial Case Files, RG 153, 157.

41. Testimony of May, General Court-Martial of Clarence A. Brittain, in Court-Martial Case Files, RG 153, 180; March 8 must be the date in question as that is the only listing showing May and Cunningham as having patrolled together; Report for Week of March 9, 1912, in Sylvan Pass Weekly Log.

42. Testimony of Mutch, General Court-Martial of Clarence A. Brittain, in Court-Martial Case Files, RG 153, 46.

43. Testimony of Brittain, General Court-Martial of Clarence A. Brittain, in Court-Martial Case Files, RG 153, 348.

44. Testimony of Winter, General Court-Martial of Clarence A. Brittain, in Court-Martial Case Files, RG 153, 320.

45. Testimony of Foy, General Court-Martial of Clarence A. Brittain, in Court-Martial Case Files, RG 153, 260.

46. Testimony of Winter, General Court-Martial of Clarence A. Brittain, in Court-Martial Case Files, RG 153, 323.

47. Testimony of May, General Court-Martial of Clarence A. Brittain, in Court-Martial Case Files, RG 153, 231–232; testimony of Brittain, General Court-Martial of Clarence A. Brittain, in Court-Martial Case Files, RG 153, 348; testimony of Foy, General Court-Martial of Clarence A. Brittain, in Court-Martial Case Files, RG 153, 260; Sylvan Pass Daily Log Book 1903–1924, March 31, 1912, Soldier Stations and Snowshoe Cabins Records, YNPA; "Insubordinate Soldiers Shot Down by Officer: Pvt. Frank Cunningham Seriously Hurt," *Park County Enterprise*, March 31, 1912.

48. Testimony of Mutch, General Court-Martial of Clarence A. Brittain, in Court-Martial Case Files, RG 153, 36.

49. Testimony of Mutch, General Court-Martial of Clarence A. Brittain, in Court-Martial Case Files, RG 153, 37; testimony of Brittain, General Court-Martial of Clarence A. Brittain, in Court-Martial Case Files, RG 153, 351.

50. The actual account of the confrontation is a conglomeration of testimony taken from the surviving members of the Sylvan Pass soldier station. On the whole, the testimony agrees with only slight variations in dialogue, which are not footnoted. The accounts can be found in the following testimony in the General Court-Martial of Clarence A. Brittain, in Court-Martial Case Files, RG 153: Mutch, 11–23; Carroll, 90–101, 107–111; May, 168–174; Brittain, 353–361, 374–379.

51. Testimony of Foy, General Court-Martial of Clarence A. Brittain, in Court-Martial Case Files, RG 153, 285.

52. Testimony of May, General Court-Martial of Clarence A. Brittain, in Court-Martial Case Files, RG 153, 201.

53. Testimony of Mutch and May, General Court-Martial of Clarence A. Brittain, in Court-Martial Case Files, RG 153, 62.

54. Testimony of Mutch and May, General Court-Martial of Clarence A. Brittain, in Court-Martial Case Files, RG 153, 191; Sylvan Pass Weekly Log, March 30, 1912, Box 126.

55. Testimony of Mutch, General Court-Martial of Clarence A. Brittain, in Court-Martial Case Files, RG 153, 30; Testimony of May, General Court-Martial of Clarence A. Brittain, in Court-Martial Case Files, RG 153, 70.

56. Testimony of Mutch, General Court-Martial of Clarence A. Brittain, in Court-Martial Case Files, RG 153, 33.

57. "Cunningham Dies from Wound and Carroll Will Lose His Left Arm," *Park County Enterprise*, April 3, 1912.

58. Testimony of Mutch, General Court-Martial of Clarence A. Brittain, in Court-Martial Case Files, RG 153, 30, 53; "Cunningham Dies from Wound," *Park County Enterprise*, April 3, 1912.

59. Testimony of Foy, General Court-Martial of Clarence A. Brittain, in Court-Martial Case Files, RG 153, 8.

60. Testimony of Foy, General Court-Martial of Clarence A. Brittain, in Court-Martial Case Files, RG 153, 9–10.

61. "One Soldier Dead and One Will Be Badly Crippled by Shot of the Sergeant," *Northern Wyoming Herald (Cody, WY)*, April 5, 1912.

62. "Cunningham Dies from Wound," *Park County Enterprise*, April 3, 1912.

63. It is not clear at exactly what time they adjourned to deliberate. The final two witness were called at 8:00 a.m. on May 13. They testified, then both sides presented their lengthy summaries. The court adjourned but reconvened at 9:07 a.m. with the verdict. It took only minutes to reach a decision. General Court-Martial of Clarence A. Brittain, in Court-Martial Case Files, RG 153, 395–409.

64. Connery, "Winter Tragedy," 147.

65. Frederick A. Cook, *Through the First Antarctic Night, 1898–1899* (Pittsburgh, PA: Polar, 1909), 282.

66. William Haythorn, "Interpersonal Stress in Isolated Groups," in *Social and Psychological Factors in Stress*, ed. J. McGrath (New York: Holt, Rinehart & Winston, 1970), 159–176; Robert Bechtel and Alan Berning, "The Third-Quarter Phenomenon: Do People Experience Discomfort after Stress Has Passed?" in *From Antarctica to Outer Space: Life in Isolation and Confinement*, ed. Albert Harrison (New York: Springer Verlag, 1991), 261–266; Jack Stuster, *Bold Endeavors: Lessons from Polar and Space Exploration* (Annapolis, MD: Naval Institute Press, 1996), 303–322; Lawrence A. Palinkas, "Psychological Issues in Long-term Space Flight: Overview," *Gravitational and Space Biology Bulletin* 14, no. 2 (June 2001): 31.

67. Palinkas, "Psychological Issues," 26.

68. Lawrence Palinkas, Lester Reed, and Nhan Do, "Association between Polar T3 Syndrome and the Winter-Over Syndrome in Antarctica," *Antarctic Journal of the United States* 32 (1997): 112–114.

69. Bechtel and Berning, "Third-Quarter Phenomenon," 266.

70. T. J. McFadden et al., "Predicting Astronauts' Effectiveness: A Multivariate Approach," *Aviation, Space, and Environmental Medicine* 65 (1994): 904–909.

71. Palinkas, "Psychological Issues," 23.

72. Palinkas, "Psychological Issues," 30.

73. P. D. Nelson, "Psychological Aspects of Antarctic Living," *Military Medicine* 130, no. 5 (1965): 488–489; G. M. Sandal, et al., "Psychological Reactions during Polar Expeditions and Isolation in Hyperbaric Chambers," *Aviation, Space, and Environmental Medicine* 67 (1995): 228; N. Kanas, et al., "Crew Member Interactions during a Mir Space Station Simulation," *Aviation, Space, and Environmental Medicine* 67 (1996): 974–975.

74. Palinkas "Psychological Issues," 26; H. S. F. Cooper, *A House in Space* (New York: Holt, Rinehart & Winston (1976), 23–25, 82–84.

75. Stuster, *Bold Endeavors*, 50–52; Bryan Burrough, *Dragonfly: An Epic Adventure of Survival in Outer Space* (New York: Harper Collins, 1995), 511–516.

76. "One Soldier Dead," *Northern Wyoming Herald*, April 5, 1912.

## CONCLUSION: "PATRIOTISM . . . AND THE LOVE OF NATURE"

1. Quoted in Haines, *Yellowstone Story*, 2: 284; R. B. Marshall, "Park Administration," in United States Department of the Interior, *Proceedings of the National Park Conference Held at the Yellowstone National Park, September 11 and 12, 1911* (Washington, DC: GPO, 1912), 116; Col. L. M. Brett, "Yellowstone National Park," in ibid., 154–155; for details, see Kiki Rydell and Mary Culpin, *Managing the "Matchless Wonders": A History of Administrative Development in Yellowstone National Park, 1872–1965* (Yellowstone National Park, WY: National Park Service, Center for Resources, 2006), 52–74; Richard Bartlett, *Yellowstone: A Wilderness Besieged* (Tucson: University of Arizona Press, 1985), 281–308; Haines, *Yellowstone Story*, 2: 279–317; H. Duane Hampton, *How the U.S. Cavalry Saved Our National Parks* (Bloomington: Indiana University Press, 1971), 169–182.

2. Chief of Staff Office, Memorandum against Troops in Park, Feb. 11, 1914; Secretary of War to Secretary of Interior, March 3, 1914, Central Files 1907–1918, Records of the National Park Service, RG 79, NARA, College Park, MD.

3. Adolph Miller, Assistant to the Secretary of the Interior to J.E.B. Seely, Secretary of War, March 21, 1914, File "Troops Required in Park and Use of," Box A-7, YNPA; Lt. Col. Lloyd M. Brett, Acting Superintendent of Yellowstone National Park to Maj. Gen. J. Franklin Bell, Chief of Staff, January 14, 1914; J.E.B. Seely, Secretary of War, to Franklin K. Lane, Secretary of the Interior, March 14, 1914, in United States Department of the Interior, Records of the National Park Service, 1939 Liquor Traffic, Parks, Reservations, and Antiquities, Yellowstone National Park, Central Files 1907–1918, RG 79, NARA, College Park, MD; Summary Court Martials, Troops 1 and 2 Yellowstone National Park Detachment, in United States Department of War, Records of United States Continental Commands 1821–1920, Fort Yellowstone, WY, Summary Court-Martial Records, Fort Yellowstone, NARA, RG 393; Summary Court-Martial of Pvt. George Miller, August 10, 1916, in Summary Court-Martial Records, RG 393.

4. Hampton, *How the Cavalry*, 181–182; General Order No. 2, October 1, 1918, in United States Department of War, Records of United States Continental Commands, Orders 1917–1918, Record Group 393, NARA, Washington, DC.

5. Chester Lindsley, *Annual Report of the Superintendent of National Parks to the Secretary of the Interior for the Fiscal Year Ended June 30, 1916* (Washington, DC: GPO, 1916), 13–14; Rydell and Culpin, *Matchless Wonders*, 57; interview with Horace Albright by Aubrey Haines, quoted in Haines, *Yellowstone Story*, 2: 289; Bartlett, *Yellowstone*, 288; Donald Swain, *Wilderness Defender: Horace M. Albright and Conservation* (Chicago: University of Chicago Press, 1968), 110–115, 117–140; John Miles, *Wilderness in National Parks: Playground or Preserve* (Seattle: University of Washington Press, 2011), 33.

6. Hampton, *How the Cavalry*, 173.

# Bibliography

## GOVERNMENT DOCUMENTS


Anderson, George S., Capt. *Report of the Acting Superintendent of the Yellowstone National Park to the Secretary of the Interior, 1893.* Washington, DC: GPO, 1893.

———. *Report of the Acting Superintendent of the Yellowstone National Park to the Secretary of the Interior, 1894.* Washington, DC: GPO, 1894.

———. *Report of the Acting Superintendent of the Yellowstone National Park to the Secretary of the Interior, 1895.* Washington, DC: GPO, 1895.

———. *Report of the Acting Superintendent of the Yellowstone National Park to the Secretary of the Interior, 1896.* Washington, DC: GPO, 1896.

———. *Report of the Acting Superintendent of the Yellowstone National Park to the Secretary of the Interior, 1898.* Washington, DC: GPO, 1898.

Boutelle, Frazier, Capt. *Report of the Acting Superintendent of the Yellowstone National Park to the Secretary of the Interior, 1890.* Washington, DC: GPO 1890.

———. *Report of the Acting Superintendent of the Yellowstone National Park to the Secretary of the Interior, 1891.* Washington, DC: GPO 1891.

Cole, Cornelius. To Secretary of the Interior Carl Schurz, Feb. 21, 1878, in 45th Cong., 2d Sess., House, Ex. Doc. No. 75, Apr. 11, 1878.

*Congressional Record,* 47th Cong., 2nd Sess., XIV, Part 4. Washington, DC: GPO, 1881.

*Congressional Record,* 47th Cong., 2nd Sess., XIV, Part 4. Washington, DC: GPO, 1883.

*Congressional Record,* 49th Cong., 1st Sess., XCII, Part 7. Washington, DC: GPO, 1886.

*Congressional Record,* 49th Cong., 1st Sess., XCII, Part 8. Washington, DC: GPO, 1887.

Crosby, J. S. "Report of the Governor of Montana Territory." In *Department of Interior Report, 1884.* Vol. 2. Washington, DC: GPO, 1885, 562.

Erwin, James B., Capt. *Report of the Acting Superintendent of the Yellowstone National Park to the Secretary of the Interior, 1898.* Washington, DC: GPO, 1898.

Harris, Moses, Capt. *Report of the Acting Superintendent of the Yellowstone National Park to the Secretary of the Interior, 1886.* Washington, DC: GPO, 1886.

———. *Report of the Acting Superintendent of the Yellowstone National Park to the Secretary of the Interior, 1887.* Washington, DC: GPO, 1887.

———. *Report of the Acting Superintendent of the Yellowstone National Park to the Secretary of the Interior, 1888.* Washington, DC: GPO, 1888.

———. *Report of the Acting Superintendent of the Yellowstone National Park to the Secretary of the Interior, 1889.* Washington, DC: GPO, 1889.

Judson, Everett. "A Report of the Sanitary Survey of the Water Supplies of Yellowstone National Park, June 1918." YELL-01528. Gardiner, MT: Yellowstone National Park Archives.

Lindsley, Chester. *Annual Report of the Superintendent of National Parks to the Secretary of the Interior for the Fiscal Year Ended June 30, 1916.* Washington, DC: GPO, 1916.

Pitcher, John, Maj. *Report of the Acting Superintendent of the Yellowstone National Park to the Secretary of the Interior, 1904.* Washington, DC: GPO, 1904.

Reade, Philip, Lt. Col. Annual Inspection Report of Fort Yellowstone 1901, Records of the Office of the Inspector General (Army), Records of the Office of the Inspector General (Army), Inspection Reports, 1891–1913, Record Group 159, United States Department of War, National Archives and Records Administration, Washington, DC.

Reynolds, Alfred, Maj. Annual Inspection Report of Fort Yellowstone 1902, Records of the Office of the Inspector General (Army), Records of the Office of the Inspector General (Army), Inspection Reports, 1891–1913, Record Group 159, United States Department of War, National Archives and Records Administration, Washington, DC.

United States Congress. *The Congressional Globe: Containing the Debates and Proceedings of the Second Session of the Forty-First Congress*, Washington, DC: John C. Rivers Publishers, 1871, 687–699.

———. H. R. Rep. No. 49-1076, at 248 (1885).

———. H. R. Rep. No. 52-1956, at 272–275 (1891).

———. S. Rep. No. 47-911 (1881).

United States Department of the Army. *Cavalry Drill Regulations, United States Army.* Adopted Oct. 3, 1891. Washington, DC: GPO, 1891.United States Department of the Interior, Patents and Miscellaneous Division, Letters Received, 1872–1882. Record Group 48. Washington, DC: National Archives and Record Administration.

———, ed. *Proceedings of the National Park Conference Held at the Yellowstone National Park, September 11 and 12, 1911.* Washington, DC: GPO, 1912.

———, ed. *Proceedings of the National Park Conference Held at Berkeley, California, March 11, 12, and 13, 1915.* Washington, DC: GPO, 1916.

———. Records of the National Park Service, 1939 Liquor Traffic, Parks, Reservations, and Antiquities, Yellowstone National Park, Central Files 1907–1918. Record Group 79. College Park, MD: National Archives and Record Administration.

———. Yellowstone National Park Army Era Records. Circulars and Other Instructions to Stations. Gardiner, MT: Yellowstone National Park Archives.

———. Yellowstone National Park Army Era Records. Complaints 1909–1914. Gardiner, MT: Yellowstone National Park Archives.

———. Yellowstone National Park Army Era Records. Employees, Jan. 1, 1898–Dec. 31, 1903. Gardiner, MT: Yellowstone National Park Archives.

———. Yellowstone National Park Army Era Records. Employees, Jan. 1, 1904–Dec. 31, 1907. Gardiner, MT: Yellowstone National Park Archives.

———. Yellowstone National Park Army Era Records. Journal of the Acting Superintendent, 1900–1903. Gardiner, MT: Yellowstone National Park Archives.

———. Yellowstone National Park Army Era Records. Letters, Employees, 1908–1917. Gardiner, MT: Yellowstone National Park Archives.

———. Yellowstone National Park Army Era Records. Letters, L–R, Jan. 1, 1892–Dec. 31, 1895. Gardiner, MT: Yellowstone National Park Archives.

———. Yellowstone National Park Army Era Records. Letters, S–Z, Jan. 1, 1894–Dec. 31, 1909. Gardiner, MT: Yellowstone National Park Archives.

———. Yellowstone National Park Army Era Records. Letters Received, Jan. 1, 1897 to May 31, 1899. Gardiner, MT: Yellowstone National Park Archives.

———. Yellowstone National Park Army Era Records. Letters Received, 1906–1909. Gardiner, MT: Yellowstone National Park Archives.

———. Yellowstone National Park Army Era Records. Letters Sent, 1886–1887. Gardiner, MT: Yellowstone National Park Archives.

———. Yellowstone National Park Army Era Records. Letters Sent, 1887–1899. Gardiner, MT: Yellowstone National Park Archives.

———. Yellowstone National Park Army Era Records. Letters Sent, 1889–1892. Gardiner, MT: Yellowstone National Park Archives.

———. Yellowstone National Park Army Era Records. Letters Sent, 1892–1894. Gardiner, MT: Yellowstone National Park Archives.

———. Yellowstone National Park Army Era Records. Letters Sent, 1894–1896. Gardiner, MT: Yellowstone National Park Archives.

———. Yellowstone National Park Army Era Records. Letters Sent, 1896–1899. Gardiner, MT: Yellowstone National Park Archives.

———. Yellowstone National Park Army Era Records. Letters Sent, 1899–1900. Gardiner, MT: Yellowstone National Park Archives.

———. Yellowstone National Park Army Era Records. Letters Sent, 1901–1902. Gardiner, MT: Yellowstone National Park Archives.

———. Yellowstone National Park Army Era Records. Miscellaneous Receipts, etc., 1900–1905. Gardiner, MT: Yellowstone National Park Archives.

———. Yellowstone National Park Army Era Records. Monthly Reports, Canyon Station, 1897. Gardiner, MT: Yellowstone National Park Archives.

———. Yellowstone National Park Army Era Records. Monthly Reports, Sylvan Pass Weekly Station Log, July 1910–January 1916. Gardiner, MT: Yellowstone National Park Archives.

———. Yellowstone National Park Army Era Records. Sylvan Pass Station Log, 1914–1924. Gardiner, MT: Yellowstone National Park Archives.

———. Yellowstone National Park Army Era Records. Property. Gardiner, MT: Yellowstone National Park Archives.

United States Department of War, Records of the Adjutant General's Office,

Letters Sent, Record Group 94. Washington, DC: National Archives and Record Administration.

———. Records of the Adjutant General's Office, Post Returns, Fort Yellowstone, WY, Record Group 94. Washington, DC: National Archives and Record Administration.

———. Records of the Office of the Secretary of War, General Correspondence, 1891–1913, Record Group 107. Washington, DC: National Archives and Record Administration.

———. Records of the Office of the Inspector General (Army), General Correspondence, 1894–1914, Record Group 159. Washington, DC: National Archives and Record Administration.

———. Records of the Office of the Inspector General (Army), Inspection Reports, 1891–1913, Record Group 159. Washington, DC: National Archives and Record Administration.

———. Records of the Judge Advocate General, Court-Martial Case Files and Related Records. Record Group 153. Washington, DC: National Archives and Record Administration.

———. Records of United States Continental Commands 1821–1920, Department of Dakota, Special Orders, 1866–1891, Record Group 393. Washington, DC: National Archives and Record Administration.

———. Records of United States Continental Commands 1821–1920, Fort Yellowstone, WY, General Orders and Memoranda 1910–1918, Record Group 393. Washington, DC: National Archives and Record Administration.

———. Records of United States Continental Commands 1821–1920, Fort Yellowstone, WY, Letters Sent, Record Group 393. Washington, DC: National Archives and Record Administration.

———. Records of United States Continental Commands 1821–1920, Fort Yellowstone, WY, Letters Received, Record Group 393. Washington, DC: National Archives and Record Administration.

———. Records of United States Continental Commands 1821–1920, Fort Yellowstone, WY, Orders 1915–1917, Record Group 393. Washington, DC: National Archives and Record Administration.

———. Records of United States Continental Commands 1821–1920, Fort Yellowstone, WY, Orders and Circulars, Record Group 393. Washington, DC: National Archives and Record Administration.

———. Records of United States Continental Commands 1821–1920, Fort Yellowstone, WY, Park Orders, Record Group 393. Washington, DC: National Archives and Record Administration.

———. Records of United States Continental Commands 1821–1920, Fort Yellowstone, WY, Special Orders, General Orders, and Circulars 1896–1902, Record Group 393. Washington, DC: National Archives and Record Administration.

———. Records of United States Continental Commands 1821–1920, Fort Yellowstone, WY, Summary Court-Martial Records, Fort Yellowstone, Record Group 393. Washington, DC: National Archives and Record Administration.

United States Military History Institute. "Army Officer—Records from the Adjutant General (Biographical Data)," Yellowstone National Park Library, Gardiner, MT. Vertical File.

United States Secretary of the Interior, *Rules, Regulations, and Instructions for the Information and Guidance of Officers and Enlisted Men of the United States Army, and of the Scouts Doing Duty in the Yellowstone National Park.* Washington, DC: GPO, 1907.

———. Office of the Secretary of Interior, Letters Received 1883–1884, National Archives and Record Administration, Washington, DC, Record Group 48.

______. National Park Service, Central Files 1907–1918, Records of the National Park Service, National Archives and Record Administration, College Park, MD, Record Group 79.

United States Statutes at Large, Vol. 17, Chap. 24, pp. 32–33. "An Act to set apart a certain Tract of Land lying near the Head-waters of the Yellowstone River as a public Park." [S. 392]

Wint, Theo J., Lt. Col. Annual Inspection Report of Fort Yellowstone 1899, Records of the Office of the Inspector General (Army), Inspection Reports, 1891–1913, Record Group 159, United States Department of War, National Archives and Records Administration, Washington, DC.

———. Annual Inspection Report of Fort Yellowstone 1900, Records of the Office of the Inspector General (Army), Inspection Reports, 1891–1913, Record Group 159, United States Department of War, National Archives and Records Administration, Washington, DC.

Young, Samuel M. B. *Report of the Superintendent of the Yellowstone National Park to the Secretary of the Interior, 1897.* Washington, DC: GPO, 1897.

———. *Report of the Superintendent of the Yellowstone National Park to the Secretary of the Interior, 1907.* Washington, DC: GPO, 1907.

## NONGOVERNMENT ARCHIVAL RESOURCES

Angelo, Herbert. Diary, Vertical File. Yellowstone National Park Library, Gardiner, MT.

Fort Yellowstone Cemetery Records. Vertical File. Yellowstone National Park Library, Gardiner, MT.

Green, Clara. Diary. Vertical File. Yellowstone National Park Library, Gardiner, MT.

Haynes-Arnold, Bessie. "Diary of Bessie Haynes Arnold, Fort Yellowstone, 1915." YNPL, VF.

———. "An Interview—1975," Vertical File. Yellowstone National Park Library, Gardiner, MT.

Marble, Charles ("Buckskin Charley"). "Fifty Years in and around Yellowstone Park." Typewritten manuscript. Theodore Roosevelt National Park. Theodore Roosevelt Digital Library. Dickinson State University. https://www.theodore-rooseveltcenter.org/Research/Collections?colID=c138.

Moorman, Edward H. "Yellowstone Park Camps History." Vertical File. Yellowstone National Park Library, Gardiner, MT.

Offley, Edward M. Diary. Vertical File. Yellowstone National Park Library, Gardiner, MT.

Whittaker, George. Diary, "Scout Diaries." Manuscript. Yellowstone National Park Archives, Gardiner, MT.

Willis, J. Frank. Letter to Son Nathan. Manuscripts (Willis), Rare Book Collection. Yellowstone National Park Archives, Gardiner, MT.

Wineman, Mode. Typed manuscript, 1908. Vertical File. Yellowstone National Park Library, Gardiner, MT.

## CONTEMPORARY NEWSPAPER AND MAGAZINE ARTICLES

Anon. "Every Inch a Soldier." *Sunset Magazine* (August 1913): 350–355.

Anon. "The Fullerton Park Criticisms." *Forest and Stream: A Journal of Outdoor Life, Travel, Nature Study, Shooting, Fishing, Yachting* 64, no. 4 (March 1905): 1.

Anon. "The Yellowstone Park." *Forest and Stream: A Journal of Outdoor Life, Travel, Nature Study, Shooting, Fishing, Yachting* 60, no. 17 (January 1903): 1.

Anon. "Scouts for Park Poachers," *Forest and Stream* 42 (June 30, 1884).

*Billings* (MT) *Gazette*, various issues.

*Butte* (MT) *Daily Post*, various issues.

Connery, Thomas M. "The Winter Tragedy of the Yellowstone." *Wide World: A Magazine for Everybody* (June 1919): 143–148.

*Fort Benton* (MT) *River Press*, various issues.

*Great Falls* (MT) *Tribune*, various issues.

Grinnell, George B. "Mr. Vest's Victory." *Forest and Stream: A Journal of Outdoor Life, Travel, Nature Study, Shooting, Fishing, Yachting* 20, no. 5 (March 8, 1883): 101.

*Helena* (MT) *Independent*, August 31, 1889.

Lindsley, Elmer. "A Winter Trip through the Yellowstone." *Harper's Weekly* 42 (January 19, 1898): 107.

*Livingston* (MT) *Enterprise*, various issues.

*Livingston* (MT) *Post*, various issues.

*Northern Wyoming Herald* (Cody, WY), various issues.

*Park County* (WY) *Enterprise*, various issues.

*Red Lodge* (MT) *Pickett*, various issues.

*Wonderland* (Gardiner, MT), various issues.

## SECONDARY SOURCES

Adams, Kevin. *Class and Race in the Frontier Army: Military Life in the West, 1870–1890*. Norman: University of Oklahoma Press, 2009.

Ammerman, David. *In the Common Cause: American Response to the Coercive Acts of 1774*. New York: Norton, 1974.

Anderson, Fred. *Crucible of War: The Seven Years' War and the Fate of Empire in British North America, 1754–1766*. New York: Vintage, 2001.

Bartlett, Richard. *Yellowstone: A Wilderness Besieged*. Tucson: University of Arizona Press, 1985.

Bechtel, Robert, and Alan Berning. "The Third-Quarter Phenomenon: Do People Experience Discomfort after Stress Has Passed?" In *From Antarctica to Outer Space: Life in Isolation and Confinement*, edited by Albert Harrison, 261–266. New York: Springer Verlag, 1991.

Becker, Theodore M. "The Place of Private Police in Society: An Area for Research in Social Sciences." *Social Problems* 21, no. 3 (1974): 438–453.

Bergey, Ellwood. *Why Soldiers Desert from the United States Army*. Philadelphia: William F. Fell, 1903.

Bradley, Mark L. *The Army and Reconstruction, 1865–1877*. Washington, DC: United States Army Center of Military History, 2015.

Brinkley, Douglas. *The Wilderness Warrior: Theodore Roosevelt and the Crusade for America*. New York: Harper Collins, 2009.

Brouse, Edwin C. *The U.S. Army and Constabulary Operations*. Leavenworth, KS: School of Advanced Military Studies, 2006.

Brucker, Gene. *Giovanni and Lusanna: Love and Marriage in Renaissance Florence*. Berkeley: University of California, 2004.

Bungaard, Axel. *Muscle and Manliness: The Rise of Sport in American Boarding Schools*. Syracuse, NY: Syracuse University Press, 2005.

Burrough, Bryan. *Dragonfly: An Epic Adventure of Survival in Outer Space*. New York: Harper Collins, 1995.

Chambers, John W., II. "The New Military History: Myth and Reality." *Journal of Military History* 55, no. 3 (1991): 395–406.

Childers, Thomas. *Soldier from the War Returning: The Greatest Generation's Troubled Homecoming from World War II*. New York: Mariner Books, 2010.

Chin, Gabrial. "The Voting Rights Act of 1867: The Constitutionality of Federal Regulations of Suffrage during Reconstruction." *North Carolina Law Review* 82 (2004): 1581–1610.

Chittenden, Hiram M. *The Yellowstone National Park: Historical and Descriptive, Illustrated with Maps, Views, and Portraits*. Cincinnati, OH: Robert Clarke, 1900.

Christie, Ian, and Benjamin Labaree. *Empire or Independence, 1760–1776*. New York: Norton, 1976.

Citino, Robert M. "Military Histories Old and New: A Reintroduction." *American Historical Review* 112, no. 4 (October 2007): 1070–1090.

Cloward, Richard. "Illegitimate Means, Anomie, and Deviant Behavior." *American Sociological Review* 24 (1959): 164–177.

Coffman, Edward M. "The New American Military History." *Military Affairs* 48, no. 1 (January 1984), 1–5.

Cohen, Albert. *Delinquent Boys*. Glencoe, IL: Free Press, 1955.

Cohen, Thomas V. *Love and Death in Renaissance Italy.* Chicago: University of Chicago Press, 2004.

Cook, Frederick A. *Through the First Antarctic Night, 1898–1899.* Pittsburgh, PA: Polar, 1909.

Cullum, George W. *Biographical Register of Officers and Graduates of the U.S. Military Academy at West Point, N.Y., from Its Establishment in 1802 to 1890; with Early History of the United States Military Academy by Brevet Major General George W. Cullum.* Vol. 6. Saginaw, MI: Seeman & Peters, 1901.

———. *Biographical Register of Officers and Graduates of the U.S. Military Academy at West Point, N.Y., from Its Establishment in 1802 to 1890; with Early History of the United States Military Academy by Brevet Major General George W. Cullum,* Vol. 5. Saginaw, MI: Seeman & Peters, 1910.

———. *Biographical Register of Officers and Graduates of the U.S. Military Academy at West Point, N.Y., from Its Establishment in 1802 to 1890; with Early History of the United States Military Academy by Brevet Major General George W. Cullum,* Vol. 6a. Saginaw, MI: Seeman & Peters, 1920.

———. *Biographical Register of Officers and Graduates of the U.S. Military Academy at West Point, N.Y., from Its Establishment in 1802 to 1890; with Early History of the United States Military Academy by Brevet Major General George W. Cullum,* Vol. 9. Saginaw, MI: Seeman & Peters, 1941.

Davis, Natalie Zemon. *The Return of Martin Guerre.* Cambridge, MA: Harvard University Press, 1983.

Degler, Carl. *In Search of Human Nature: The Decline and Revival of Darwinism in American Social Thought.* New York: Oxford University Press, 1991.

Dodd, David J. "Police Mentality and Behavior." *Issues in Criminology* 3, no. 1 (1967): 47–67.

Fantina, Robert. *Desertion and the American Soldier, 1776–2006.* New York: Algora, 2007.

Felson, Lawrence, and Marcus Cohen, "Human Ecology and Crime: A Routine Activity Approach." *Human Ecology* 8, no. 4 (1980): 380–406.

Fine, Gary A. "Enacting Norms: Mushrooming and the Culture of Expectations and Explanations." In *Social Norms,* edited by Michael Hechter and Karl-Dieter Opp, 139–164. New York: Russell Sage Foundation, 2001.

Foner, Eric. *Reconstruction: America's Unfinished Revolution, 1863–1877.* New York: Harper Collins, 1988.

Gigerenzer, Gerd, and Dan Goldstein. "Reasoning the Fast and Frugal Way: Models of Bounded Rationality." *Psychological Review* 103, no. 4 (1996): 650–669.

Ginzburg, Carlo. *The Cheese and the Worms: The Cosmos of a Sixteenth-Century Miller.* Translated by John and Anne Tedeschi. Baltimore: Johns Hopkins Press, 1980.

———. "The Philosopher and the Witches: An Experiment in Cultural History," *Acta-Ethnographica-Academiae-Scientiarum-Hungaricae* 37 (1991–1992): 283–292.

_______. "Just One Witness." In *Probing the Limits of Representation: Nazism and the "Final Solution."* Cambridge, MA: Harvard University Press, 1992.

Grant, Robert M. "Prospering in Dynamically-Competitive Environments: Organizational Capability as Knowledge Integration." *Organization Science* 7(4): 375–387.

Gruber, Ira. "The American Revolution as a Conspiracy: The British View." *William and Mary Quarterly* 26, no. 3 (1969): 360–372.

Haines, Aubrey L. "A Review of Certain Attempts to Make Adverse Use of Yellowstone National Park." Vertical File. Yellowstone National Park Library, Gardiner, MT. Undated.

———. *The Yellowstone Story.* 2 vols. Boulder: Yellowstone Library and Colorado Associate University Press, 1977.

Hampton, H. Duane. *How the U.S. Cavalry Saved Our National Parks.* Bloomington: Indiana University Press, 1971.

Harris, James R. "'What Really Interests Me Are the People': Edward M. Coffman on Soldiers, Scholars, and the New Military History." *Register of the Kentucky Historical Society* 99, no. 2 (Spring 2001): 123–152.

Haynes, Jack Ellis. *Haynes Official Guide: Yellowstone National Park: Descriptive, Geological, Historical.* St. Paul, MN: F. Jay Haynes, 1912.

———. *Yellowstone Stage Holdups.* Denver, CO: Brand Books, 1952.

Hays, Samuel. *Conservation and the Gospel of Efficiency: The Progressive Conservation Movement, 1890–1920.* Pittsburgh: University of Pittsburgh Press, 1959.

Haythorn, William. "Interpersonal Stress in Isolated Groups." In *Social and Psychological Factors in Stress*, edited by J. McGrath, 159–176. New York: Holt, Rinehart & Winston, 1970.

Haywood, C. Robert. *Victorian West: Class and Culture in Kansas Cattle Towns.* Lawrence: University Press of Kansas, 1991.

Holsinger, M. Paul. "Senator George Graham Vest and the 'Menace' of Mormonism, 1882–1887." *Missouri Historical Review* 65 (October 1970): 23–26.

Howe, Daniel. *Victorian America.* Philadelphia: University of Pennsylvania Press, 1976.

Hutton, Paul A. *Phil Sheridan and His Army.* Lincoln: University of Nebraska Press, 1989.

Iggers, George G. *Historiography in the Twentieth Century: From Scientific Objectivity to the Postmodern Challenge.* Hanover, NH: Wesleyan University Press, 1997.

Jacoby, Karl. *Crimes against Nature: Squatters, Poachers, Thieves, and the Hidden History of American Conservation.* Berkeley: University of California Press, 2001.

Jensen, Joan M. *Army Surveillance in America, 1775–1980.* New Haven, CT: Yale University Press, 1991.

Joffe, Joseph. "John W. Meldrum." *Annals of Wyoming* 13, no. 2 (April 1941): 105–140.

Kahl, Joseph. *The America Class Structure: A New Synthesis.* Chicago: Dorsey Press, 1987.

Kahneman, Daniel, and Dale Miller. "Norm Theory: Comparing Reality to Its Alternatives." *Psychological Review* 93, no. 2 (1986): 136–153.

Kanas, N., D. S. Weiss, and C. R. Marmar, "Crew Member Interactions during a Mir Space Station Simulation." *Aviation, Space, and Environmental Medicine* 67 (1996), 969–975.

Kane, Robert. "The Social Ecology of Police Misconduct." *Criminology* 40, no. 4 (2002): 867–896.

Karsmizki, Kenneth. *Fountain Soldier Station (48YE727): Report of Research and Mitigation Prepared for the National Park Service, Rocky Mountain Region.* Bozeman, MT: Museum of the Rockies, 2001.

———. *Soda Butte Soldier Station (48YE88): Report of Research and Testing Prepared for the National Park Service Intermountain Region.* Bozeman, MT: Museum of the Rockies, 1998.

———. *Tower Falls Soldier Station (48YE163): Historical Archaeology, Report of Research Prepared for the National Park Service Intermountain Region.* Bozeman, MT: Museum of the Rockies, 2000.

Kasson, John F. *Rudeness and Civility: Manners in Nineteenth-Century America.* New York: Hill & Wang, 1990.

Keegan, John. *The Face of Battle: A Study of Agincourt, Waterloo, and the Somme.* New York: Penguin Books, 1983.

K.H.A. "Obituary, Frank Porter Amos, No. 3968, Class of 1900." In *Sixty-Second Annual Report of the Association of Graduates of the United States Military Academy at West Point, New York,* United States Military Academy, 369. Chicago: R. R. Donnelley & Sons, 1931.

Kipling, Rudyard. *From Sea to Sea: Letters of Travel.* Vol. 2. New York: Doubleday & McClure, 1899.

Knight, Oliver. *Life and Manners in the Frontier Army.* Norman: University of Oklahoma Press, 1978.

Kohn, Richard. "The Social History of the American Soldier: A Review and Prospectus for Research." *American Historical Review* 86, no. 3 (June 1981): 553–567.

Kuhr, Manuel I. "How George Vest Came to Missouri." *Missouri Historical Review* 59 (April 1965): 424–427.

Levine, Lawrence. *Highbrow/Lowbrow: The Emergence of Cultural Hierarchy in America.* Boston: Harvard University Press, 1990.

Loftus, Bethan. "Police Occupational Culture: Classic Themes, Alter Times." *Policing and Society: An International Journal of Research and Policy* 20, no. 1 (2010): 1–20.

Magnusson, Sigurdur G. "The Singularization of History: Social History and Microhistory within the Postmodern State of Knowledge." *Journal of Social History* 36 (Spring 2003): 701–735.

Mason, Kathy. *Natural Museums: U.S. National Parks, 1872–1916.* East Lansing: Michigan State University Press, 2004.

McChristain, Douglas C. *Regular Army O!: Soldiering on the Western Frontier, 1865–1891.* Norman: University of Oklahoma Press, 2017.

McFadden, T. J., R. L. Helmreich, R. M. Rose, and L. F. Fogg, "Predicting Astronauts' Effectiveness: A Multivariate Approach." *Aviation, Space, and Environmental Medicine* 65 (1994): 904–909.

McPherson, James. *For Cause and Comrades: Why Men Fought in the Civil War.* New York: Oxford, 1998.

Messner, Steven, and Richard Rosenfeld, *Crime and the American Dream.* Belmont, CA: Wadsworth, 1997.

Meyerson, Harvey. *Nature's Army: When Soldiers Fought for Yosemite.* Lawrence: University Press of Kansas, 2001.

Middlekauff, Robert. *The Glorious Cause: The American Revolution, 1763–1789.* New York: Oxford University Press, 2005.

Miles, John. *Wilderness in National Parks: Playground or Preserve.* Seattle: University of Washington Press, 2011.

Miller, Char. *Seeking the Greatest Good: The Conservation Legacy of Gifford Pinchot.* Pittsburgh, PA: University of Pittsburgh Press, 2013.

Millet, Allan, and Peter Maslowski. *For the Common Defense: A Military History of the United States from 1607–2012.* 3rd ed. New York: Free Press, 2012.

Mitchell, Reid. *Civil War Soldiers.* New York: Penguin Books, 1997.

Morn, Frank. *The Eye That Never Sleeps: A History of the Pinkerton National Detective Agency.* Bloomington: Indiana University Press, 1982.

Morris, Roy, Jr. *Sheridan: The Life and Wars of General Phil Sheridan.* New York: Crown Publishing, 1992.

Muir, Edward, and Guido Ruggiero, eds. *Microhistory and the Lost People of Europe.* Translated by Eren Branch. Baltimore, MD: Johns Hopkins University Press, 1991.

National Research Council. *The Context of Military Environments: An Agenda for Basic Research on Social and Organizational Factors Relevant to Small Units.* Washington, DC: National Academies Press, 2014.

Nelson, P. D. "Psychological Aspects of Antarctic Living." *Military Medicine* 130, no. 5: 485–489.

Nye, Robert. "Western Masculinities in War and Peace." *American Historical Review* 112, no. 2 (April 2007): 417–438.

Oriard, Michael. *Reading Football: How the Popular Press Created an American Spectacle.* Chapel Hill: University of North Carolina Press, 1993.

Palinkas, Lawrence A. "On the Ice: Individual and Group Adaptation in Antarctica." Unpublished manuscript, 2000. www.bec.ucla.edu/papers/Palinkas_On_The_Ice.pdf.

———. "Psychological Issues in Long-Term Space Flight: Overview." *Gravitational and Space Biology Bulletin* 14, no. 2 (June 2001): 25–33.

Palinkas, Lawrence, Lester Reed, and Nhan Do. "Association between Polar T3 Syndrome and the Winter-Over Syndrome in Antarctica." *Antarctic Journal of the United States* 32 (1997): 112–114.

Post, Emily. *Etiquette in Society, in Business, in Politics and at Home.* New York: Funk & Wagnalls, 1922.

Reade, Philip H. *Epochs in U.S. History: A Series of Military, Historical, Educational and Interesting Lectures, Replete with Narrative and Personal Reminiscences.* Lowell, MA: Courier Citizen, 1906.

Reed, H. Lester, E. D. Silverman, K. M. Shakir, R. Dons, K. D. Burman, and J. T. O'Brian. "Changes in Serum Triodothyronine (T3) Kinetics after Prolonged

Antarctic Residence: The Polar T3 Syndrome." *Journal of Clinical Endocrinology & Metabolism* 70, no. 4 (1990): 965–974.

Rickey, Don. *Forty Miles a Day on Beans and Hay.* Norman: University of Oklahoma Press, 1963.

Rodenbough, Theophilus F., Bvt. Brig. Gen., and Maj. William L. Haskin, eds. *The Army of the United States: Historical Sketches of Staff and Line with Portraits of Generals-in-Chief.* New York: Maynard, Merrill, 1886.

Rust, Thomas C. *Lost Fort Ellis: A Frontier History of Bozeman.* Charleston, SC: History Press, 2015.

Rydell, Kikki L., and Mary S. Culpin. *Managing the "Matchless Wonders": A History of Administrative Development in Yellowstone National Park, 1872–1965.* Yellowstone National Park, WY: National Park Service, Center for Resources, 2006.

Sandal, G. M., R. Vaernes, T. Bergan, M. Warncke, and H. Ursin. "Psychological Reactions during Polar Expeditions and Isolation in Hyperbaric Chambers." *Aviation, Space, and Environmental Medicine* 67 (1995): 227–234.

Schlereth, Thomas J. *Victorian America: Transformations in Everyday Life, 1876–1915.* New York: Harper Perennial, 1991.

Schmidt, Carl E. *A Western Trip.* Detroit, MI: Herold Press, 1901.

Scott, Carole E. "Racism and Southern Anti-Imperialists: The Blounts of Georgia." *Atlanta History* 31, no. 3 (June 1987): 24–29.

Sefton, James. *The United States Army and Reconstruction, 1865–1877.* Baton Rouge: Louisiana State University Press, 1967.

Sosin, Jack. "The Massachusetts Acts of 1774: Coercive or Preventative?" *Huntington Library Quarterly* (1963): 235–252.

Steele, Ian. "Governors or Generals?: A Note on Martial Law and the Revolution of 1689 in English America." *William and Mary Quarterly* 46, no. 2 (April 1989): 304–314.

Stuster, Jack. *Bold Endeavors: Lessons from Polar and Space Exploration.* Annapolis, MD: Naval Institute Press, 1996.

Swain, Donald. *Wilderness Defender: Horace M. Albright and Conservation.* Chicago: University of Chicago Press, 1968.

Sykes, Richard, and John Clark. "A Theory of Deference Exchange in Police-Civilian Encounters." *American Journal of Sociology* 81, no. 3 (November 1975): 584–586.

Synge, Georgina. *A Ride through Wonderland.* London: Sampson, Low, Marston, 1892.

Talbert, Roy, Jr. *Negative Intelligence: The Army and the American Left, 1917–1941.* Jackson: University Press of Mississippi, 1991.

Trask, David F. "The 'New Military History' and Army Historians." *Army Historian* 5 (Fall 1984): 7–10.

Tuckman, B. W. "Developmental Sequence in Small Groups." *Psychological Bulletin* 63, no. 6 (1965): 384–399.

Turrill, Gardner S. *A Tale of the Yellowstone, or, In a Wagon through Western Wyoming and Wonderland.* Jefferson, IA: G. S. Turrill, 1901.

United States Military Academy. *Sixteenth Annual Report of the Association of*

*Graduates of the United States Military Academy at West Point, New York.* Newburgh, NY: Moore Printing Co., 1929.
Upton, Richard. *Fort Custer on the Big Horn, 1877–1898: Its History and Personalities as Told and Pictured by Its Contemporaries.* Glendale, CA: Arthur H. Clark, 1973.
Utley, Robert. *Frontier Regulars: The United States Army and the Indian, 1866–1991.* Lincoln, NE: Bison Books, 1973.
———. *Life in Custer's Cavalry.* New Haven, CT: Yale University Press, 1977.
Walker, Danny. *Faunal Remains from Three Military Soldier Stations, Yellowstone National Park, Wyoming*. Bozeman, MT: Museum of the Rockies, 1999.
Warhauser, Mathew. *Andrew Jackson and the Politics of Martial Law: Nationalism, Civil Liberties, and Partisanship.* Knoxville: University of Tennessee Press, 2007.
Watry, Elizabeth, and Lee Whittlesey. *Images of America: Fort Yellowstone.* Charleston, SC: Arcadia 2012.
Wells, Collin D. "Social Darwinism." *American Journal of Sociology* 12, no. 5 (1907): 687–706.
Whittlesey, Lee. "In Yellowstone Park, 1886–1889: George Tutherly's Reminiscences." *Montana: Magazine of Western History* 33, no. 1 (Winter 1983): 2–13.
———. "'Music, Song, and Laughter': Yellowstone National Park's Fountain Hotel, 1891–1916." *Montana Magazine of Western History* 53, no. 4 (Winter 2003): 22–35.
———. *Yellowstone Album: A Photographic Celebration of the First National Park.* Boulder, CO: Robert Rinehart, 1997.
———. *Yellowstone Place Names.* Helena, MT: Montana Historical Society, 1988.
Wister, Owen. "Old Yellowstone Days." *Harper's Magazine* 157 (March 1936): 37–48.
Woodward, William H. "The Citizen-Soldier Historian and the 'New Military History.'" *Army Historian* 9 (Fall 1995): 13–15.
Wright, Robert K., Jr. *Military Police.* Washington, DC: United States Army Center of Military History, 1992.

# Index